A Hydra of Business and Men

Library of Economic History

VOLUME 21

The titles published in this series are listed at *brill.com/lehi*

A Hydra of Business and Men

The Habsburg Asiento de Negros *in Structuring the European Transatlantic Slave Trade*

By

Cátia Antunes, Alejandro García-Montón
Elisabeth Heijmans, Gerhard de Kok
Susana Münch Miranda, Edgar Pereira
João Paulo Salvado and Julie Svalastog

BRILL

LEIDEN | BOSTON

This publication is part of the project 'Exploiting the Empire of Others: Dutch Investment in Foreign Colonial Resources, 1570–1800' with file number VI.C.191.027 of the research program NWO-Talent Program, financed by the Dutch Research Council (NWO). The Dutch Research Council (NWO) has furthermore financed the open access publication of this book (file number 36.201.140).

Cover illustration: Juan de Herrera, *Plano de Cartagena de las Indias – por el Sargento Mayor Don Juan de Perrera y Sotto Mayor, Ingeniero Militar*, 18th century. Map. Bibliothèque Nationale de France, département Cartes et plans, GE SH 18 PF 161 DIV 9 P 36 D: FRBNF44221034.

The Library of Congress Cataloging-in-Publication Data is available online at https://catalog.loc.gov

Typeface for the Latin, Greek, and Cyrillic scripts: "Brill". See and download: brill.com/brill-typeface.

ISSN 1877-3206
ISBN 978-90-04-74508-7 (hardback)
ISBN 978-90-04-74509-4 (e-book)
DOI 10.1163/9789004745094

This book is printed on acid-free paper and produced in a sustainable manner.

Contents

Tables

Introduction

The Spanish colonies in the Americas were the destination of the majority of enslaved Africans that crossed the Atlantic between the sixteenth and the beginning of the eighteenth century. Alex Borucki, David Eltis and David Wheat claim that before 1640, the Spanish American market imported a total of 529,800 men, women and children, compared to half this amount for Brazil in the same period.[1] By 1640, the plantation complex was still unable to rival the Spanish Main for the import of enslaved Africans. According to these authors, after 1640 and until 1700, the number of enslaved Africans in the Spanish West Indies rapidly decreased to less than one eighth of the total before 1640, while the same data points to an explosion in the import of enslaved Africans into the British and the Dutch Caribbean, amounting to 308,000 for the former and 124,200 for the later.[2]

Borucki, Eltis and Wheat's data for the period between 1640 and 1700 is problematic for three reasons. It is generally acknowledged that the second half of the seventeenth century witnessed the beginning and crystallisation of cash crop production in the British and French Caribbean, although this development remained well below the levels of Brazil at the onset of the plantation complex during the 1590s. If Brazil imported, at the pick of its sugar production about 261,400 enslaved Africans, it is difficult to conceive that Barbados and Jamaica could, between 1640 and 1700, have put 308,000 enslaved Africans to work as start-up plantation complex economies. The question then arises: why did the British Caribbean, particularly Jamaica, witness such a steep rise in the imports of enslaved Africans when the British plantation complex was still on its early stages?

The second problem that arises with this data is that, like the British West Indies, the Dutch West Indies also appear as major importers of enslaved Africans, 124,200 in total for the period between 1640 and 1700. Since the Dutch Caribbean was reduced to Curaçao at the time, and lacking a serious planta-

---

1 Alex Borucki, David Eltis and David Wheath, "Atlantic History and the Slave Trade to Spanish America", *The Americal History Review*, 120, no. 2 (2015), 440, see table. António de Almeida Mendes, "The Foundations of the System : A Reassessment of the Slave Trade to the Spanish Americas in the Sixteenth and the Seventeenth centuries", in *Extending the Frontiers : Essays on the New Transatlantic Slave Trade Database*, edited by David Eltis and David Richardson, New Haven : Yale University Press, 2008, 63–94. Lutgardo García Fuentes, "Licencias para la introducción de esclavos en Indias y envíos desde Sevilla en el siglo XVI", *Jahrbuch für Geschichte von Staat, Wirtschaft und Geselschaft Lateinamerikas* 19 (1982), 1–46.

2 Borucki, Eltis and Weath, 'Atlantic Hitory', p. 440, see table.

 | DOI:10.1163/9789004745094_002

tion colony either in the Caribbean or in the Wild Coast, and given Curaçao did not produce much in terms of agriculture or manufacturing, it is difficult to place this number of enslaved Africans within a specific economic sector on the island.

The third problem is that the number of enslaved Africans transported to Brazil increased between 1640 and 1700 from 261,400 in the earlier period to 523,000, during what historiography considers a time of Brazilian economic decline due to the Dutch-Portuguese wars in sugar-producing areas and the challenging recovery of the Brazilian economy after the Dutch retreat in 1654. If the second-largest market for enslaved Africans was still growing after 1640, how can one explain the fact that the first market at the time, that of the Spanish West Indies, could settle for only 61,700 enslaved Africans?[3]

The short answer to these three problems lies in the organisation of the Spanish *asiento de Negros*. The involvement of the Dutch West India Company (henceforth WIC) and the English companies in the subcontracting of the *asiento* facilitated the development of Curaçao first and Jamaica later as hubs for the distribution of enslaved Africans to the Spanish Main. This legal arrangement allowed Dutch and English companies, restricted by their charters to trade only with their own colonies, to participate in the Spanish *Asiento* by enabling Spanish or Dutch and English private ships to transport enslaved Africans from their Caribbean hubs to the Spanish Main. When adding the total of enslaved Africans who entered the British and Dutch West Indies to those who went directly to the Spanish Main, the total number of imported slaves rises from 61,700 to 493,000. Of the latter, not all would have been re-exported from Curaçao and Jamaica to Spanish America, as some were distributed to the start-up plantation complexes in Barbados, the French and the lesser islands in the Caribbean.

The slave trade was thus essential to the survival and maintenance of the Spanish American empire. While before 1640 the Spanish American colonies constituted the largest single slave market on the American continent, they became second only to Brazil, a society centred on the plantation complex, between 1640 and 1700. Despite these numbers, Spain did not have a foothold in West Africa and Spanish merchants, bound by the rules of the *consulado* in Seville, a merchant guild with exclusive access for Castilians, do not appear to have been actively interested in the opportunities presented by this abhorrent trade. The gains to be made via the *consulado* in the *Carrera de Indias,* which monopolised trade between Spain and its American territories, were more

3 Borucki, Eltis and Weath, 'Atlantic Hitory', p. 440, see table.

attractive than the risks involved in participating in the transatlantic slave trade.

In this context, from very early of Spanish colonial expansion in America, the importation of slaves was left to men, firms and companies that operated within the orbit of the Spanish Monarchy but officially stood outside the interests and the privileged rights of the *consulado*. This course of action created a unique opportunity for non-Castilian subjects of the Spanish kings and foreigners to participate in this trade. Their involvement resulted in the development of a myriad of business organisations, ran by a transnational group of slave traders who served first the licenses and, later, the *asiento* and, by doing so, helped the Spanish Habsburg Monarchy to implement, frame and structure the transatlantic slave trade for over a hundred years.

Asientos were instruments of 'Spanish public law (...) for the purpose of public utility, (...) the administration of a public service between the Spanish government and private individuals'. The Monarchy understood as public service to include 'the administration of a tax, an enterprise of colonization, of public works, or recruiting the militia, of providing manual labour or materials'.[4] All *asientos,* including the *asiento de Negros,* encompassed the possibility of facilitating various types of transactions such as 'lending, transferring money, farming out tax-revenue and chartering monopolies. A single contract would often involve two or more of these transaction types'.[5]

As *asientos* were contracts between the King and private entrepreneurs (individual or collective), they were open for the participation of non-subjects of the Castilian Crown and to foreigners – an opportunity particularly welcome in the context of the *asiento de Negros*. This transnational participation in the slave trade to Spanish America has been acknowledge, and even overemphasised, by current scholarship, to the extent that the periodisation of the slave trade to Spanish America is often organized according to the different involvement of different 'merchant nations'. This periodisation is frequently referred to as the 'Portuguese period', the 'Dutch period', or the

4 Georges Scelle, "The Slave Trade in the Spanish Colonies of America : the Asiento", *The American Journal of International Law*, 4–3 (1910), 614–615. Georges Scelle, *La traite négrière aux Indes de Castille, contrats et traités d'assiento*, 2 vols. Paris : Librairie de la Société du Recueil J.-B. Sirey & Du Journal du Palais, 1906, p. 24. Edgar Pereira, *A Contractor Empire. Public-Private Partnerships and Overseas Expansion in Habsburg Portugal (1580–1640)*, PhD diss. Leiden: Leiden University, 2020, 8–25, for definitions and difference between the Spanish *asiento* and the Portuguese *contrato*.

5 Mauricio Drelichman and Hans-Joachim Voth, *Lending to the Borrower from Hell : Debt, Taxes, and Default in the Age of Philip II*, Princeton : Princeton University Press, 2014, 100.

'French period'.[6] This particular focus has left current scholarship with three important gaps. The first is the lack of knowledge and critical analysis regarding the participation of Spanish and Spanish American subjects of the Habsburg kings in slave trading activities. The second is the portrayal of non-Castilian merchant nations involved in the *asiento* as self-contained merchant communities that simply replaced each other according to the whims of the Spanish Monarchy. The third is the lack of attention to the development of entanglements between different types of business organisations (partnerships, firms, chartered companies, joint stock companies) forced into cooperation, a phenomenon first tested within the purview of the *asiento*.

The issue with conceiving foreign merchant communities as contained interest groups in the context of the Spanish slave trade is that it overlooks the entanglement of these communities before, during and after their engagement with the *asiento*. The end of an *asiento* with one group did not necessarily mean the exclusion of that group, nor did it signal the end of the trade for previous *asentistas*. This is not surprising in view of the fact that the *asiento* was a personal contract between an individual and the Crown, rather than the Crown and a merchant community as a collective. Continuities emerged in the administration of the contract through ongoing contacts and the exchange of ventures between old and new *asentistas,* rather than between old and new merchant communities. This book departs from the given that the *asiento* was transnational, but bond to individuals rather than merchant nations. We explore the complex entanglements between the multiple business groups, not necessarily connected by cultural or communal affinity that participated in the slave trade destined for the Spanish American markets. In this decision, we position this book as complementary to already existing studies about these 'communal approaches'.[7] Exploring this complexity simultaneously deepens our understanding of the structuring of the European slave trade during the long seventeenth century and moves beyond traditional perspectives of transnational history (in contrast to national historiographies).[8] Fur-

---

6 José Maria Delgado Ribas, "The Slave Trade in the Spanish Imperial System, 1500–1800", in *Slavery and Antislavery in Spain's Atlantic Empire,* edited by Josep Maria Fradera and Christopher Schmidt-Nowara (New York: Berghahn, 2013), 13–42. Scelle, *La traite négrière.*

7 Alejandro García-Montón, *Genoese Entrepreneurship and the Asiento Slave Trade, 1650–1700.* London and New York: Routledge, 2022. Miguel Geraldes Rodrigues, *Between West Africa and America. The Angolan Slave Trade in the Portuguese and Spanish Atlantic Empires (1560–1641)* PhD diss. (Florence: European University Institute, 2019).

8 This book has been greatly inspired by the discussions initiated by Bartolomé Yun Casallila, " 'Localism', Global History and Transnational History: A Reflection from the Historian of Early Modern Europe", *Historisk Tidskrift* 127 (2007), 659–678; Gunilla Budde, Sebastian

thermore, by focusing our interest in the intersection of individual transnationalism, in contrast with communal transnationalism, in a context of diverse business organisations, we follow the lead of David Hedinger and Nadin Heé by emphasising the role business relationships fostered by connectivity, cooperation and competition framed and structured the trade in enslaved Africans to the Spanish American colonies.[9]

The lack of an overview of entanglements between *asiento* holders under the Habsburgs can partially be explained by the difficulty of combining archives from different countries, written in different languages, and containing different typologies of archival materials – a challenge that is hard for a single historian to undertake. Furthermore, the wealth of information in some archives is met with a lack of sources in a different archival context, leaving historians with unequal quantitative and qualitative information. This explains the decision to write this co-authored book with a group of early modernists whose approaches, focuses, and interests differ, but whose insights into de establishment, development, and consequences of the *asiento* align. This multifaceted team has accessed a range of archives in different countries, from institutional to personal collections, to answer the following question: how was the largest single slave market in the Americas supplied in the period between the 1590s and 1713? How did a nationally bound contract evolve into a transnational, pluricultural and interconnected entrepreneurial endeavor that affected the lives of millions of human beings in Africa, the Americas and Europe? The answers to these questions contribute to a better understanding of the *asiento de negros* as an instrument of colonial exploitation, as a key framework for structuring the transatlantic slave trade, and a source of business opportunities for merchants, agents, entrepreneurs, and companies who would otherwise have been excluded from participating in the largest single slave market in the Atlantic before 1715.

The reconstruction of the transnational and intertwined nature of the *asiento* challenges current perceptions in scholarship regarding European overseas empires, which are often seen as accommodating transnationality

Conrad, Oliver Janz (eds.), *Transnationale Geschiechte : Themen, Tendenzen und Theorien* (Gottingen: Vandenhoek & Ruprecht, 2006) ; Christopher A. Bayly *et al.*, AHR Conversation: On Transnational History, in *American Historical Review* 111 (2006), p. 1441–1464. Dipesh Chakrabarty, *Provincializing Europe: Postcolonial Thought and Historical Difference* (Princeton: Princeton University Press, 2000).

9 David Hedinger and Nadin Heé, 'Transnational History – Connectivity, Cooperation and Competition', *Journal of Modern Eurpean History*, 16–4 (2018), 429–452.

only at the fringes or the peripheries of the Atlantic.[10] In this historiography, exchanges between people of different countries and cultures were thought to take place primarily in areas where state power, through its various colonial governments, was unable to impose the legal and sovereign boundaries often enshrined in laws and political economies. Places such as the Caribbean are often portrayed as spaces of entanglement in the periphery of many empires, although the Caribbean remained largely a Spanish sphere well into the first quarter of the eighteenth century.[11] In this book we demonstrate that transnationality of empire was not spatially bound to the peripheries but welcomed and structured within the centrers of empire in Europe.

The idea that transnationality is spatially bound to specific peripheries is often associated with illegal practices.[12] The argument is frequently that colonial empires were nationally oriented spaces that operated within a specific set of rules and institutions, limiting them to particular types of exchanges, only conceivable within the framework of exclusive access to the subjects (or carefully selected privileged groups) of each European state. The underlying consequence of this argument is that potentially, all cross-colonial, cross-imperial, and transnational exchanges in the so-called peripheries were almost certainly illegal. The illegal nature of transnational exchanges in the peripheries has also cast a shadow of suspicion to the 'who', 'where', 'when' and 'how much' of the colonial exploitative projects actually known to historians through surviving archives, as accountability for this illegal enterprises remains elusive in many contemporary accounts.[13]

Even if we do not dispute the fact that illegal exchanges fostered by transnational networks were a reality in many colonial peripheries in the Atlantic,

10 Gert Oostindie and Jessica Roitman (eds.), *Dutch Atlantic Connections, 1680–1800. Linking Empires, Bridging Borders* (Leiden: Brill, 2014) ; Alison Games, *The Web of Empire. English Cosmopolitans in an Age of Expansion, 1560–1660* (Oxford: Oxford University Press, 2008).

11 Wim Klooster, *The Dutch Moment: War, Trade, and Settlement in the Seventeenth-Century Atlantic World* (Ithaca: Cornell University Press, 2016).

12 Markus A. Denzel, Jan de Vries, and Philipp Robinson Rössner (eds.), *Small Is Beautiful? Interlopers and Smaller Trading Nations in the Pre-industrial Period: Proceedings of the XVth World Economic History Congress in Utrecht* (Stuttgart: Franz Steiner Verlag, 2011); Alan L. Karras, *Smuggling: Contraband and Corruption in World History* (Lanham, MD: Rowman & Littlefield, 2010); Wim Klooster, "Inter-imperial Smuggling in the Americas, 1600–1800", in *Soundings in Atlantic History: Latent Structures and Intellectual Currents, 1500–1830,* edited by Bernard Bailyn and Patricia L. Denault (Cambridge, MA: Harvard University Press, 2009), 141–180; Gregorio de Robles, *América a fines del siglo XVII: Noticia de los lugares de contrabando* (Valladolid: Casa-Museo de Colón, 1980).

13 Sophus Reinert and Pernille Røge (eds.), *Political Economy of Empire in the Early Modern World* (New York: Palgrave Macmillan, 2013).

we argue that transnationality was just as much, if not more, spatially located at the centre of the empires in early modern Western Europe, framed by European states within the constraints imposed by laws and regulations.[14] In this way, transnationality was not only spatially central but also legal. In this context, transnationality becomes a key characteristic of European colonial expansion and exploitation.

A transnational perspective on the study of the *asiento* also challenges current views regarding the transatlantic slave trade. Historiography has been inclined to associated the slave trade primarily with the plantation complex, and within this framework, there is debate as to whether the Anglophile experience of the slave trade and the enslavement of Africans offers a direct link between cash crop exploitation based on enslaved labour, the roots of the Industrial Revolution, and global inequalities in postcolonial states such as the United States.[15] In this selective approach to understanding slavery in the Americas, Spanish America has often been overlooked in the debate, as the only plantation complex of note in the Spanish context was Cuba, which did not rival with the British cash crops in the Caribbean and in North America. This legacy of international debate has excluded the largest market for enslaved Africans before the 1700s – namely, the Spanish American colonies – from discussions about the transatlantic slave trade.

This disengagement with the Spanish experience in the slave trade has consequently contributed to a misunderstanding of the *asiento* as an international, rather than Spanish, framework for human trafficking in the Atlantic. Within this framework, different business organisations (partnerships, firms, chartered and joint stock companies) and diverse economic agents (merchants, skippers, agents, tax farmers, among others) connected, cooperated and competed while shaping it. Since the interaction between the Spanish

14 Delgado Ribas, "The Slave Trade in the Spanish Empire".

15 The discussion arises with Eric Williams, *Capitalism and Slavery* (Chapel Hill: The University of North Carolina Press, 1944) and takes multiple iterations (supporters: Richard Sheridan, "The Plantation Revolution and the Industrial Revolution, 1625–1775", *Caribbean Studies* 9, no. 3 (1969), 5–25. Critics: Roger Anstey, "Capitalism and Slavery: a Critique", *Economic History Review* 21, no. 2 (1968), 307–320. Stanley Engerman, "The Slave Trade and British Capital Formation in the Eighteenth Century: a Comment of the Williams Thesis", *Business Studies Review* 46, no. 4 (1972), 430–443. Howard Temperley, *British Anti-Slavery, 1833–1870* (London: Longmans, 1972). Keith Aufhauser, "Profitability of Slavery in the British Caribbean", *Journal of Interdisciplinary History* 5, no. 1 (1974), 45–67. Robert Thomas and Richard Bean, "The Fishers of Men: Profits of the Slave Trade", *The Journal of Economic History* 34, no. 4 (1974), 885–914). More recently, Williams' thesis was revived and critically reflected on by Sven Beckert, *Empire of Cotton : A Global History* (New York: Alfred A. Knopf, 2014).

Monarchy, the *asiento* (as a legal framework), and *asentistas* (holders of the *asiento*) changed over time, the *asiento* became a laboratory for European institutions and traders to learn, through trial and error, how to transform the trade in enslaved Africans into a venture that served commercial interests in Europe, West Africa and the Americas.

Licences to introduce enslaved people of African and other origins in the Americas predate the royal favour bestowed upon a servant of a Spanish king. This occurred when Emperor Charles V (Charles I of Spain after 1516) granted his servant Laurent de Gouvenot (Lourenzo de Gorrevod in Spanish documents), a Burgundian, governor of Bressa (Italy), and *majordomo* of the king, a privilege for a period of nine years after 1518.[16] This allowed Gouvenot to import enslaved Africans from the West Coast of Africa into the Spanish Caribbean ports, creating the first *de facto* Crown monopoly over the slave trade. Coincidently, 1518 was also the year in which the *Casa de la Contratación* began to supervise and systematically organise the slave trade. This was particularly necessary in Gouvenot's case, as he did not engage in the trade himself. Instead, he used his royal privilege to sell licences to prominent merchants, such as the Genoese partnership of Adamo Vivaldo, Tomasso de Fornari & Co., which included other notable Genoese traders like Gaspare Centurione, a resident of Seville. However, the Genoese did not operate alone or independently. They associated and partnered, separately or as members of the original partnership, with prominent Spanish merchants from Seville, Burgos and Toledo.[17] This successful first trial with a system of licences resulted in

16 Marc Eagle and David Wheat, "The Early Iberian Slave Trade to the Spanish Caribbean, 1500–1580", in *From the Galleons to the Highlands: Slave Trade Routes in the Spanish Americas*, edited by Alex Borucki, David Eltis and David Wheat (Albuquerque: University of New Mexico Press, 2020), 53–54. Germán Santana Pérez, "Mercaderes hispanos en África subsahariana antes de la Unión Ibérica, 1503–1580", in *Los negocios de la esclavitud: tratantes y mercados de esclavos en el Atlántico Ibérico, siglos XV-XVIII*, edited by José Luis Belmonte Postigo, Manuel F. Fernández Chaves and Rafael M. Pérez García (Sevilla: Universidad de Sevilla, 2019), 74–75. Rafael M. Pérez García, "Metodología para el análisis y cuantificación de la trata de esclavos hacia la América española en el siglo XVI", in *Los vestidos de Clío: métodos y tendencias recientes de la historiográfica modernista española (1973–2013)*, edited by Ofelia Rey Castelao and Fernando Suárez Golán (Santiago de Compostela: Universidad de Santiago de Compostela, 2013), 829–830.

17 Manuel Francisco Fernández Chaves and Rafael M. Pérez García, "La élite mercantil judeoconversa andaluza y la articulación de la trata negrera hacia las Indias de Castilla, ca. 1518–1560", *Hispania* 76, no. 253 (2016), 399. Manuel Francisco Fernández Chaves and Rafael M. Pérez García, "La penetración económica portuguesa en la Sevilla del siglo XVI", *Espacio Tiempo y Forma, serie IV, Historia Moderna*, 25 (2012), 206–207. Statements in these works are based on Enrique Otte, *Sevilla, siglo XVI: materiales para su historia económica* (Sevilla: Centro de Estudios Andaluces, 2008).

three features that were to continue and dominate the licences until the 1590s, and the *asiento de Negros* thereafter. The first feature was the realisation, on the part of the Monarchy, of its ability to mobilise financial liquidity through the issuing of licences.[18] The second feature was the successful subcontracting of the different stages of the business process to different individuals, in single liability or in partnerships, of different geographical and social origins, to participate in the commercialisation of the licences. The last feature was the acceptance of the licences as a means to legally penetrate the exclusive political economy of the Spanish Empire, introducing human beings as commodity in exchange for the much coveted American silver, an essential means of payment in Western Europe, the Mediterranean, but more acutely in East Asia.

Although the personal privilege granted to Gouvenot is not legally an *asiento,*[19] all the main characteristics and actors involved in this early slave trade persisted into the seventeenth-century *asientos*. Gouvenot, Vivaldo or Fornari were not Spanish.[20] The latter, together with their Spanish associates, maintained close business relationships with Portuguese traders and administrators in West Africa.[21] Even though the first slaving ships carrying Gouve-

18 Donoso Anes, Rafael, "Algunos aspectos relacionados con el control administrativo y contable de la renta de los esclavos enviados a Hispanoamérica (hasta el final del período de las licencias en 1595)", *Revista Española de Financiación y Contabilidad* 110 (2001), p. 1093–1136; Delgado Ribas, "The Slave Trade", 16–17.

19 Scelles, *La traite négrière*, vol. 1, 121–162.

20 Manuel Gimenez Fernandez, *Bartolomeo de las Casas. Capellan de S.M. Carlos I. Poblador de Cumana (1517–1523)*, vol. II, Madrid : Consejo Superior de Investigaciones Cientificas – Escuela de Estudios Hispanoamericanos, 1984, 561.

21 António de Almeida "Portugal e o tráfico de escravos na primeira metade do século XVI", *Africana Studia* 7 (2004), 13–30. Francisco Bethencourt, "Iberian Atlantic: Ties, Networks, and Boundaries", in *Theorising the Ibero-American Atlantic,* edited by Harald E. Braun, Lisa Vollendorf (Leiden and Boston: Brill, 2013), 15–36; Sanjay Subrahmanyam, "Holding the World in Balance: The Connected Histories of the Iberian Overseas Empires, 1500–1640", *The American Historical Review* 112, no. 5(2007), 1359–1385; Serge Gruzinski, *Les quatre parties du monde. Histoire d'une mondialisation* (Paris: Éditions de la Martinière, 2004); Serge Gruzinski, *The Eagle and dragon: Globalization and European Dreams of Conquest in China and America in the Sixteenth century* (Cambridge: Cambridge Polity Press, 2014); Sanjay Subrahmanyam, "Connected Histories: Notes Toward a Reconfiguration of Early Modern Eurasia", *Modern Asian Studies* 31, no. 3 (1997), 735–762. P. E. H. Hair, "Columbus from Guinea to America", *History in Africa* 17 (1990), 113–129; Toby Green, *The Rise of the Trans-Atlantic Slave Trade in Western Africa, 1300–1589* (New York: Cambridge University Press, 2012). Linda Heywood, "Slavery and its transformations in the Kingdom of Kongo, 1492–1800", *The Journal of African History* 50, no 1 (2009), 1–22; Isabel Castro Henriques, "A Rota dos Escravos. Angola e a rede do comércio negreiro (sécs. XV a XIX)", in *A rota dos escravos. Angola e a rede do comércio negreiro*, edited by João Medina and Isabel Castro Henriques (Lisbon: Cegia, 1996). Robert W. Harms, *River of Wealth, River of*

not's licences arrived in Cuba as early as 1519,[22] the peak of the transports was organised from São Tomé and arrived in Puerto Rico after 1524.[23] Finally, the grantee of the royal privilege did not directly utilise the privilege but issued permissions (licences) to third parties, thereby broadening the network of participants in the Spanish slave trade.

Charles v's needs to further secure the support of merchants and bankers to finance his many European wars opened the door for slave trade privileges to be granted to German banking houses, particularly those of the Fuggers and the Welsers.[24] As bankers to the king, these families were not deeply acquainted with the requirements of the slave trade but participated in *asientos* related to mining in the Americas, where the demand for enslaved labour was high. This need for labour prompted the Welsers to petition for licences for the slave trade.[25] Following the traditional course of action, the Welsers sub-licenced their privilege to another party, returning to the Genoese nation of Seville to once again handle the shipping and contacts with Portuguese and African merchants in West Africa, with the Genoese remaining the active party in the banker's licences and sharing in the profits.[26] In addition to the Genoese, the Basques also took a central role in the licensing and sub-licensing of the slave trade for most of the sixteenth century,[27] along with a close-knit network of Andalusian New Christians.[28] Once again, non-Castilian subjects of Charles v were the direct beneficiaries of the king's magnanimity and the profits derived from the trafficking of enslaved Africans.[29]

Sorro: The Central Zaire Basin in the Era of the Slave and Ivory Trades, 1500–1891 (New Haven: Yale University Press, 1981); George Brooks, *Landlords and Strangers: Ecology, Society, and Trade in Western Africa, 1000–1630* (Boulder: Westview, 1993); Maria da Graça Mateus Ventura, *Negreiros Portugueses na rota das Indias de Castela: 1541–1556* (Lisbon: Colibri, Instituto de Cultura Ibero-Atlântico, 1998), p. 39–42.

22 Chaves Fernández and Pérez García, "La penetracion económica", 206.

23 Eagle and Wheat, "The Early Iberian Slave Trade", 53.

24 Donoso Anes, "Algunos Aspectos", pp. 1099–1100

25 Demetrio Ramos Pérez, "El negocio negrero de los Welser y sus habilidades monopolistas", *Revista de Historia de América* 81 (1976), 7–81.

26 José Luis Cortés López, *Esclavo y colono* (Salamanca : Universidad de Salamanca, 2004), 28.

27 Javier Ortiz Arza, "Introducción al estudio de los navegantes vascos de la carrera de Indias y su participación en la trata atlántica de esclavos del siglo xvi", *Brocar. Cuadernos de Investigación Histórica*, 43 (2019), 41–72. Javier Ortiz Arza, "Los libros-registro de esclavos, el sistema de licencias y la trata con Hispanoamérica en el siglo xvi: análisis y aspectos metodológicos a través del caso vasco", *Anuario de Estudios Americanos*, 77–2 (2020), 579–611.

28 Fernández Chaves and Pérez García, "La élite mercantil", 385–414.

29 Cortés López, *Esclavo y colono,* 28 and 76.

After 1536 and until the incorporation of Portugal into the Habsburg domains between 1580 and 1640, privileges and licences for the importation of enslaved Africans into Spanish America were sporadic, and our knowledge of them is patchy or, at times, fragmented.[30] However, Portuguese and Spanish sources consistently point to the presence of Genoese and Spanish slave traders of various origins operating in the Portuguese sphere in West Africa.[31] The destination of this trade was overwhelmingly Spanish America, where agents and commissioners of Spanish and Genoese communities collaborated, resulting in trans-communal entanglements, which turn into individual transnational alliances in later periods.[32]

The Union of the Crowns, with brought about the inclusion of Portugal and its empire under the rule of Philip II and his descendants, albeit as separate sovereign entities, opened more sustained and intensive Portuguese participation in the supply of the Spanish colonies with enslaved Africans. Portuguese involvement in the trade dated back to the early sixteenth century, although evidence shows that after the 1560s, Portuguese traders, governors, and their African partners intensified their involvement in the trade, with fleets commissioned by Genoese slave traders using Portuguese ports in São Tomé, Cape Verde, Guinea and Castelo da Mina to load their ships.[33] After 1590, however, the Portuguese, Luso-Africans, and Africans were not only supplying Basque, Genoese, and Portuguese ships, but also were commanding a large number of slaving fleets that supplied the plantation complexes in São Tomé and Brazil (under Portuguese jurisdiction) as well as the Spanish

30 Rafael M. Pérez García and Manuel Francisco Fernández Chaves, "Sevilla y la trata negrera atlántica: envíos de esclavos desde Cabo Verde a la América española, 1569–1579", León Carlos Álvarez y Santaló (ed.), *Estudios de historia moderna en homenaje al profesor Antonio García-Baquero*, Sevilla: Universidad de Sevilla, 2009, 597–622. Manuel Francisco Fernández Chaves and Rafael M. Pérez García, "Las redes de la trata negrera: mercaderes portugueses y tráfico de esclavos en Sevilla (c. 1560–1580)", in *La esclavitud negroafricana en la historia de España siglos XVI y XVII*, edited by Aurelia Martín Casares and Margarita García Barranco (Granada: Editorial Comares, 2010), 5–34. Eagle and Wheat, "The Early Iberian Slave Trade", 47–72.

31 Ruth Pike, *Enterprise and Adventure. The Genoese in Seville and the Opening of the New World* (Ithaca: Cornell University Press, 1966), 48–83 and 128–144. Heather Dalton, "Into Speyne to Selle for Slavys: English, Spanish, and Genoese Merchant Networks and Their Involvement with the 'Cost of Gwynea' Trade before 1550", in *Brokers of Change: Atlantic Commerce and Cultures in Pre-Colonial Western Africa*, edited by Toby Green (Oxford: Oxford University Press, 2012), 89–124. Santana Pérez, "Mercaderes hispanos en África", 71–92.

32 Eagle and Wheat, "The Early Iberian Slave Trade", 60–61.

33 Pérez García and Fernández Chaves, "Sevilla y la trata negrera", 604. Fernández Chaves and Pérez García, "Las redes de la trata negrera", 10.

American colonies in the Caribbean and on the mainland. The period of Portuguese dominance over the Spanish *asiento de negros* is addressed in detail in Chapter 2.

The period between Portugal's regained independence (1640) and the new *asiento* (1662) provided an opportunity for private partnerships from all over Europe, but in particular from the Dutch Republic to continue supplying the Spanish colonies with enslaved Africans. With the Portuguese excluded from the *Asiento* after 1640, it was the Portuguese Nation of Amsterdam, along with their Dutch partners and their family connections in West Africa and Lisbon, that were able to meet the demands of the Spanish American markets. Building on networks of information and knowledge developed between the fifteenth and the mid-seventeenth centuries, and supported by the cultural framework (including diverse religious practices) of the Portuguese (often referred to as) Sephardic Jewish diaspora, fleets departing from Amsterdam were able to service the Spanish American ports, with significant assistance from family members and coreligionists based in (Dutch) Curaçao and (English) Barbados.[34]

The next a*siento* was contracted by Domenico Grillo and Ambrosio Lomellino in 1662. After being granted the privilege of becoming the treasurers of the Holy Crusade in 1654, thereby gaining partial access to Spanish silver, the Genoese partnership was able to secure a contract with the King for the supply of enslaved Africans for the period between 1662 and 1674. The new *asentistas* introduced significant changes to the a*siento*: they opened up the trade to non-subjects of the king, employed a new business model by contracting with Dutch and English chartered and joint-stock companies, brough an end to the direct African-Spanish American trade by introducing a Caribbean port of call or 'storage' as redistribution hub for enslaved Africans destined to the Spanish American ports, as detailed in Chapters 3, 4 and 5.

Grillo and Lomellino's contract with the king ended in 1674 as stipulated, although the partnership's reputation suffered as, after the death of one of the

---

34 Wim Klooster, "Slavenvaart op Spaanse kusten. De Nederlandse slavenhandel met Spaans Amerika, 1648–1701", *Tijdschrift voor de Zeegeschiedenis* (1997), 121–140. Wim Klooster, *Illicit Riches: Dutch Trade in the Caribbean, 1648–1795* (Leiden: KITLV Press, 1998), particularly chapter 2. Wim Klooster, "Curaçao and the Caribbean Transit Trade", in *From Atlantic Commerce: Dutch Transatlantic Trade and Shipping*, 1585–1817, edited by Johannes Postma and Victor Enthoven (Leiden: Brill, 2003), 203–218. Cátia Antunes and Filipa Ribeiro da Silva, "Windows of Global Exchange: Dutch Ports and the Slave Trade, 1600–1800", *International Journals of Maritime History* 30, no. 3 (2018), 422–441. Peter Mark and José da Silva Horta, *The Forgotten Diaspora. Jewish communities in West Africa and the Making of the Atlantic World* (New York: Cambridge University Press, 2011).

partners, the company became insolvent.[35] Insolvency prevented the partnership from securing a new *asiento*, which was then taken upon by the Portuguese António Garcia, in partnership with Sebastián Silíceo, who planned to continue the contract with Charles II of Spain.[36] However, Garcia and Silíceo were unable to take up the trade as they failed to provide the required collateral demanded by the king. By 13 August 1675, they still had not provided the necessary guarantees, leading the Council of the Indies to cancel the *asiento* altogether. Nevertheless, under the false pretence of being the *asentista*, Garcia sought support from old acquaintances in Amsterdam, including the WIC and the Coymans family. He aimed to involve these two partners in securing the trade in enslaved Africans between the West Coast of Africa and the Caribbean. Once in the Caribbean, WIC fleets were to deliver the enslaved Africans to Curaçao, and from there, Garcia would ensure their distribution to various Spanish ports.[37]

The brief arrangement between Garcia, the Coymans, and the WIC faced a downward spiral. The French invasion of the Low Countries in 1672, known in Dutch historiography as the *Rampjaar* (Year of Catastrophe), and the bankruptcy of the WIC between 1672 and 1674 hindered Garcia's ability to deploy a significant amount of enslaved Africans to the Spanish Caribbean ports.[38] Complains from the Spanish colonies to the court in Madrid followed, leading to a proposal by Manuel Hierro de Castro and Manuel José Cortizos to supply the Spanish American slave markets by importing enslaved Africans from the Portuguese in Cape Verde and selling them in Curaçao, from where they

---

35 Hugh Thomas, *The Slave Trade : the Story of the Atlantic Slave Trade, 1440–1870* (New York: Simon & Schuster, 1999), p. 213. This book is not unproblematic, although it offers a panoramic view of the trade in enslaved Africans to Spanish America, but it contains several problematic assertions.

36 Klooster, *Slavenvaart op Spaanse kusten*, p. 127.

37 Pedro van Belle, *Pertinent en Waarachtig Verhaal van alle Handelingen en Directie van Pedro van Belle omtrent Den Slavenhandel, ofte, het Assiento de Negros, eerst door D. Juan Barosso y Posso, bij zijn overlijden door D. Nicolas Porsio, en daar na door Balthasar Coijmans met den Koning van Spangien aangegaan, zoo in Spangien, de West-Indijes, als op Curaçao: Dienende tot onderrichtinge van alle die gene, die bij het voorsz. Assiento, ofte de Compagnie van Coijmans en Van Belle tot Cadix, eenigsints zouden mogen wezen geinteresseert* (Rotterdam: Reinier Leers, 1689). Van Belle's self-ingratiating and defensive statements need to be critically appraised. Linda Rupert, *Creolization and Contraband : Curaçao in the Early Modern Atlantic World* (Athens and London: The University of Georgia Press, 2012), 78.

38 Erik Odegard, "Recapitalization or Reform? The Bankruptcy of the First Dutch West India Company and the Formation of the Second West India Company, 1674", *Itinerario* 43, nr. 1 (2019): 88–106.

would be redistributed throughout the Spanish American ports.[39] This solution was difficult to accept, as Curaçao was unable to transaction enslaved Africans acquired outside the charter of the WIC, as was the case with Cape Verde.[40] In light of this obstacle, the WIC instead suggested importing enslaved Africans from anywhere in West Africa and supplying of the Spanish American markets from Hispaniola, rather than Curaçao, or trading directly with the Spanish Main. In the end, the *asiento* was placed under the 'management' of the *consulado* in Seville between 1676 and 1681, as those seeking to contract were not sufficiently prepared to meet the legal obligations upon signature.[41]

As the 1670s came to a close, it became clear that Dutch shipping (both WIC and private merchants) could not deliver enough enslaved Africans annually to the Caribbean. This resulted in shortages in the Spanish American markets, driving up the price of enslaved Africans and increasing incentives for their illegal introduction into Spanish America. To counteract this and partially recover some of the original investment of the early 1670s, the Coymans family, mostly Balthazar (nephew of Joseph and Balthazar mentioned earlier), chose to finance the shipping fleets of Juan Barroso del Pozo from 1679

39 Carmen Sanz Ayán, "Consolidación y destrucción de patrimonios financieros en la Edad Moderna: Los Cortizos (1630–1715)", in *Fortuna y negocios: formación y gestión de los grandes patrimonios (siglos XVI-XX)*, Hilario Casado Alonso y Ricardo Robledo Hernández (Valladolid: Universidad de Valladolid, 2002), 73–98. Carmen Sanz Ayán, "Procedimientos culturales y transculturales de integración en un clan financiero internacional: los Cortizos (siglos XVII y XVIII)", in *Las redes del imperio: élites sociales en la articulación de la Monarquía Hispánica, 1492–1714*, edited by Bartolomé Yun Casalilla (Madrid: Marcial Pons, 2009, 65–94. Antonio José Rodríguez Hernández, 'Los judeoconversos y el negocio de la guerra: la leva de Manuel Cortizos por vía de Factoría (1648)', *Hispania* 76–253 (2016), 473–510.

40 Johannes Postma, *The Dutch in the Atlantic Slave Trade, 1600–1815* (Cambridge: Cambridge University Press, 1992), 40.

41 Enriqueta Vila Vilar, "El consulado de Sevilla, asentista de esclavos: una nueva tentativa para el mantenimiento del monopolio comercial", *Primeras Jornadas de Andalucía y América*, edited by Angél Perez Guerra, vol. 1 (La Rábida: Instituto de Estudios Onubenses, 1981), 181–96.

onwards.[42] As Barroso del Pozo's fleet proved successful, he was able, together with his son-in-law Nicolàs Porcio, a Venetian, to run the a*siento* after 1680.[43]

The a*siento* of Barroso and Porcio, following a two-year test period between 1680 and 1682, was officially signed with Charles II until 1688, granting the partners over six years to fulfil the contract's clauses.[44] After Pozo's death in 1683, Porcio was left to run the contract alone. He faced regular losses of ships and high mortality rates among the enslaved Africans. These difficulties often led to liquidity problems, and when visiting Portobelo, he was arrested, likely because of his debts. There personal setbacks significantly influenced Porcio's ability to manage the *asiento,* and he accused the royal authorities in Cartagena as making his life impossible, blaming them for his losses and his failure to meet the contract's requirements.[45]

In light of Porcio's inability to fulfil the a*siento* and honour the contract with the king, Madrid allowed for the early reallocation of the contract to a different party, namely Balthasar Coymans, who initially offered to take on the debts left by Pozo and Porcio.[46] Charles II only agreed to Coymans' participation on the condition that he could swiftly provide the first payment required to activate the contract. This payment was facilitated by the Coymans House in Amsterdam, which financed the settlement of debts owed to the Monarchy

42 Jonatán Orozco Cruz, "Barroso, Porcio y Coymans: redes y entramados mercantiles en la articulación de los asientos de negros de finales del siglo XVII (1675–1692)", in *Tratas atlánticas y esclavitudes en América, siglos XVI-XIX*, edited by Manuel Fernández Chaves and Rafael Pérez García (Sevilla: Editorial Universidad de Sevilla, 2021), 125–140; Scelle, *La traite négrière*, vol. 1, 831–836.

43 C. M. Shaw, "The Overseas Spanish Empire and the Dutch Republic Before and After the Peace of Munster", *De Zeventiende Eeuw* 13 (1997), 131–139. Thomas, *The Slave Trade.* Jonatán Orozco Cruz, "Redes transnacionales de comercio en el asiento de negros: La compañía de Juan Barroso del Pozo y Nicolás Porcio (1675–1682)", *Hacer historia moderna: Líneas actuales y futuras de investigación*, edited by Juan José Iglesias Rodríguez y Isabel María Melero Muñoz (Sevilla: Editorial Universidad de Sevilla, 2020), 319–31.

44 *Coleccion de los tratados de paz, alianza, neutralidad, garantía, protección, tregua, mediación, accesión, reglamento de limites, comercio, navigacion, etc. hechos por los pueblos, reyes, y príncipes de España con los pueblos, reyes príncipes, republicas, y demás potencias de Europea, y otras partes del mundo, y entre sì mismos, y con sus respectivos adversarios, y juntamente de los hechos directa, ò indirectamente contra ella,* part 2 (Madrid: Diego Peralta, Antonio Marin y Juan de Zuñiga, 1740), 478 and 681.

45 J. E. Wills, *1688. A Global History* (New York: W. W. Norton, 2001) p. 50 ; Delgado Ribas, "The Slave Trade in the Spanish Imperial System", 25.

46 Violet Barbour, *Capitalism in Amsterdam in the Seventeenth Century* (Ann Arbor: University of Michigan Press, 1963), 110–111; Kenneth Gordon Davies, *The Royal African Company,* London : Taylor & Francis, 1957. Scelle, *La traite négrière*, 641–676, where he places particular emphasis om the Coymans administration as a means to take over Barroso and Porcio's debts.

and funded the construction of a Spanish fleet in the city's shipyards. In addition to paying for the fleet, the Coymans family also advanced the taxes that Balthasar was required to pay to import European goods into Spanish America.[47] The news of Coymans' success spread quickly, and by 1685, the highest Spanish colonial administrators were aware of his achievements in manning the a*siento*.[48]

Despite the initial success of Balthasar Coymans as *asentista*, his relationship with certain members of the court in Madrid soured, partly due to the influence of some members of the *consulado* of Seville. In 1686, the Council of Castile initiated an hostile campaign against Coymans by investigating whether the *asiento* he had received three years earlier had been legally signed.[49] As the investigation progressed during the summer of 1686, and with his trade activities paralysed until a conclusion was reached, Coymans and his Dutch partners refused to acknowledge the jurisdiction of the Council and the *Junta de Asiento de Negros* to rule on the validity of the *asiento*. They continued to trading with the Caribbean,[50] arguing that ceasing the importation of enslaved Africans would not only ruin their firm by making them unable to meet the contract's obligations and payments to the Crown, but it would also end Curaçao's prominence as a hub for Caribbean distribution of enslaved Africans. English traders had already developed Jamaica for the same purpose, and without the Coymans' business, Curaçao would lose its advantage to Jamaica.[51]

Further complicating matters, the exclusivity agreement with the WIC for the supply of the enslaved Africans to Curaçao, along with difficulties in meeting the supply quotas stipulated by the *asiento,* left Coymans and his partner, Pedro van Belle, in a precarious position. They were squeezed between financiers (Coijmans House and their partners) and exclusive suppliers (WIC) in

47 Wills, *1688. A Global History*, 85; Barbour, *Capitalism in Amsterdam*, 111.

48 AHNOB/1//OSUNA,CT.106,D.12 : *Carta de Rodrigo Gómez a [Manuel Diego López de Zúñiga Mendoza Sotomayor, X] Duque de Béjar informando de la concesión de un asiento de negros en el Río de la Plata a favor de Baltasar Coymans y pide recomendaciones personales para que su hijo Pedro sea empleado en ese negocio. Menciona también a Gaspar de Rebolledo, Juan Pimentel como Gobernador de Buenos Aires y a [Carlos José Gutiérrez de los Ríos Roha, VI] Conde de Fernán-Núñez.*, Antwerp, 17 April 1685.

49 James A. Rawley and Stephen D. Behrend, *The Transatlantic Slave Trade : A History, revisited edition* (Lincoln and London: University of Nebraska Press, 1981), particularly chapter 4.

50 I. A. Wright, "The Coymans Asiento (1685–1689)", *Bijdragen voor Vaderlandse Geschiedenis en Oudheidkunde* 6 (1924), 38.

51 Silva Mazagalli, Paul Butel, Hubert Bonin, eds., *Négoce, ports et océans, XVIe–XXe siècles*: mélanges offerts à Paul Butel (Bordeaux: Presses Universitaires de Bordeaux, 2000).

Amsterdam, the demands of the contract as dictated by Madrid, and a vast network of agents in Jamaica, Curaçao and Spanish America.[52]

The death of Balthasar Coymans in 1686, leaving his partner Pedro van Belle as his presumptive successor, gave the Spanish authorities an opportunity to review the terms of the Coymans *asiento.* Van Belle's delayed return from the Caribbean to Spain, combined with the Spanish authorities' seizure of the assets and management records of Van Belle & Coymans, led to the proposal that Jan Carcau, one of Coymans' former employees, should continue the *asiento*. However, Carcau was arrested in March 1688 in Cadiz, accused of robbery and fraud.[53] In light of his arrest, the *Junta* seized the opportunity to terminate the *asiento* contracted with Balthasar Coymans by forcing the remaining partners to acknowledge the *Junta*'s jurisdiction over the legality of the original agreement.[54] Despite the continued refusal of the Coymans partners to recognise this jurisdiction, with Balthasar deceased, Pedro travelling between the Caribbean, Madrid, Cadiz and Amsterdam, and Carcau arrested, the *asiento* was returned to Nicolàs Porcio in 1688 and remained under his control until 1691, following his release from detention in Portobelo by the authorities in Cartagena de las *Indias*. Chapter 6 will explore the complexities of the Coymans's tenure of the *Asiento*.

The end of the Dutch direct participation in the *asiento* brought about yet another shift in the contract, as it entered a phase in which the trade in enslaved Africans was to be organised by merchants in the Spanish American colonies and the Portuguese possessions in West Africa. From 1692, Bernardo Francisco Marín de Guzmán, a prominent merchant in Caracas contracted the *asiento*. What he failed to disclose while negotiating with Madrid was his plan to enter the slave trade by forming partnerships with African traders of Portuguese descent and Portuguese traders in Guinea. The negotiations with the *Companhia de Cacheu e Cabo Verde* (Company of Cacheu and Cape Verde), represented by Manuel Ferreira de Carvalho, began before the end of 1692, but Marín de Guzmán's early death not only endangered the conclusion of these negotiations but the *asiento* itself.[55] For this reason, and citing the advanced stage of the negotiations, the *Companhia de Cacheu e Cabo Verde* petitioned

52 Wright, "The Coymans Asiento", 23–62. For a first hand account of Van Belle's precarious situation Van Belle, *Pertinent en Waarachtig Verhaal*; Ramona Negron goes into further detail on Van Belle's predicament in *Dutch Entrepreneurship in the Spanish Empire, 1580–1700*, PhD diss. (Leiden: Leiden University Press, 2025).

53 Postma, *The Dutch in the Atlantic Slave Trade*, 41; Wright, "The Coymans Asiento", 51.

54 Wills, *1688. A Global History*, 51–52.

55 Rolando Melaffe, *Negro Slavery in Latin America*, Berkeley : University of California Press, 1975, 52.

the court in Madrid and was recognised as the new legal *asentista*. Fifty-six years after being excluded from the direct trade in enslaved Africans to the Spanish Main, the Portuguese took once again the initiative to exploit the slave trade. The *asiento* continued until 1703, despite the need to renegotiate the position of the *Companhia de Cacheu e Cabo Verde* after 1699, particularly following the death of Charles II in 1700, when Spain was left without a royal successor. With the end of the Spanish Habsburg line, Manuel de Belmonte, with the implicit support of Francisco de Schonenberg, sought to cooperate with Luis and Simão Rodrigues de Sousa, representatives of the *Companhia*, following their vested interests in the Coymans' *asiento* of the 1680s, as discussed in Chapter 7.

The death of Charles II and the presumed succession of Phillip, Duke of Anjou (the future King Philip V of Spain), the first of the Bourbon dynasty, brought about a somewhat chaotic end to the Habsburg *asiento de negros*. While the *Companhia de Cacheu e Cabo Verde* remained as *asentista* under the contract signed with Charles II, Philip V also granted the same *asiento* to one of his supporters during his bid for the Spanish throne in the War of Spanish Succession (1700–1713), a figure known to historians as Jean-Baptiste du Casse.

Jean du Casse had been a loyal supporter of Philip's ascension to the Spanish throne, as he was seen as one of the enforcers of the testament of Charles II's testament, which had named Philip as his successor. Along with other supporters, including Louis XIV, King of France, Jean devised a series of preemptive attacks on Spanish American ports in an attempt to disrupt the flow of silver to Europe. The aim was to deprive Philip's enemies of the bullion needed to oppose his claim. Louis XIV supported the plan, seeing these attacks as an integral part of the Nine Years' War (1688–1697). In this context, the French raided and plundered Cartagena in May 1697, against Du Casse's advice to target Portobello, which was then the main port of bullion export. The end of the war in September 1697, saw Spain's recognition of French sovereignty over Tortuga and Saint-Domingue, while the ports in the Spanish American Main, which had been plundered and besieged earlier that spring, were left largely intact. However, the post-Nine Years War world saw Spain's growing dependence on French shipping, not only for the importation of silver but also for maintaining the slave trade.[56] In this new context, all negotiations surrounding the War of Spanish Succession were deeply affected by the

56 Kenneth R. Maxwell, "Hegemonies Old and New : the Ibero-Atlantic in the Long Eigthteenth Century", in *Colonial Legacies : The Problem of Persistence in Latin American History*, edited by Jeremy Adelman (New York and London: Routledge, 1999), 73.

ambitions of the countries involved, each seeking to secure the *asiento de Negros* for themselves. Portugal was unwilling to relinquish its acquired rights to the *asiento* with the contract signed between Charles II and the *Companhia de Cacheu e Cabo Verde*, while the English, Dutch and French eagerly vied for the contract.

Despite the interventions of Manuel de Belmonte and Francisco de Schonenberg in favour of the Portuguese, the French managed to assert their dominance, as Spain's dependence on French shipping and military forces to enforce Charles II's testament after 1700 was crucial for a Spanish victory against the allied Protestant forces of William V, stadholder of the Dutch Republic, who became William III, King of England, after 1689.[57] Philip, Duke of Anjou, already using the title and royal prerogatives as Philip V, signed a new *asiento de Negros* with his loyal supporter, Jean-Baptiste du Casse, for the duration of the War of Spanish Succession.

As the signatory of the *asiento*, Du Casse worked not in his own name, but on behalf of the *Compagnie de Guinée et de l'Assiente des Royaume de France*, a company created in 1684. Since the 1680s, the company's main goal had been to import enslaved Africans from Guinea to Saint-Domingue and export sugar onto the port of Nantes.[58] This relatively small company would have been unable to fulfil the *asiento* had it not been for the reorganisation that took place after 1701, whereby the company became the first and only charted company in the history of the Atlantic to have, simultaneously, the King of France and the King of Spain as shareholders, together holding one-quarter of the company's total capital, as will be discussed in detail in Chapter 8.

The end of the War of Spanish Succession in 1713 marked the conclusion of the Spanish Habsburgs' involvement in the slave trade. However, the repercussions of the Habsburg *asientos de Negros* did not end in 1713. For the *Compagnie de Guinée*, the conclusion of the *asiento* marked the end of French slave trading organised by chartered companies. After 1713, French private traders from Nantes, Bordeaux, La Rochelle, Le Havre, and Saint Malo were permitted to participate in the slave trade south of Sierra Leone. This free trade involved transporting enslaved Africans to the French West Indies and paying taxes for

---

57 Jutta Wimmler, *The Sun King's Atlantic : Drugs, Demons and Dyestuffs in the Atlantic World* (Leiden: Brill, 2017), 149.

58 Colin A. Palmer, "The Company Trade and the Numerical Distribution of Slaves to Spanish America, 1703–1739", in *Africans in Bondage : Studies in Slavery and the Slave Trade. Essays in Honor of Philip D. Curtin on the Occasion of the Twenty-Fifth Anniversary of African Studies at the University of Wisconsin*, edited by Philip D. Curtin and Paul E. Lovejoy (Madison: University of Wisconsin African Studies Program, 1986), 27–42.

each enslaved person traded upon their return to Europe.[59] The Portuguese slave trade continued with the broad participation from investors and merchants in Portugal, Brazil, Angola, and Cape Verde. However, it was the end of the Habsburg *asientos* that inaugurated an era of rapid growth in British participation in the slave trade, particularly after the South Sea Company signed the *Real Asiento de Inglaterra* for a period of thirty years. Even though the ruling monarch changed from a Habsburg to a Bourbon, the jurisdictional boundaries of the contract remained as they had been for most of the seventeenth century. The transnational nature of the *asiento* also continued well into the eighteenth century, although by mid-century, subjects of the Spanish King were given the licences, privileges, and small *asientos* to actively participate in and organise the slave trade into the Spanish Americas,[60] such as Miguel de Uriarte, who signed the contract as representative of Aguirre, Aristegui, Enrile & Co., in what historians refer to as the *Compañia Gaditana*.[61] However, even here, capital was drawn from various international investors, marking a return of Genoese businessmen to the supply of enslaved Africans to the Americas.[62]

Voiced in this co-authored endeavour, our aim of portraying the diversity of business organisations, and the individual rather than communal transnationality associated with the *asiento* and its development over more than a century, has, however, precluded us from engaging meaningfully with the business organisations, transnational networks, and structural transformations that the introduction of the *asientos* in Europe triggered in the coastal regions of West and West Central Africa. The available archival materials merit a central role in future research, wherein scholars may wish to investigate the networks of investors and traders involved in the enslavement of human beings along the West African coast and its immediate hinterlands.

---

59 Elisabeth Heijmans, *The Agency of Empire : Personal Connections and Individual Strategies in the Shaping of the French Early Modern Expansion (1686–1746)*, PhD diss. Leiden: Leiden University, 2018,. 47 and 49; for a revised version see Elisabeth Heijmans, *The Agency of Empire: Connections and Strategies in French Overseas Expansion (1686–1746)* (Leiden: Brill, 2020).

60 Alex Borucki, "From Asiento to Spanish Networks. Slave Trading in Río de La Plata, 1700–1800", in *From the Galleons to the Highlands: Slave Trade Routes in the Spanish Americas*, edited by Philip D. Curtin and Paul E. Lovejoy (Albuquerque: University of New Mexico Press, 2020), 177–200.

61 Bibiano Torres Ramirez, *La Compañia Gaditana de negros* (Seville : Escuela de Estudios Hispano-Americanos de Sevilla), 1973.

62 Catia Brilli, "Los genoveses en el comercio americano de esclavos (segunda mitad del siglo XVIII)", *Rivista storica italiana*, 127, no. 1 (2015), 159–82.

CHAPTER 1

Direct Management of the 'Portuguese' *Asientos*

Two decades after Colombus' pioneering the transatlantic voyage to the Caribbean, permission to take slaves into Spanish America directly from West Africa was first granted by emperor Charles V to a selected few. These first shipments were followed by nearly eight decades of licences and *ad hoc* permits to market enslaved labour in the Spanish West Indies before the Hispanic Monarchy adopted a more systematised and tightly regulated framework of supply.[1] As the sixteenth century progressed, and the transatlantic trade became an economically strategic and lucrative activity, the Monarchy sought new ways to regulate and derive income from it. This lead to the creation, right at the turn of the century, of an exclusive mercantile supply contract for the provisioning of enslaved Africans to the entirety of its American domains, the *asiento de negros*.[2]

Starting in 1595, Portuguese merchant-bankers took advantage of being subjects of the Spanish Habsburg monarchs to secure all of the first six *asientos*, which allowed them to licence all transatlantic slave voyages to Spanish America. Their grip on the transatlantic trafficking circuits grew tighter because they were also tax-farmers on Portuguese areas in the West Coast of Africa, and therefore able to regulate the access to the supply markets and to tax the purchase of slaves. At the same time, while government contracts for supply and distribution were ratified in Lisbon and Madrid respectively, merchants and shipmasters who also hailed from Portugal acquired many of the *asiento*'s export licences. Bearing these legal permits, they dispatched from the West African coast a great number of human beings to Spanish America.

This provision system, whereby Portuguese merchant elites controlled the licensing and taxation of the trade, and the middle tier of colonial traders managed the transport and exchanges necessary to acquire and distribute African enslaved labour, collapsed forty-five years after its inception. In December 1640 the Kingdom of Portugal seceded from the Hispanic Monarchy, turning the Spanish empire's leading slave traders into rebels overnight. As a result,

1 And also of sporadic of one-off government contracts to deliver a predetermined number of Africans captives Eagle and Wheat, "The Early Iberian Slave Trade", 53–54.

2 For more details see the introduction to this book and the secondary literature quoted therein.

Portuguese financiers lost their grip on the *asiento* contracts, and legal access to Spanish American ports was denied to Portuguese slaving ships. Concomitantly, Spanish traders who wished to barter for slaves had to look elsewhere than the Portuguese offshoots on the coasts of Upper Guinea and West Central Africa. The implosion of the Union of the Crowns lead to the severing of all official ties between West African slave provenance zones controlled by the Portuguese and the consumption markets in Spanish America.[3]

Transatlantic slave trade during the era of the so-called Portuguese *asientos* has long attracted the interest of historians of different backgrounds and specialisations.[4] More than a century ago, Georges Scelle pioneered the juridical analysis of the legally binding contracts between the Spanish monarchs and a range of private traders, subjects and non-subjects of the king. In his work, Scelle saw these *asiento* contracts as forerunners of international law and economic diplomacy.[5] On the other hand, scholars of the Spanish Atlantic viewed the *asiento de negros* as an eloquent example of the inbuilt flaws of the Hispanic colonial system. According to them, the *asiento* gave foreign interlopers legal footing to trade manufactured goods and other non-Spanish exports to Spain's colonies, using foreign ships to do so, in an exchange that resulted in the siphoning of bullion away from Spain.[6]

Until recently, Spanish America was the great blind spot in the estimations of the numbers of Africans trafficked to the Americas. The launching of the Transatlantic Trade Database, or TSTD, now ongoing in one of his many iterations, along with the work of Spanish-speaking scholars who had previously attempted to quantify the number of enslaved individuals brought to Spanish America, was aided by the database as a means to see many of their claims corroborated. The availability of this so-called 'Spanish data' has also enabled American or British-trained scholars to overcame their linguistic shortcom-

3 Enriqueta Vila Vilar, "La Sublevacion de Portugal y La Trata de Negros", *Ibero-Amerikanisches Archiv* 2, no. 3 (1976), 171–92.

4 Roquinaldo Ferreira and Tatiana Seijas, "The Slave Trade to Latin America: A Historiographical Assessment", in *Afro-Latin American Studies: An Introduction*, edited by Alejandro de la Fuente and George Reid Andrews (Cambridge: Cambridge University Press, 2018), 27–51.

5 Scelle, *La traite négrière*. For a more recent survey on the asiento from the perspective of international law, Andrea Weindl, "The Asiento de Negros and International Law", *Journal of the History of International Law/Revue d'histoire Du Droit International* 10, no. 2 (2008), 229–57.

6 For a representative example of a study that espouses this idea, Stanley J. Stein and Barbara H. Stein, *Silver, Trade, and War: Spain and America in the Making of Early Modern Europe* (Baltimore: The Johns Hopkins University Press, 2000).

ings and engage with more up-to-date knowledge regarding the slave exports to Spain's New World colonies.[7]

Social and cultural historians, for their part, have noted that the a*siento de Negros* was the legal framework that enabled Spanish officials and merchant capitalists from the metropole to capitalise on the 'Africanisation' of Spanish American societies.[8] More recently, the movement of slave traders, skippers and crews operating under the auspices of the *asientos* (or openly circumventing them) have become a staple of the connected histories of Iberian societies, as they embodied the more intense exchanges between Portuguese and Spanish territories, including their respective overseas offshoots, in the lead-up to and during the Union of the Crowns.[9]

While these different surveys have covered a lot of ground, several key aspects of the first *asientos* remain misunderstood, with particular gaps regarding the bureaucratic procedures that took place in West Africa, the funding of Atlantic slaving operations, and its profitability remaining unresolved. Also unclear is the way in which the "metropolitan state", understood here as the Hispanic Monarchy, benefitted from the slave trade of its American domains. Miguel Rodrigues offers the most comprehensive examination of the 'Portuguese' *asientos* to date, finally clarifying some of these matters and, for the first time, firmly linking the demand side in Spanish America to the political and economic developments in Western Central Africa.[10] Drawing on some

7 David Wheat, "The First Great Waves: African Provenance Zones for the Transatlantic Slave Trade to Cartagena de India, 1570–1640", *The Journal of African History* 52, no. 1 (2011), 1–22; Borucki, Eltis and Wheat, "Atlantic History", *American Historical Review* 120, no. 2 (2015), 433–61; Enriqueta Vila Vilar, *Hispanoamérica y el comercio de esclavos: los asientos portugueses* (Seville: Estudios Hispanoamericanos de Sevilla, 1977).

8 Emily Berquist Soule, "From Africa to the Ocean Sea: Atlantic Slavery in the Origins of the Spanish Empire", *Atlantic Studies* 15, no. 1 (2018), 16–39; Sherwin K. Bryant, Rachel Sarah O'Toole, and Ben Vinson, eds., *Africans to Spanish America: Expanding the Diaspora* (Urbana/Chicago/Springfield: University of Illinois Press, 2012); Gwendolyn Midlo Hall, *Slavery and African Ethnicities in the Americas: Restoring the Links* (Chapel Hill: University of North Carolina Press, 2009); Frederick P. Bowser, *The African Slave in Colonial Peru, 1524–1650* (Stanford: Standford University Press, 1974).

9 Tamar Herzog, "Una Monarquía, Dos Territorios. La Frontera Entre Españoles y Portugueses: España y Portugal Durante (y Después) de La Unión", in *Espanã y Portugal En El Mundo (1581–1668)*, edited Carlos Martínez Shaw and J. A. Martínez Torres (Madrid: Polifemo, 2014), 139–155; Sanjay Subrahmanyam, "Holding the World in Balance: The Connected Histories of the Iberian Overseas Empires, 1500–1640", *The American Historical Review* 112, no. 5 (2007), 1359–85.

10 Miguel Geraldes Rodrigues, *Between West Africa and America. The Angolan Slave Trade in the Portuguese and Spanish Atlantic Empires (1560–1641)* PhD diss. (Florence: European University Institute, 2019).

of Rodrigues' proposals, as well as reference studies on the slave trade to colonial Spanish America, this chapter re-examines the contours, and re-contextualises the purpose and outcomes of the *asiento de negros* during its first iteration (1595–1640), with particular attention to the transnational character of the actors involved and the diversity of business organisations that stood at the core of these contracts.

1 The Lead up to the 'Portuguese' *Asientos*

In the aftermath of the dynastic crisis that followed the death of Cardinal-King Henrique of Avis, who left the Portuguese throne without an heir, Phillip II, King of Spain, claimed the vacant Portuguese throne in 1580, through a combination of legitimate inheritance claims, support of the kingdom's elite groups, and armed force. Although Spanish troops were dispatched across the border to subdue a rival claimant, the union between Portugal, its overseas domains, and Philip II's Monarchy did not occur under the normative framework of the *right of conquest*. As such, Portuguese political institutions and governing bodies continued to uphold the kingdom's pre-existing laws and customs and were not absorbed by, or subordinated to, their Spanish counterparts. *De jure,* and for the most part *de facto* too, Portugal and its empire remained under the jurisdiction of its native governing bodies and administrative apparatus.[11]

By the same token, however, the subjects of the Portuguese Crown continued to be treated as foreigners in the other kingdoms and territories under Philip II's sovereignty. Portuguese *naturais* were legally barred from pursuing economic opportunities (such as trade) and political careers (by taking posts in the royal or municipal administration) in other Habsburg polities, including in its colonies. In this sense, the Habsburg Atlantic empire, the so-called Indies of Castile (*Indias de Castela*), was under the aegis of the Castilian Crown and was to be economically exploited by its *naturales* only, through the *consulado* of Seville, whereas Brazil and the West Coast of Africa fell

11 Pedro Cardim, "Portugal's Elites and the Status of the Kingdom of Portugal within the Spanish Monarchy", *Monarchy Transformed: Princes and Their Elites in Early Modern Western Europe,* edited by Robert von Friedeburg and John Morrill (Cambridge: Cambridge University Press, 2017), 212–43; John H. Elliott, "The Spanish Monarchy and the Kingdom of Portugal, 1580–1640", in *Conquest and Coalescence. The Shaping of the State in Early Modern Europe,* edited by Mark Greengrass (London: Edward Arnold, 1991), 48–67.

under the authority of the Crown of Portugal. Portugal's territories and overseas interests answered directly to the Council of Portugal, set up at the court of Madrid (but comprised of Portuguese aristocrats and jurists), and other councils of government and administration that convened in Lisbon, rather than to Castile's *Consejo de Hacienda* and *Consejo de Indias*.[12]

While the Union of the Iberian Crowns was a watershed moment in the history of the Iberian empires, historians believe it is more accurate to view those sixty years as the culmination of a process long in the making. The break with what came before was less pronounced than previously thought, as the Portuguese and Spanish empires were already becoming more tightly entangled well before 1580, thanks to Portuguese commercial inroads and immigration into Spain and Spanish America, and due to Spain's diplomatic and cultural influence over Portuguese court circles.[13] If formal political aggregation was preceded by the interpenetration of individuals, goods, artistic forms, and ideas, the Dual Monarchy did not bring political, institutional or cultural uniformity to the peoples of Iberia.[14] This opposition between the principle of institutional separation between the different constituent polities of the same Monarchy and the economic and demographic interdependence played a major part in the politics and practice of the first *asientos*. One of the areas where the tension between these push-and-pull factors was clearest was precisely the Portuguese involvement in the slave trade to the Spanish empire.[15]

Before the creation of the *asiento*, the holders of *licencias de negros* – permits required by the state for the shipment of enslaved Africans to Spanish

12 Pedro Cardim, Antonio Feros, and Gaetano Sabatini, "The Political Constitution of the Iberian Monarchies", in *The Iberian World. 1450–1820*, edited by Fernando Bouza Alvarez, Pedro Cardim, and Antonio Feros (London and New York: Routledge, 2020), 34–61; Jean-Frédéric Schaub, *Portugal na Monarquia Hispânica* (*1580–1640*) (Lisbon: Livros Horizonte, 2001).

13 Daviken Studnicki-Gizbert, *A Nation upon the Ocean Sea: Portugal's Atlantic Diaspora and the Crisis of the Spanish Empire, 1492–1640* (New York: Oxford University Press, 2007); Maria da Graça Mateus Ventura, *Os Portugueses no Peru ao tempo da União Ibérica: mobilidade, cumplicidade e vivências*, vol. 1 (Lisbon: Imprensa Nacional-Casa da Moeda, 2005); Subrahmanyam, 'Holding the World in Balance'; Fernando Bouza Alvarez, *Portugal en la Monarquia Hispanica* (*1580–1640*). *Felipe II, las Cortes y la genesis del Portugal catolico,* PhD diss. (Madrid: Universidad Complutense de Madrid, 1987).

14 Brian Hamm, "Constructing and Contesting Portuguese Difference in Colonial Spanish America, 1500–1650", *Anais de História de Além-Mar* XVII (2016), 303–336.

15 Kara D. Schultz, "Interwoven: Slaving in the Southern Atlantic under the Union of the Iberian Crowns, 1580–1640", *Journal of Global Slavery* 2, no. 3 (2017), 248–272; António de Almeida Mendes, Carlos Martínez Shaw, and J. A. Martínez Torres, "Sueños y invenciones en el Atlántico en la ocasión Africana y Ibérica. Estrategias de unión y desunión de los imperios de España y Portugal en los viejos mundos (Siglos XV–XVII)', in *España y*

America – were often granted them as rewards for loyalty and service to the Crown, including for renegotiating the Monarchy's short-term debt with German and Genoese merchant bankers. In most cases, the recipients had little exposure to, or practical knowledge of, the Atlantic slave trade and opted to sell the licences to individuals who had extensive experience in the heinous trade of enslaved Africans and,[16] moreover, had access to the trading outposts of their King.[17] Unsurprisingly, a large number of the licences issued prior to 1580 ended up in the hands of Portuguese merchants, their skippers, and their ships.

Since the early 1520s, Portuguese slave traders, operating out of their country of origin or already based in Andalusia, purchased licences from their original recipients (on a secondary market of sorts),[18] or were commissioned by the *Casa de Contratacíon* (at the request of the Crown) to supply a specific number of slaves to certain regions of Spanish America.[19] This extensive reliance on these slavers was opposed from early on by the *consulado de cargadores*, the merchants' guild and commercial court of Seville,[20] whose members saw direct trade between Africa and the Americas as a threat to their commercial privileges. They strongly objected to non-members trading with the Spanish West Indies in general, and specifically to slave-carrying vessels sailing directly from the West Coast of Africa to Spanish America and not joining the fleets of the *Carrera de Indias* (sailing under the status of *navios sueltos*). The *consulado*'s pleas for the Monarchy to demand that all slave voyages

---

Portugal En El Mundo (1561–1668), edited by edited by Carlos Martínez Shaw and José Antonio Martínez Torres (Madrid: Polifemo, 2014), 195–218.

16 García Fuentes, "Licencias para la introducción de esclavos", 1–46.

17 Toby Green, *The Rise of the Trans-Atlantic Slave Trade in Western Africa, 1300–1589* (New York: Cambridge University Press, 2012), 248–52; Maria Manuel Ferraz Torrão, "Rotas Comerciais, Agentes Económicos, Meios de Pagamento", in *História Geral de Cabo Verde*, edited by Maria Emília Madeira Santos, vol. 2 (Lisbon and Praia: Instituto de Investigação Científica Tropical and Instituto Nacional de Cultura de Cabo Verde, 1995), 17–124; Rafael Donoso Anes, "Algunos aspectos relacionados con el control administrativo y contable de la renta de los esclavos enviados a Hispanoamérica', *Revista Española de Financiación y Contabilidad* 30, no. 110 (2001), 1103.

18 Fernández Chaves and Pérez Garcia, 'La penetración económica', 199–222; Enrique Otte and Conchita Ruiz-Burruecos, "Los portugueses en La trata de esclavos negros de las postmerias del siglo XVI", *Moneda y Crédito*, no. 85 (1963), 3–31.

19 Mendes, "The Foundations of the System", 74; There were also Portuguese financiers who having received licenses as collateral and compensation for their state loans, actually made use of them to launch slave voyages, opting not selling them on the "secondary market". The Nunes Caldeira in the 1550s and 1560s are a case in point. See: Rodrigues, *Between West Africa and America*, 229ss.

20 And likewise a frequent money lenders to the crown and tax farmer.

return to Andalusia and join the armed convoy naturally fell on deaf hears because of the longer duration of the voyages (which had the potential to sharply increase mortality rates on board), higher shipping costs, fewer opportunities to import exclusive American commodities and bullion, and slower turnover of capital for investors.[21] Despite the staunch opposition of Seville's *consulado de cargadores*, and fears that Portuguese merchants would defraud the royal treasury by engaging in widespread smuggling, Philip II turned to his new subjects when it came to reform the system of *ad hoc licencias*.

By 1580 it had become clear that the system in place was ill-suited to meet Madrid's goals for the transatlantic slave trade. Incidental licences failed to satisfy the labour force demands of the mining sector (which relied not on the native American powered extraction of silver and gold), urban manufacturing, public works, and the elite household economies of Spanish America.[22] Furthermore, this haphazard system of labour export permits did not generate the steady revenue streams that the royal exchequer needed to forecast its military and redistributive expenses, and which could equally be earmarked to public debt servicing.[23] These dysfunctions partially stemmed from the preference of many holders of *licencias* to delay selling them, waiting for the market value of slaves to rise in America before making more licences available, leading to a continuous valuation of the enslaved as commodities in the buying markets in the Spanish Caribbean and elsewhere in Spanish America. The result of these speculative practices was a disturbance in the supply

21 For an overview of the community of merchants that received the prerogative to conduct most of Spain's commercial exchanges with the American colonies, Jeremy Baskes, *Staying Afloat: Risk and Uncertainty in Spanish Atlantic World Trade, 1760–1820* (Stanford University Press, 2013) chapter 3; Xabier Lamikiz, *Trade and Trust in the Eighteenth-Century Atlantic World: Spanish Merchants and Their Overseas Networks* (Woodbridge: The Boydell Press, 2013).

22 Labour intensive cultivation of cash crops would only become a mainstay of Spain's colonial economy well into the eighteenth century, when the Cuban and Puerto Rico sugar cycles began. Therefore, it was not in plantations, but in the activities listed above, that the vast majority of enslaved Africans were put to work in the sixteenth and seventeenth centuries. Pablo Miguel Sierra Silva, *Urban Slavery in Colonial Mexico* (Cambridge: Cambridge University Press, 2018); Kris Lane, "Africans and Natives in the Mines of Spanish America", in *Beyond Black and Red. African-Native Relations in Colonial Latin America*, edited by Matthew Restall (Albuquerque: University of New Mexico Press, 2005), 156–86; Herman L. Bennett, *Africans in Colonial Mexico: Absolutism, Christianity, and Afro-Creole Consciousness, 1570–1640* (Bloomington: Indiana University Press, 2003); Luz María Martínez-Montiel, "The Influence of Blacks in the Americas", in *From Chins to Bonds. The Slave Trade Revisited*, edited by Doudou Diène (New York-Oxford: Berghahn, 2001), 376–94.

23 Drelichman and Voth, *Lending to the Borrower from Hell.*

chains and a shortage of labour in the Spanish West Indies, which negatively impacted the colonial economy.

The royal purse was also directly affected by speculative trade in the licences. Once speculators decided to place the licences on the market, the value of the new *licencias* issued by the Crown decreased, affecting the exchequer's ability to extract income from their sale. Simultaneously, the economic downturn caused by fewer slaves being imported into Spanish America meant diminishing returns in tax collection on mining (the net income of the royal fifth was smaller), production in the Americas, as well in tariffs levied on colonial trade and shipping.[24] But the main problem besetting the provision of colonial slave labour before 1580 was Spain's dependency on supply markets and traders outside its empire.

The Treaty of Alcáçovas (1479), ratified by the Portuguese monarch and the Catholic kings of Castile and Aragon, saw the soon-to-be united Spanish Crowns relinquish all claims to trade and settlement on the West African coast in favour of Portugal.[25] As a result, Spain became reliant on subjects of the Portuguese Crown who bartered for slaves on West Africa to supply its American colonies with enslaved labour. In practice, however, Alcáçovas was unable to create a 'national' barrier that would effectively prevent or hinder the bilateral trade between West Africa and Spanish America. Extensive Portuguese-Spanish investments and logistics led to operational cooperation, established early on by Portuguese and Spanish (as well as Italian and Flemish) financiers, insurers, traders and ship-owners.[26] Portuguese subjects undersigned the official paperwork that enabled a group of silent transnational investors to barter for slaves in West Africa, while a Castilian associate could serve as the legal front for that same partnership to sell those captives in Spanish America. As far as the Iberian-Atlantic slaving was concerned, the Union of the Crowns may have had political and diplomatic implications for the central government of the Monarchy, but it did not fundamentally change the organisational practices or investment structures. Although Spanish merchants and skippers continued to be denied access to the trading stations and offshore bartering areas controlled by the Portuguese Crown, after 1580 the Monarchy

24 Rodrigues, *Between West Africa and America*, 134, 228–229, 234–235.

25 Bailey W. Diffie and George Winius, *Foundations of the Portuguese Empire: 1415–1580* (Minneapolis: University of Minnesota Press, 1977); Ivana Elbl, "Cross-Cultural Trade and Diplomacy: Portuguese Relations with West Africa, 1441–1521", *Journal of World History* 3, no. 2 (1992), 165–204.

26 Eagle and Wheat, "The Early Iberian Slave Trade", 60; Fernández Chaves and Pérez Garcia, "La Penetración Económica Portuguesa".

no longer had to rely on diplomatic agreements with foreign jurisdictions regarding subjects of foreign rulers, but could rather trust in its new vassals to provision Spanish America with enslaved Africans.

To ensure a steady outflow of African slaves into the Spanish Indies and an influx of related revenues into the Monarchy's treasury, while respecting the principle of institutional and economic separation between the two empires, Phillip II turned to the *contratadores*. These individuals were the tax-farmers of slaving duties and leaseholders of trade monopolies in the Western African outposts of the Portuguese Crown.[27] Since the fifteenth century, the Portuguese Crown had claimed comprehensive monopolies on the trade with West Africa, reserving the right to tax transactions conducted by its subjects in its official settlements.[28] Rather than entrusting the local bartering activities with African and Luso-African middlemen to royal factors, or assigning treasury officials to levy tariffs on all commercial exchanges, the Crown opted to farm out the monopolies and tax collection to private merchants, usually organised in partnerships, who bid on public auctions organised by the royal exchequer in Lisbon. Every three or six years, temporary partnerships of affluent metropolitan merchants leased from the Portuguese Crown three separate revenue farms for West Africa – the Cape Verde-Guinea, São Tomé, and Angola contracts – each named after a district of the Portuguese empire where slaves were procured.[29]

Upon securing the Portuguese throne, Phillip II decreed that licences for the export of enslaved Africans to Spanish America would be added to the clauses of the *contratos* (the royal farms for the licensing of the trade and the

27 Maria Manuel Ferraz Torrão, "Os Portugueses e o trato de escravos de Cabo Verde Com a América Espanhola no fim do século XVI. Os contratadores do trato de Cabo Verde e a Coroa, uma relação de conveniência numa época de oportunidades (1583–1600)", in *Portugal Na Monarquia Hispânica: Dinâmicas de Integração e Conflito*, edited by Pedro Cardim, Leonor Freire Costa, and Mafalda Soares da Cunha (Lisbon: CHAM, 2013), 93–106; José Gonçalves Salvador, *Os magnatas do tráfico negreiro* (São Paulo: Pioneira-Edusp, 1981).

28 Filipa Ribeiro da Silva, *Dutch and Portuguese in Western Africa: Empires, Merchants and the Atlantic System, 1580–1674* (Leiden and Boston: Brill, 2011), 82–96; Ivana Elbl, *The Portuguese Trade with West Africa, 1440–1521*, PhD diss. (Toronto: University of Toronto, 1986); António Carreira, *Notas sobre o tráfico português de escravos*, 2a ed. rev (Lisbon: Faculdade de Ciências Sociais e Humanas da Univ. Nova, 1983).

29 Revenue farming and other forms of government contracts in Habsburg Portugal are surveyed in Edgar Pereira, *A Contractor Empire;* Zelinda Cohen, "Subsídios para a História Geral de Cabo Verde: os contratos de arrendamento para a cobrança de rendas e direitos reais das ilhas de Cabo Verde (1501–1560)", *Stvdia*, no. 53 (1994), 317–364.

collection of slaving duties on the West African outposts).[30] The new clauses of the *contratos* granted the leaseholders the right to sub-contract the supply of 300 to 500 slaves to Spanish America every year for the duration of their leases, which normally lasted six years. In return, the *contratadores* paid the Spanish royal exchequer one-quarter of their reported profits from the slave sales derived from their *licencias.* Alternatively, it was stipulated that between one quarter to one third of all captives shipped from their respective districts would be earmarked to the Spanish American markets, with the remaining being exported to Brazil.[31]

While including the *licencias* in the tax farm contracts of the Portuguese Crown proved highly lucrative for the *contratadores*, this arrangement failed to live up to Madrid's financial expectations and was staunchly opposed by Seville's *consulado* and other government agencies. For example, the *Casa de la Contratacíon* was displeased with losing control over the sale of licences and being relegated to the role of a mere certification and monitoring institution. Meanwhile, the Castilian *Consejo de Hacienda* warned that the income generated by the licences had been diverted to the treasury of the Portuguese Crown, to whom the *contratadores* paid a percentage on each enslaved African sold upon disembarkation in the Spanish Indies. If the Monarchy truly hoped to place the Spanish American slave trade at the service of government borrowing, diverting the income generated from the sale of *licencias* to one of the Monarchy's peripheral treasuries, which was not involved in the annual state loans negotiated at the court, did not serve the interests of the Monarchy.

It was against this backdrop that the idea of an exclusive contract, entrusting the entire distribution of slave licences for the whole of Spanish America – and not only to a specific port, as had previously been the case – to a single concessionaire, began to gain traction at court. While the concept of an *asiento de negros* was not unheard off, it was only during the 1590s that Phillip II and his closest advisers seemed truly committed to the idea.[32]

---

30 An example is the arrangement made with the leaseholder of the *contrato* of São Tomé, the Milanese Giovanni Battista Rovellasca and the Portuguese Álvaro Mendes de Castro, who agreed to supply the Indies of Castile with slaves acquired in the adjacent West Central Africa coast (Loango, Kongo and Angola) in 1582. There were also contacts made with the *contratadores* of Cape Verde-Upper Guinea and those of Angola (a royal farm that had had been created around this time, in 1587). Rodrigues, *Between West Africa and America*, 239.

31 Rodrigues, *Between West Africa and America*, 241–47; Vilar, *Hispanoamérica*, 23–27; Scelle, *La traite négrière*, vol. 1, 324–331.

32 Eagle and Wheat, "The Early Iberian Slave Trade", 54ss; Vilar, *Hispanoamérica*, 28–32; Scelle, *La traite négrière*, vol. 1, 799–809.

The creation of the *asiento de negros* reflects Madrid's new priorities for the slave trade to Spanish America. As this trade increased in volume and value, the monarch no longer viewed it as an instrument for redistributive policies and reduced the number of grants.[33] The export of enslaved colonial labour became a strategic sector requiring close regulation – meaning the Monarchy set and enforced the terms under which private actors could participate – in order to generate income for the Spanish exchequer. Hard-pressed to raise new funds to service its short-term debt to international bankers and consolidated treasury bondholders, the Monarchy opted to entrust the wholesale distribution of the licences to royal financiers in exchange for a flat sum, rather than handle the sale of the licences to slave traders directly.[34]

At the same time, the *asiento* was intended to provide the Portuguese and Spanish subjects of the Hispanic Monarchy with an opportunity to earn a living, and potentially make a fortune, as the *asentistas* were required to sell licences to anyone who requested them. Madrid also aimed to supply the colonial governments and their subjects in the Indies with enslaved labour, while ensuring they were not overly-supplied. It was in the Crown's interest – even if to the detriment of slave buyers in the Americas – to ensure that colonial markets were never at risk of being glutted, as this would cut into the profits of the slave traders and royal contractors in Iberia. To prevent this, the Monarchy decided early on to establish annual export limits. These limits could not be too low as to jeopardise colonial production and trade, and the taxation thereof, nor so high that slave prices would deflate and merchants would no longer be willing to purchase *licencias*. A reduction in the real value of the *licencias* would drive merchant-bankers away from taking on the *asiento*, thus leaving the flat sums that the Monarchy earmarked for debt service and other royal expenditures unpaid.

The entanglement between the a*siento de negros* and the central treasury of the Spanish Monarchy followed. The royal *hacienda* welcomed the additional

33 The value of a *licencia* increased an astonishing 1,400% since they were first issued in the 1510s, and the prices of slaves on the Upper Guinea coast had also greatly increased during the second half of the sixteenth century; Rodrigues, *Between West Africa and America*, 227.

34 The political economy of Spain's early modern overseas empire is unpacked in Regina Grafe and Alejandra Irigoin, "A Stakeholder Empire: The Political Economy of Spanish Imperial Rule in America", *Economic History Review* 65, no. 2 (2012), 609–651; John H. Coatsworth, "Political Economy and Economic Organization", in *The Cambridge Economic History of Latin America*, edited by Victor Bulmer-Thomas, John H. Coatsworth, and Roberto Cortés-Conde (Cambridge: Cambridge University Press, 2005), 235–274.

revenues generated by the lump sums and taxes paid by the *asentistas,* in exchange for the prerogative to licence an expanding slave trade, the so-called *renta de esclavos negros*. These revenue streams could be allocated for the payment of interests on loans owed to court bankers, or used as disposable income when renegotiating the complex mechanisms of public debt.[35]

2 *Asientos de Negros*: The Standard Contractual Provisions

In 1594, after several years of uncertainty, the king instructed the *Consejo de Indias* to advertise and negotiate the first-ever *asiento de negros*. Several bidders expressed interest in the new slave export contract, but the choice came down to two prominent Portuguese merchant bankers, António Nunes Caldeira and Pedro Gomes Reinel, with the latter emerging as the winner.[36]

Starting with Gomes Reinel and all the way to Melchior Gomes and Cristovão Mendes de Sousa (see Table 1.1), the recipients of all six *asientos* and the lease prices were determined by a competitive system of ascending bids. This process combined public auctions with direct, but often confidential, negotiations with the *Consejo de Indias,* the *Junta de Negros,* and members of the king's entourage. Each of these entities discussed the details and practicalities of the royal contracts and provided counsel to the king, who had the final say over who would become *asentista*. The negotiations between the Crown and the various contenders for the *asiento de negros*, particularly the final round of

35 In 1617 the Spanish Monarchy renegotiated its floating, short-term debt to the Genoese banker Ottavio Centurione by assigning him with government bonds whose interests would be paid from different revenue streams. Among the new sources of income that service the interests of his newly contracted debt instrument, 3,750,000 *maravedis* (principal at an interest of 5%) from the *renta de los esclavos negros.* Centurione proceeded to parcel out smaller portions, which he sold in a "secondary market". This example shows how revenues that slave trade to the American colonies generated for the crown were embroiled in the management of Spain's public debt. Carmen Sanz-Ayan, *Un Banquero en el Siglo de Oro. Octavio Centurion, el financier de los Austrias* (Madrid: La Esfera de los Libros, 2015), 132–133.

36 Francisco Bethencourt argues for the importance and centrality the *asientos* played in the business life of Portuguese New Christians, with a particular emphasis for the first half of the seventeenth century. Francisco Bethencourt, *Stangers Within. The Rise and Fall of the New Christian Trading Elite* (Princeton : Princeton University Press, 2024), 234–279. However, he insists in the overall importance of the *asiento* for the group before 1600 and after the 1640s as well.

talks with the successful applicant, culminated in a written contract specifying the reciprocal rights and obligations of the two parties that ratified the *asiento*.

In exchange for the right to exploit the *asiento de negros*, the contractors owed the royal treasury a lump sum to be paid in Spain in different instalments, the value of which was determined by an auction and subsequent negotiations with the Monarchy. The annual price of the Portuguese *asientos* varied between 95,000 and 170,000 ducats, but if the *asiento* of João Rodrigues Coutinho is excluded due to its unique features,[37] their average value was close to 115,000 ducats (see Table 1.1). This placed the *asiento de negros* as a middle-tier government contract, as far as its revenue-generating potential for the Crown. In addition to the monetary deposit for the contract, the *asentistas* had to pledge chattels (collateral) and appoint warrantors (guarantors), whose assets, like the contractor's, would be seized if the latter failed to meet the financial obligations of the *asiento*. As with other revenue farms, the value of the collateral generally varied between one-fourth to one-third of the annual value of the *asiento*.

While the value of the tenders and the financial resources available to the candidates were the main factors considered, their reputation as capable and trustworthy businessmen, as well as their previous dealings with the Monarchy, were also taken into account. On some occasions, the *asiento* negotiations were used by the Monarchy to settle a debt with a creditor, who was offered the opportunity to operate the *asiento de negros* as payment for an outstanding debt from a previous supply contract. Finally, public-private partnerships like the *asiento de negros* were also ratified with individuals with whom the monarch and his closest circle hoped to continue doing business in the future. In such cases, the *asiento de negros* represented another step in what the Crown and the contractor hoped would be a long and mutually beneficial relationship. The strategic partnership between the two was based on the *asentista* performing a task of public utility (in this case, advancing funds through concession fees and administering the provision of enslaved labour to the American colonies), for which he would receive a return that was unattainable in non-state-related investments. Moreover, if both parties were satisfied with the management of the *asiento*, more demanding but more

37 This high value for concession fee was negotiated at the very first decade of the seventeenth century, at a time when the *asiento* was purposely granted to the Coutinho Brothers, as a collateral for leading an armed campaigns of territorial conquest in Angola, and were combined with the lease of the Angola *contrato*, which explains the significantly higher value that the concession fee reached.

TABLE 1.1 Holders of the first six *asiento de negros* (1595–1640)

Years	Asentista	Yearly concession fee (ducados)	Number of licenses allotted
1595–1600	Pedro Gomes Reinel	100,000	4,250
1600–1603	João Rodrigues Coutinho	170,000	4,250
1604–1609	Gonçalo Vaz Coutinho	140,000	4,250
1615–1623	António Fernandes d'Elvas	115,000	3,500
1624–1631	Manuel Rodrigues Lamego	120,000	3,500
1632–1640	Melchior Gomes, Cristovão Mendes de Sousa	95,000	3,500

SOURCE: MIGUEL RODRIGUES, *BETWEEN WEST AFRICA AND AMERICA. THE ANGOLAN SLAVE TRADE IN THE PORTUGUESE AND SPANISH ATLANTIC EMPIRES (1560–1640)*, PHD DISS. (FLORENCE: EUROPEAN UNIVERSITY INSTITUTE, 2019), 281.

profitable government contracts would follow, along with highly coveted honours and privileges for the *asentista*.[38]

The most important aspect of the *asiento de negros* was the exclusive right to issue permits (*licencias*) authorising traders to export and distribute enslaved Africans in ports across Spanish America for the duration of the contract, which typically lasted eight or nine years. Without these licences, slave ships were not legally cleared to call at Spanish American ports and sell their human cargos, previously acquired in West Africa. The *licencias* were, therefore, subcontracts between the holder of the government contract, the *asentista,* and the third parties who actually conducted the transatlantic slave trade to Spanish America.

Each contract set a cap on the maximum number of licences to be sold each year, or alternatively, the total number of licenses for the entire duration of the contract. During the period of the "Portuguese *asientos*", the number of licences sold annually ranged between 3,500 and 5,000.[39] These export quotas reflected the Crown's understanding of what it deemed the appropriate num-

38 For the political economy of government contracting in *Ancien Régime* Spain; Rafael Torres Sánchez, *Military Entrepreneurs and the Spanish Contractor State in the Eighteenth Century* (Oxford: Oxford University Press, 2016).

39 Vilar, *Hispanoamérica,* 54–58.

ber of enslaved workers for the Indies. As previously mentioned, from the Crown's perspective, appropriate meant meeting the needs of the colonial economy without oversupplying the market, which would cause the price of enslaved people to drop, but at the same time maintaining a stable income for the exchequer.

In addition to selling the *licencias* to third parties, the *asentista* was allowed to retain some for his own ventures and launch his own voyages. Trading in enslaved Africans could be an enticing prospect for *asentistas*, as they enjoyed certain competitive advantages over other traders, such as tax exemptions (for instance, the fee paid to the physicians who inspected the enslaved), not to mention the fact they did not have to pay for licences to operate within legal boundaries.

Besides limiting the number of *licencias* allotted to each *asentista,* the Crown fixed the price at which they should be marketed to third-parties, and determined how much should be paid to the royal treasury in taxes. The *asentistas* were permitted to sell licenses on credit, meaning they accepted deferred payments rather than requiring payment upfront. Different sale prices and duties depended on whether the licences were paid upfront in *comptoirs* in Iberia or later in Spanish America, after the slaves were disembarked and sold. A slave licence purchased on credit was more expensive than one paid upfront, but most merchants preferred the latter option, as the proceeds from the sale in Spanish America were expected to cover the licencing fee, other administrative costs, and yield a profit. The *asientos* stipulated that in Iberia, an individual *licencia* cost 30 ducats plus an additional 20 ducats of *aduanilla,*[40] while in Spanish America, slave traders were required to pay 40 ducats for the licence and 30 ducats for the *aduanilla*.

After requesting *licencias* and receiving a favourable reply from the *asentista,* those seeking permits were required to register each licence with the *Casa de Contratacíon,* which produced an official registry certifying the *licencias,* known as the *registro*. Marc Eagle has defined the *registro* as "the general list of goods, shippers and consignees, approved destinations, and royal imposts, issued after physical inspection of the ship by the Casa de Contratación in Seville".[41] It was against this *registro* that Spanish magistrates and treasury officials in the West Indies reviewed the human cargoes and proceeded to

40 Direct contribution to the taxation office.

41 Marc Eagle, "Chasing the Avença: An Investigation of Illicit Slave Trading in Santo Domingo at the End of the Portuguese Asiento Period", *Slavery & Abolition* 35, no. 1 (2014), 101.

levy taxes and tariffs accordingly. It should be noted that, since the *registro* was created before the departure of the slaving vessels for West Africa, it often did not reflect the actual number of enslaved individuals ultimately sold in the Spanish Caribbean or mainland America.

Although the *asentista* was the only entity allowed to market *licencias* for profit on the primary market, the *asiento de negros* cannot be regarded as a complete monopoly, because the king did not relinquish his customary prerogative to award licences to his vassals at his discretion. These direct permits significant for the total volume of slave exports, as they enabled their recipients to export hundreds of enslaved Africans to the Indies of Castile. Awarded in large lots, these grants were, for all intents and purposes, mini-*asientos*. In the *asiento* negotiations, the Monarchy and the prospective contract holder agreed on the maximum number of export permits the king could grant each year, which tended to be around one thousand. According to a recent estimation, the licences issued outside the *asiento* accounted for one-quarter to one-third of the annual export quotas managed by the *asentistas*. In addition to serving as a tool of royal patronage, granting *licencias* also provided the Monarchy with a way to check the extensive economic powers it had granted to the *asentistas*, and to compensate rival bidders who had been left out during the bidding process.[42]

Aware of the risks involved in the slave trade, including the high mortality rates among captives as they awaited embarkation and during the Middle Passage, the Crown included mortality discount rates in the contracts. Based on these rates, *asentistas* were allowed to issue additional permits to account for the number of casualties that occurred before the captives were sold in the American markets. The calculation of death rates was particularly significant to the balance sheet of all *asientos*, as it created a grey area that *asentistas*, licence holders and shipmasters could exploit to increase the number of captives per licence without being formally accused of defrauding the Crown. The issue of mortality compensation further complicates the already ambiguous equivalence between *licencias* and *pieza de Indias*, which was not synonymous with one individual slave. A *pieza de Indias* referred to an adult male in his prime years, typically aged between 15 and 40, excluding female captives and those from other age groups. For this reason, a conversion rate was established, whereby a certain number of women, elderly males, children, and infants were considered to have the same worth as one *pieza de Indias*.

42 Rodrigues, *Between West Africa and America*, 260–262.

These classifications allowed *asentistas* and licence holders to push beyond the export limits imposed by each individual licence.[43]

The ports where enslaved Africans could be disembarked in the Americas were specified in the written clauses of the *asiento*, which identified Veracruz, the main Atlantic port of New Spain and Central America, and Cartagena de las *Indias*, the gateway for enslaved Africans bound for South America, including major colonial markets in the viceroyalties of New Granada and especially Peru.[44] Other major slaving ports of Spanish America were conspicuous for their absence from the *asiento* provisions, none more so than Buenos Aires. Although shipments to Buenos Aires were consistently excluded from the contracts and deemed off-limits by the Crown, they were highly coveted by the *asentistas* and licence holders, as the slave transactions taking place there and at the neighbouring ports in the Rio de la Plata were paid for in untaxed silver syphoned from the Peruvian mines.[45]

To insure that the *asentistas* fulfilled the contract to the best of their ability, the Monarchy pledged to support them in various ways. This included granting permission for the *asentistas* to receive the proceeds of the sale of their *licencias* in Spanish American bullion, transported to Europe via the *Carrera de Indias*. Equally beneficial was the appointment of a royal judge to adjudicate disputes related to the implementation of the contract, particularly if these disputes directly involved the Crown or the royal institutions responsible for granting residence permits to those acting as factors of the *asiento* in Spanish American ports.

A range of additional benefits was extended to the *asentista*, including symbolic rewards designed to enhance the contractor's social standing, which made these business ventures appealing beyond purely economic considerations. Financial incentives were also significant, as the *asentistas* were

---

43 Linda A. Newson and Susie Minchin, *From Capture to Sale: The Portuguese Slave Trade to Spanish South America in the Early Seventeenth Century* (Leiden: Brill, 2007), 63–64.

44 During the period under study Cartagena de Indias was, overall, the main gateway for enslaved Africans into the Indies of Castille, and not only for Spain's South American possessions, ahead of Veracruz. Wheat, "The First Great Waves".

45 Exports via the River Plate also allowed merchants to reach customers in the southernmost parts of Spanish America faster than by sending goods on the *Tierra Firme* fleet, given that merchandise would then have to be redistributed via the great fairs held every year at the isthmus of Panama. For the River Plate trade, in slaves and other merchandises, Kara D. Schultz, "'The Kingdom of Angola Is Not Very Far from Here': The South Atlantic Slave Port of Buenos Aires, 1585–1640", *Slavery & Abolition* 36, no. 3 (2015), 424–444; Zacarías Moutoukias, *Contrabando y control colonial en el siglo XVII: Buenos Aires, el Atlántico y el espacio peruano* (Buenos Aires: Centro Editor de América Latina, 1988).

entitled to two-thirds of the value of all contraband cargoes their agents managed to apprehend, with the remaining one-third split between the prosecutor assigned to the case and the individual who reported the illegal transaction.[46] This clause demonstrates how the *asiento* was designed to involve the *asentistas* in combating fraud and smuggling in cooperation with the royal authorities, making the *asentista* a direct enforcer of the empire's political economy.

Every two years, the *asentista* was contractually obliged to inform the *Consejo de Indias* of the number of licences he had sold or used for his own benefit, and to report the operational results of *the asiento* to the *Casa de la Contratación*. The contractors had to submit copies of their ledgers to the *Consejo de Indias*, which would compare them with the records of the *registros* made by the *Casa de la Contratacíon*. The written clauses also made it clear that if the *asentistas* deviated too much from the number of *licencias* they were supposed to market, whether by over- or underselling, or if they failed to pay the contract's lump sums to the Crown, their contracts could be terminated. In such cases, the *asentista* could be immediately stripped of the right to issue additional licences, and the proceeds from sales made up to that point would be seized. Additionally, the *asentista*'s collateralised assets would be confiscated, and he would face judicial proceedings, with the risk of arrest of assets and/or potential imprisonment.

The *asentistas* were more than wholesale slave traffickers trading in large numbers of enslaved Africans for profit based on price differentials on both sides of the Atlantic. Even if they occasionally engaged in this nefarious trade themselves, they were primarily fiscal intermediaries for the Crown, ensuring that the export quotas set by the Crown were met by subcontracting the *licencias*. At the same time, they facilitated the movement and sale of enslaved Africans by others, as most of the export permits were paid only after the human cargoes had been sold in the Americas, rather than when the *licencia* was requested and the *registro* was certified in Seville. The scheme of deferred-payments, i.e., sale of *licencias* on credit, was crucial for the stability of the transatlantic trade, and explains why the trade suffered whenever government agencies took over the marketing of licences (i.e. *administracíon* rather than *asiento*).[47] The role of enabler was better performed by a merchant-banker that was solvent, well-connected to creditors who could lend money to bridge temporary cash flow gaps, and well-versed in transatlantic trade, than by an official from the royal treasury.

46 Enriqueta Vila Vilar, "Los asientos portugueses y el contrabando de negros", *Anuario de Estudios Americanos*, no. 30 (1973), 24.

47 Rodrigues, *Between West Africa and America*, 307 and 354.

3 The Organisation and Implementation of the *Asientos*

Even though the *asiento* established detailed provisions regulating nearly all aspects of the shipment and trade of enslaved Africans to Spanish America, there was nonetheless a glaring omission. No mention was made of how to access the West African slave markets where the holders of the *licencias* could acquire their human cargoes. This omission arose from the fact that the West African coast fell outside the jurisdictional scope of the Crown of Castile. As previously mentioned, it was the *contratadores,* the tax-farmers of the Portuguese Crown, who regulated the access of slave ships to the two main slave markets at the time: the greater Senegambia and Upper Guinea coast,[48] and the vast stretch of the West Central Africa from Loango to Angola. Like the *asentistas,* the *contratadores* held government contracts granting them exclusive rights to issue licences permitting others to trade in slaves, but unlike the *asiento,* their *contratos* did not grant access to the import markets in Spanish America, but rather to the export markets in West Africa.

Although the possibility of merging the Spanish *asiento de negros* with a Portuguese *contrato* into a large, all-encompassing public-private partnership was never seriously considered by the Monarchy, as it infringed on the jurisdictions of the Spanish and Portuguese Crowns, some means of coordination between the two contracts were necessary to insure the smooth provisioning of enslaved people and the collection of the revenues under both contracts. This coordination was essential for the effective functioning of the *asiento* and the *contratos* and a guarantee of their success in fulfilling obligations towards the Monarchy. Madrid facilitated and encouraged this coordination in two ways. On the one hand, the Crown sought to entice the *asentista de negros* and the *contratador* of one of the Portuguese *contratos* to cooperate in maximising their respective earnings by facilitating the entanglement of their shipping, trading and financial networks. Alternatively, the King allowed the same partnership, firm or family to act as both *asentista* and *contratador* simultaneously, an option that increased efficiency and even enabled market coordination and integration in West Africa and in Spanish America.

There were two occasions when the Monarchy allowed, and even fostered, the concentration of the *asiento* and one of the *contratos* in the hands of a business family. The first case pertained to João Rodrigues and Gonçalo Vaz Coutinho, brothers who combined the *asiento* with the Angola *contrato.* The second case was that of António Fernandes d'Elvas and his family mem-

48 This area of extraction was known in the official sources as the "Rivers of Guinea", and comprised the mouths of the Gambia, São Domingos, Geba and Casamance rivers.

bers, who secured the *asiento* and the extensive *contratos* for Angola and Cape Verde-Guinea. Despite the successful deployment of these coordinated efforts, the Monarchy was wary of having the administration of the *asiento* and the *contratos* in the hands of the same familial and commercial groups, as the King feared losing control over private parties, even when they were willing to pay and generate substantial and predictable revenues for the royal treasury.[49]

When *asiento* and *contratos* were held by different networks of traders, the system required Portuguese and Spanish merchants to secure a *licencia* from the *asentista* giving them permission to sell slaves at Spanish American ports. They also had to acquire a similar permit sold by the *contratadores,* the so-called *avença,* which authorised traders to procure slaves in West Africa, in the region covered by the *contrato* that had issued the *avença*.[50] Upon arrival in the Upper Guinea coast or in Loango/Angola, skippers or supercargoes of the slave ships were tasked with overseeing the loading of the number of captives stated in the *licencia* that had been purchased beforehand.[51] Once loaded and before departure, slaving ships had to pay the tariffs specified in the *avença* to the agents of the *contratador* in Africa, and undergo inspection to confirm the legality of the number of enslaved people on board.[52] On the African coast, skippers and supercargoes sent by the holders of the *licencias* and *avenças* relied on Luso-African networks that ensured that men, women and children in bondage were acquired in the hinterland slave markets and brought to the coast. These local networks were also instrumental for supplying water and food to both crews and the enslaved while waiting permission to depart for the Caribbean or Spanish America, as well as for restocking the ships with provisions for the Middle Passage.[53]

---

49 Rodrigues, *Between West Africa and America*, 265–266, 274, 304 and 322.

50 Eagle, "Chasing the Avença"; Silva, *Dutch and Portuguese*, 91.

51 Arlindo Manuel Caldeira, "Angola and the Seventeenth-Century South Atlantic Slave Trade", in *Networks and Trans-Cultural Exchange: Slave Trading in the South Atlantic, 1590–1867*, edited by Filipa Ribeiro Da Silva and David Richardson, (Leiden and Boston: Brill, 2015), 101–42; Linda A. Newson, "Africans and Luso-Africans in the Portuguese Slave Trade on the Upper Guinea Coast in the Early Seventeenth Century", *The Journal of African History* 53, no. 1 (2012), 1–24.

52 Rodrigues, *Between West Africa and America*, 322–42; Silva, *Dutch and Portuguese*, 90–92; Maria Manuel Ferraz Torrão, "De Santiago para a costa da Guiné: a transferência do centro geográfico dos negócios e a manutenção da elite comerciante. As transacções da companhia de António Fernandes Landim e de Francisco Dias Mendes de Brito (1629–1630)', *Arquipélago* 2 (1997), 83–118.

53 Fernando Jorge Cruz Mouta, " 'Por Virtud Del Asiento": The Naval Logistics of the Slave Trade to the Spanish Indies (1604–1624)', *International Journal of Maritime History* 31, no. 4 (2019), 707–728; Caldeira, "Angola and the Seventeenth-Century".

To monitor the operations of slave traders and ensure they paid what was due to the administration of the *asiento* in Spanish America, *asentistas,* who very rarely travelled to America themselves, appointed a number of correspondents to represent them at the various ports of arrival in the Caribbean, as well as in Iberia. There were two types of correspondents. On the one hand, correspondents could be factors of the *asentista* in Spanish America and earned a fixed salary for their services. On the other hand, correspondents could be individuals holding powers of attorney issued by the *asentista,* who were paid a commission for every transaction they oversaw on behalf of the *asentista.*[54] Among the tasks of factors and representatives was the issuing of licences to all those requesting them in the Iberian *comptoirs* of the *asiento* in Lisbon, Seville, and Madrid. They were also responsible for recording in account books the payments made by the majority of slave traders who, having requested *licencias* on credit in one of the Iberian *comptoirs*, only repaid the *asentista* in America. Factors and representatives at the Spanish American ports were also expected to confirm that the number of captives disembarked matched the *registro* of the *Casa de la Contratacíon.* They were present during inspections to newly arrived slaving vessels by the Crown's revenue and custom officials, ensuring that the interests of the *asentista* were not compromised by overzealous royal administrators or shipmasters.[55]

According to the provisions of the *asiento*, the proceeds of the sale of the *licencias* paid in Spanish America were not remitted to Spain by Crown officials, as part of the Monarchy's attempt to monitor and tax the treasury's remittances from the West Indies. The money earned from the *licencias* was handed over by the factors or representatives of the *asentista* to officials of the exchequer in Spanish America, who deposited it in the royal coffers where the colonial remittances bound for Iberia were secured. The coffers were dispatched to Spain via the *Carrera de Índias*, and the funds were handed over to the *asentista* in Seville by the agents of *Casa de la Contratacíon*, after deducting the royal fifth that generally applied to the cargoes in the *Carrera.*[56]

54 For the differences between the remunation of these two types of agents in the South Atlantic, Daniel Strum, *The Sugar Trade: Brazil, Portugal and the Netherlands (1595–1630)* (Stanford, California, Rio de Janeiro: Stanford University Press-Versal Editores, 2013).

55 Upon arriving at the ports of the Indies of Castile the slave ships were inspected by crown magistrates and treasury officials. These inspections centred around the *registro,* which was cross-checked with the *avença,* the Portuguese equivalent to the *licensia* that was issued by the *contratadores* to allow ships to call at the slave embarkation points in Western Africa. Eagle, "Chasing the Avença"; Newson and Minchin, *From Capture to Sale*, 18–21.

56 Rodrigues, *Between West Africa and America*, 259.

It was fairly common for *asentistas* to dispatch members of their family, their networks, or a highly recommended and reputable acquaintance to the various slave-trading ports and *comptoirs* of the *asiento* to serve as factors or representatives. For the West Coast of Africa, *asentistas* and *contratadores* preferred to appoint long-time residents at slaving entrepôts like Cacheu or Luanda, usually of Luso-African descent, to look after their interests. These individuals were valued for their knowledge of the trade, local embeddedness in both African and European societies, and their extensive familial networks in the hinterland. This preference for local long-term residents as factors and representatives later extended to the Circum-Caribbean ports. In both cases, long-term residents had the advantage of being locally attuned to social and commercial practices, and their permanent presence in the ports facilitated the transition of the *asiento* or *contrato* from one administration to the next, providing institutional memory and continuity.[57] As many of these men represented different *asentistas* and *contratadores* at various points in their careers and occasionally even simultaneously, they became pivotal for the structuring of the transatlantic slave trade. Ultimately, the competent, effective and trustworthy performance of factors and representatives was crucial for the success of *asientos* and *contratos* and the outcome thereof.

4 Costs and Benefits of the *Asientos*

In 1595, Pedro Gomes Reinel emerged as the winner of the contract negotiations for the first formal *asiento de negros* thanks to a last-minute bid that surpassed the financial offer of his main competitor, António Nunes Caldeira. Although Caldeira was highly regarded as a solvent and trustworthy businessman with first-hand experience in the slave trade as a merchant and tax-farmer for the Portuguese Crown (*contratador*), it was Reinel who became the first *asentista*. His winning bid of 100,000 Spanish ducats annually far exceeded Caldeira's final tender of 72,000 Spanish ducats.[58]

The first auction and *asiento* negotiations set the trend for the years to come. Although the decision-making bodies at court tended to select the highest bidder at the expense of more knowledgeable candidates with solid financial credentials, this did not mean that the *asiento* was a ruinous investment

57 Studnicki-Gizbert, *A Nation upon the Ocean Sea*; Rodrigues, *Between West Africa and America*, 308; Vila Vilar, *Hispanoamérica*, 50 and 70.

58 Rodrigues, *Between West Africa and America*, 255; Vilar, *Hispanoamérica* 28–32, 65–76.

for its recipients, as is often believed. For a long time, historians have argued that all *asentistas* between 1595 and 1623 became insolvent or went bankrupt because of, or as a result of, the *asiento*. Furthermore, historiography claims that only the last two *asentistas* were able to meet their quotas of *licencias* and pay the instalments of the contracts before their expiration date. However, Rodrigues has recently demonstrated that the overwhelming majority of the Portuguese *asentistas* were able to honour their financial commitments to the Monarchy. Only in one case did the King rescind the contract with an *asentista de negros* consequently initiating judicial proceedings against him for failing to meet the financial clauses of the contract.[59]

The confusion in the debate arises from the fact that several *asientos* prior to the 1620s were terminated before their expiration, although this did not occur because the *asentistas* were unable or failed to make the payments to the royal exchequer. The reason why *asientos* were rescinded and advertised anew was that recipients were found to be involved in malfeasance, fraud or tax evasion. Common arguments made by the Monarchy included that *asentistas* sold more licences than their contracts allowed, that they marketed each licence at higher prices than those fixed by the Crown, or that they claimed as their proceeds the licences sold under the tenure of their predecessors.[60]

António Fernandes d'Elvas was the only *asentista* who became insolvent and was consequently declared bankrupt, as he was unable to meet the financial obligations of the *asiento de negros* and the *contratos* of Cape Verde and Angola. The fact that he held simultaneously all the Portuguese slaving contracts and the Spanish *asiento* provided him with the opportunity to derive administrative and fiscal gains from slave voyages and slave imports that no other contractor, before or after, could have imagined. However, Elvas was unable to accumulate the necessary revenues to cover the costly concession fees of the *asiento* and of the two *contratos*, essentially because of the late capitalisation of these contracts and their tight payment schedules, which were due simultaneously in Lisbon and Madrid. Ironically, the end of Elvas's *asiento* and his downfall as *asentista* coincided with a period when the volume of the slave trade had vastly exceeded the contract's initial export limit, largely because of a steep increase in unregistered, contraband voyages from Angola and West Central Africa. While there are indications that António Fernandes

59 Rodrigues, *Between West Africa and America*, 280, 307–10.

60 Such was the case of the first *asentista de negros*, Pedro Gomes Reinel. Germán Peralta Rivera, *Los mecanismos del comercio negrero* (Lima: Kuntur Editores, 1990), 282 and 325–27.

d'Elvas consented to and actively participated in some of this illicit trade, he was neither alone nor the primary beneficiary of this illegal trade.[61]

For a long time, historians have been puzzled by the apparent lack of judgement of merchant-bankers who risked their fortunes and reputations on a business that, while appearing very profitable, invariably seemed to drive many to financial ruin or ultimate insolvency. The assumption that the *asentistas* grossly miscalculated their chances by neglecting to understand the intricacies of the contracts they signed is, however, inconsistent with the knowledge and behaviour of the same group of men when engaged in other forms of fiscal intermediation, provision of contracts to the military, or wholesale colonial trade.[62]

There was certainly much that could go wrong with the implementation of the *asiento de negros*. Problems included, but were not limited to, the lengthy cycle of capitalisation caused by the deferred payments of the export permits, or the fact that the investors in slaving voyages could take years to actually formalise the *registro* and dispatch their ships.[63] Moreover, even when voyages were launched not long after the *licencia* was procured, the uncertainty and risks of the Atlantic slave trade also loomed over the *asentista*. If a slave ship ran aground, was caught in a storm, was attacked by hostile naval forces, or if the enslaved perished or were not profitably sold in the American ports, contractors risked not being paid for the corresponding *licencias*. In turn, while the yields of the *asiento* could take some time to be realised and remitted to the *asentista*, the lease payments to the royal exchequer had to be met regularly, requiring contractors to remain solvent while they waited for the proceeds from the sale of the *licencias* – a process that could take years. Furthermore, the *asentistas* relied on the goodwill and cooperation of Crown agents in Seville and Spanish America to collect and repatriate the income, revenue, and profits of the *asiento*. Complaints by contractors that the wind-

61 Rodrigues and Alencastro have both drawn attention to the existence of other magnates of the slave trade to Latin America, beyond the government contractors. Their respective research has emphasized the colonial governors of Angola, who made use of their political and military authority not only to ship slaves in large numbers without paying royal licenses, but to become involved in the actual "production" of slaves, by wars against mainland societies that produced captives. Rodrigues, *Between West Africa and America*, 307–309, 358–362; Luiz Felipe de Alencastro, *The Trade in the Living: The Formation of Brazil in the South Atlantic, Sixteenth to Seventeenth Centuries* (Albany: State University of New York Press, 2018).

62 Bowser, *The African Slave in Colonial Peru, 1524–1650* (Stanford: Stanford University Press, 1974, 31–33.

63 Vilar, *Hispanoamérica*, 80–81.

falls of the *asiento* were withheld by officials and (mis)used for unrelated purposes were frequent.[64]

Calculating the gross returns or net gains (when administrative and operational costs are taken into consideration) of the *asiento* is a challenging task, due to the Crown's difficulties in defining the exact number of licences from which the *asentistas* received payment, the complex exchange operations involving American and Spanish currencies, and the patchy and conflicting primary sources available. Still, Miguel Rodrigues has recently attempted to calculate such gains. According to his estimation, the first *asentista,* Pedro Gomes Reinel, reportedly made a 30% turnover in a favourable year. A favourable year was defined as one in which Reinel was able to collect payment on all or almost all of the licenses he had marketed in a given year.[65] This turnover was greatly reduced by considerable administrative costs, which, at least in the case of António Fernandes d'Elvas, eclipsed a quarter of the *asiento*'s yearly returns. These costs included a multitude of fees that were levied on the income remitted from the Americas.[66]

As result, in the years that the *asentistas* did not receive the entire proceeds of the *licencias* they sold in Spanish America, and after depositing the annual lump sums and subtracting the administrative expenses, they suffered a net loss, as evidenced by the case of the third *asentista,* Gonçalo Vaz Coutinho (1609).[67] In the cases of losses, the *asentistas* hoped to recover in subsequent years, relying on alternative incomes, slave-trade related or otherwise, driving many to a state of temporary insolvency. In such cases, trust in the *asentista,* his family, friends, and networks in the market facilitated the continuation of business and the survival of the merchant-banking houses behind the *asientos.*

Notwithstanding the heavy price to pay – financially, socially, and personally – for the permission to trade in enslaved Africans to the Spanish West Indies, the slave trade boomed after the 1590s.[68] This significant increase pro-

64 Rodrigues, *Between West Africa and America,* 267, 279–280.

65 Peralta Rivera, *Los mecanismos del comercio,* 379–399.

66 Rodrigues, *Between West Africa and America,* 257, 280, 283–286.

67 From 133,696 ducats remitted from Spanish America, this *asentista* netted a loss of 24,708 ducats after paying a 140,000 ducats in yearly lump sum plus 18,405 ducats in administrative expenses to the *Casa de la Contratacíon.*

68 According to the latest estimates, between 1501 and 1641, 1,843 recorded voyages brought nearly 530,000 enslaved men, women and children to the shores of Spanish America directly from their continent of origin, but. out of these, 83% (444,900 individuals) allegedly made it through the Middle Passage (in the 1,544 slave voyages completed) during the Union of the Iberian Crowns. Alex Borucki, David Eltis, and David Wheat,

vided a positive incentive for many to bid for the *asiento* each time the Monarchy advertised one of the contracts.[69] The supply of Spanish America with enslaved labour proceeded smoothly for the most part during the first thirty years of the *asiento,* except for a brief period in the 1610s (1609–14) when the Crown decided to change course and experiment with *administracíon* (direct administration), a move that had disastrous results. The significant drop in the number of licences during those five years can be explained by the inability of the administrators appointed by the Crown to manage the system of deferred payments favoured by most slave traders, as they required payment for the *licencias* upfront. The need to pay for the licences upfront, contrary to the practice of sales on credit, became an obstacle for many to engage in the trade. The sudden removal of the possibility for delayed payment pushed many out of the legal trading routes and into the smuggling circuits or towards non-slave-related trade and investments.

The *asiento* showed the first signs of weakness during the contract between the Crown and Manuel Rodrigues Lamego (1624–1631), which coincided with the start of the Dutch offensive against the Iberian Atlantic. After the Twelve Years Truce (1609–1621), Zealand privateers systematically plundered Portuguese and Spanish merchant ships sailing across the Atlantic, including many *navios sueltos* licensed by the *asentista.* At the same time, the Dutch West India Company (WIC) targeted Spain's silver fleets, Piet Heyn's capture of the Spanish fleet off the bay of Matanzas in 1628 being a landmark in this violence, and attacked colonial possessions in Latin America and West Africa, briefly conquering São Salvador da Bahia in 1624, and then Pernambuco, the centre of Brazil's sugar plantation complex, in 1630.[70]

"The Size and Direction of the Slave Trade to the Spanish Americas", in *From the Galleons to the Highlands: Slave Trade Routes in the Spanish Americas*, edited by Alex Borucki, David Eltis, and David Wheat (Albuquerque: University of New Mexico Press, 2020), 15–46.

69 The same assumption on the profitability of the *asiento de negros* was made by García-Monton for a latter period. Alejandro García-Monton, *Génova y el Atlántico (c. 1650–1680). Emprendedores mediterráneos frente al auge del capitalismo del Norte,* PhD diss. (Florence: European University Institute, 2014).

70 Wim Klooster, *The Dutch Moment: War, Trade, and Settlement in the Seventeenth-Century Atlantic World* (Ithaca, NY: Cornell University Press, 2016); Leonor Freire Costa, *O transporte no Atlântico e a Companhia Geral do Comércio do Brasil, 1580–1663,* 2 vols. (Lisbon: Comissão Nacional para as Comemorações dos Descobrimentos Portugueses, 2002); Evaldo Cabral de Mello, *Olinda restaurada: guerra e açúcar no Nordeste, 1630–1654* (Rio de Janeiro: Topbooks, 1998).

The economic effects of war between European empires were compounded by the collapse of slave supply networks in West Central Africa caused by the military campaigns of Portuguese colonial governors in Luanda. Initially, the Portuguese military intervention in the West Central African kingdom of Ndongo had generated an outpouring of captives that supported much of the Angolan slave trading boom of the early 1600s and the high numbers of slaves from that region that reached Spanish America. However, years of armed conflict and plundering eventually destabilised the traditional procurement systems in the hinterlands of Central Africa. When the wars subsided, the traditional hinterland slave fairs had ceased to convene, and African and Luso-African go-betweens no longer ventured inland to acquire captives to take to the coast.[71]

This combination of adverse factors led, among other things, to the *asentistas* of the mid-to-late 1620s and 1630s struggling to market all the licences allowed by their contracts. While their predecessors had regularly disregarded the terms of their *asientos* by selling too many licences and exceeding the annual export limits, the *asentista* Manuel Rodrigues Lamego requested a reduction in the number of *licencias* allotted to his contract. The Monarchy acquiesced, and the export limits were lowered, initially from 4,500 *licencias* to 3,500, but later in the 1630s to 2,500.[72]

5 Conclusion

Except for a five-year interlude (1609–14), between 1595 and 1640, the *asiento de negros* was entrusted to Portuguese merchant-bankers, who ran the licensing of transatlantic slave trade to colonial Spanish America on behalf of the Monarchy, taking on associated risks and benefits. This forty five-year period represents a low-point in the abhorrent history of the transatlantic slave trade, as it marked the first major peak in the four centuries of forced trafficking of Africans to the Americas as whole. While historians continue to reassess the number of voyages and displaced Africans, expanding and refining the Transatlantic Slave Trade Database (TSTD), there is a consensus that the period of the "Portuguese *asientos*" was characterised by an extraordinary volume of slave exports, a level only to be seen again in the last quarter of the eighteenth century, with the development of the sugar plantation complexes of Cuba and

71 Rodrigues, *Between West Africa and America*; Silva, *Dutch and Portuguese.*

72 Rodrigues, *Between West Africa and America*, 292–293.

Puerto Rico, did the numbers of enslaved Africans headed for Spanish America surpass the volume reached during the Union of the Iberian Crowns.[73]

The *asiento de negros* was the instrument through which the Crown and economic elites derived financial and political benefits from the slave trade between West Africa and Spanish America. This alignment of royal and merchant-banking interests led to the imposition of entry barriers on private participation in the trade, and the extraction of rents and additional administrative revenues from this business. The Monarchy viewed the *asiento de negros* primarily as a means to maximising revenues for the metropolitan *Real Hacienda*, rather than as a tool to support the colonial economies.

Even though the *asentistas'* control over the entirety of the trade was limited by the licensing system, the volume of legal exports they administered is nonetheless a testament to the capacity of the Portuguese merchant class to tap into West African regions of enslavement. This was achieved through the Portuguese *contratos*, the channelling of large numbers of individuals to the American markets, under the *asientos*, their ability to collect deferred payments over long distances and extended periods of time, and their proficiency in remaining solvent while awaiting remittances from Spanish America to fulfil the payments contracted with the Monarchy.

The *asiento* was an attractive business venture, allowing rents to be extracted from a potentially lucrative colonial trade, with the added advantage that these profits came in the form of American silver. Although further research is required to more clearly determine the profit margins of the *asiento de negros*, this contract appears to have provided high returns on investment, potentially greater than those made from individual slave voyages and other purely private commercial ventures. However, to realise a profit from the *asiento, asentistas* needed to remain solvent for long periods, due to the late capitalisation of the Bcontract, contrasting with tight payment schedules and numerous administrative expenses. Even the gross returns from the *asiento* – those resulting from the difference between the number of *licencias* sold and the lump sums paid to the Crown – were uncertain for many reasons. Speculation by licence holders, the dangers of maritime navigation, high mortality rates among the enslaved at port and during sea voyages, as well as the rampant smuggling, all posed risks to the *asentistas*, even if they acted more as fiscal intermediaries than as traders.

A final indicator of the importance of the Portuguese *asentistas* within the system of slave provisioning and rent extraction is the state of the transatlan-

73 Borucki, Eltis, and Wheat, "The Size and Direction"; Borucki, Eltis, and Wheat, 'Atlantic History".

tic slave trade after 1640. With Portugal's newly regained independence from the Hispanic Monarchy, the volume of African slave exports to the Spanish West Indies plummeted, and the Crown's ability to derive revenues from this trade branch was temporarily lost. In the following decades, the lack of a permanent presence on the West Coast of Africa meant that Spanish America had to be supplied, both lawfully and illegally, through ports of call in the Caribbean, by slave traders, who, unlike the Portuguese, were neither subjects of the King, nor organised in familial networks or partnerships. Instead, they were foreigners, often aligned with Protestant believes and organised in partnerships, chartered companies, and joint-stock enterprises. The age of the "Portuguese *asientos*" gave way to a phase dominated by the intra-Caribbean slave trade.

CHAPTER 2

Indirect Management of the *Asiento*

In December 1640, Portugal rebelled against Philip IV. From that point until 1668, Portugal and Spain were engaged in a global-scale war that precipitated a drastic reconfiguration of the Atlantic world. One of the boldest decisions taken by the Spanish Empire during this period was the suspension of the transatlantic slave trade.[1] This measure aimed to obstruct the primary channel through which Portuguese subjects infiltrated the economies of Spanish America. However, this decision against the Portuguese slave traders did not occur in isolation. Rather than being a radical measure enacted solely within the context of war, it should be understood as the culmination of a process rooted in developments from the 1630s. During this earlier period, royal institutions and officials, both in the Iberian Peninsula and the Americas, increasingly resorted to the Inquisition as a tool to constrain the economic ascendancy of Portuguese *asentistas*. This was achieved through actions such as seizing their fortunes, threatening their families, or compelling them to collaborate with the Crown.[2]

The suspension of the official transatlantic slave trade had a profound impact on the Spanish Caribbean. Until the early 1650s, only a small number of enslaved Africans reached these colonies. In the absence of new enslaved African labour force, Spanish American colonists resorted to intra-colonial purchases to fill the labour gap. Simultaneously, indigenous enslavement became increasingly significant, both in terms of territorial scope and number of individuals enslaved. This development was accompanied by an intensification of the trade in locally born enslaved people of African descent, as well as older acculturated African slaves who had been transported to Spanish America before the suspension of the trade.[3] Although the suspension initially appeared effective, in the short and medium term, the high demand for

1 Bethencourt, *Strangers Within*. Vila Vilar, "La sublevación de Portugal", 171–192.

2 Alfonso W. Quiroz, "The Expropiation of Portuguese New Christians in Spanish America, 1635–1649," *Ibero-Amerikanisches Archiv* 11, no. 4 (1985), 407–465; Bernardo López Belinchón, *Honra, libertad y hacienda: hombres de negocios y judíos sefardíes* (Alcalá de Henares: Instituto Internacional de Estudios Sefardíes y Andalusíes – Universidad de Alcalá, 2001); Newson and Minchin, *From Capture to Sale*.

3 Tatiana Seijas and Pablo M. Sierra, "The Persistence of the Slave Market in Seventeenth-Century Central Mexico," *Slavery & Abolition* 37, no. 2 (2016), 307–333; Alejandro García-Montón, "The Rise of Portobelo and the Transformation of the Spanish American Slave

labour, coupled with mounting dissatisfaction in the Spanish American colonies, ultimately prompted the Crown to re-open the transatlantic slave trade in 1651 – seventeen years before the conclusion of the war with Portugal in 1668.

For Portuguese slave traders, the consequences of the suspension of the Spanish transatlantic slave trade were far from uniform and varied by region. By the end of the first decade of suppression, Portuguese slaving networks had lost their dominant role in controlling the distribution of slaves to the Spanish Caribbean. The vacuum created by their diminished presence was gradually filled by private Dutch traders, who aligned their interests with those of Spanish American slave traders and local officials in the Caribbean.[4] By the time the ban was lifted, Portuguese networks had largely lost their prominence in the slave trade to the Spanish Caribbean. Their primarily familial networks had been replaced by business partnerships organised out of Amsterdam and Middelburg. Nevertheless, Portuguese networks were not uniformly affected. In the South Atlantic, they managed to maintain their dominance, significantly increasing their participation in the slave trade between Angola, the Rio de la Plata region, and Brazil, a circuit that had previously been off-limits under the legal framework of the Monarchy prior to 1640.[5]

The specific reasons that led the Spanish Monarchy to re-open the slave imports into Spanish American markets in 1651 remain unclear, though a constellation of imperatives appears to have influenced this decision. The first imperative was fiscal. The decline in slave imports to the Spanish Caribbean had significantly reduced the revenue of local institutions and the Monarchy itself. Traditionally, the high demand for enslaved labour ensured that major Spanish Caribbean ports facilitated the cyclical provision of markets, becoming efficient hubs for tax collection and generating a steady stream of revenue. The second imperative arose from Spanish America itself. The Crown faced mounting pressure from most Spanish American cities, which issued a continuous wave of complaints to the *Consejo de Indias* in Madrid from 1645 onwards, emphasising the detrimental effects of labour shortages on local and regional economies. The third imperative, though historiographically

---

Trade, 1640s–1730s: Transimperial Connections and Intra-American Shipping," *Hispanic American Historical Review* 99, no. 3 (2019), 407–410.

4 Klooster, *Illicit Riches*, 41–43, 59–61, 65–67, 73–74, 105–109; Cátia Antunes and Filipa Ribeiro da Silva, "Amsterdam Merchants in the Slave Trade and African Commerce, 1580s-1670s," *Tijdschrift Voor Sociale En Economische Geschiedenis* 9, no. 4 (2012), 22–24.

5 Moutoukias, *Contrabando y control;* Silva, *Dutch and Portuguese*; Shultz, "'The Kingdom of Angola", 424–444.

contested, may have been the need for a political rapprochement between the Spanish Empire and the United Provinces following the Peace of Münster (1648) and the conclusion of the Eighty Year's War. The end of the war brought an increased presence of Dutch fleets and mariners in the Caribbean, raising concerns among Spanish colonial officials about unregulated Dutch penetration of the Spanish Caribbean markets, a phenomenon that had developed since the 1630s.[6]

The Spanish Empire's position towards Dutch merchants remained ambiguous. While formal trade between the colonies of both countries in the Caribbean was prohibited in 1651, new legislation introduced loopholes that allowed for legal trade. Most notably, from 1648 onwards, Dutch ships were granted the right to call at Spanish Caribbean ports in cases of emergency or distress. For Dutch captains and shipmasters, this clause provided a convenient pretext to call at Spanish Caribbean ports under the guise of distress, sell their cargoes, and receive payment in silver or commodities such as indigo, cochineal, sugar, or tobacco. For the local population, the arrival of Dutch ships offered valuable opportunities to barter locally produced goods for enslaved Africans and European or Asian merchandise. Over the following decades, this system, known as *arribada forzosa*, became endemic.[7]

While *arribada forzosa* provided some relief for the growing demand for enslaved labour, it was insufficient. Consequently, the Crown was compelled to explore alternative means to supply the Spanish American markets. From 1651 to 1663, the Monarchy opted to organise the official slave trade through a licensing system overseen by the *Consejo de Indias* and the *Casa de la Contratación.* The reasons why the *Consejo* chose direct administration over an *asiento* with an *asentista* or a commercial partnership remain unclear. However, this licensing reflected a balancing act: on the one hand, the Crown sought to maintain political and economic exclusion while incorporating fiscal revenues; on the one hand, it aimed to address growing competition in the Atlantic, particularly from Dutch and English traders, by encouraging merchants to invest directly in the official slave trade through legal means.

During the licensing period, the Crown sought to maximise the premiums collected for each licence. However, prices for licences remained at 1640 levels. As was customary before the 1640s, licences could be paid for in installments. Unlike earlier practices, however, payments during this period could only be made in Spain, rather than across the Iberian Peninsula and in Spanish America. This measure was likely designed to hinder the circulation and trans-

6 Klooster, *The Dutch Moment*, 56.

7 Moutoukias, *Contrabando y control*, 105–11; Klooster, *Illicit Riches*, 41–43, 52–56.

fer of capital between Spanish American colonies, as well as between these colonies and Caribbean towns beyond the territorial control of the Spanish Empire, and between Spanish Caribbean ports and Spain.[8]

The restructured framework for the slave trade was designed to prevent inter- and intra-imperial interactions in the Caribbean. To achieve this primary objective, licence holders were permitted to sail to the West Coast of Africa to purchase enslaved Africans. Spanish captains were authorised to enlist up to six Portuguese subjects as part of their crews, a measure aimed at facilitating the procurement of captives in Africa, given that Portuguese and Luso-Africans controlled specific slave markets along the coast, often beyond the reach of Portuguese-controlled territories. In effect, the importation of enslaved Africans into the Spanish Caribbean after 1651 became a Spanish enterprise mediated by Portuguese brokers aboard Spanish ships. These brokers served as intermediaries between Spanish captains and Africa-based Portuguese and Luso -African merchants, operating within a legal framework. However, the apparent choice to trade directly with Portuguese subjects in Africa is misleading. Neither the Spanish Crown, nor the licensed captains had a genuine alternative. By the 1650s, the English presence in Africa was weak, and the Dutch had lost significant ground following defeats in São Tomé and Angola to the Portuguese in 1641 and 1647, respectively. The WIC retained only Elmina (former Castelo da Mina) as its sole noteworthy African outpost.[9]

To make the licensing system more attractive to slave traders and other investors, the *Consejo de Indias* allowed licence holders to name their preferred port of disembarkation in Spanish America, submitting requests to the *Conselho* for approval. This flexibility regarding Caribbean ports resulted in significant losses for Cartagena and Veracruz, which had traditionally been the privileged and exclusive destinations for slaving ships. Alongside the loss of trade came diminished fiscal revenue, reduced local employment, and a decline in these ports' prominence as redistributive hubs of enslaved labour to the Spanish American hinterlands. Ultimately, the erosion of Cartagena's and Veracruz's privileged positions marked a transition from a system of concentrated markets for the trade and distribution of enslaved Africans to one of more diffused markets. This shift reshaped local and regional social and economic networks of distribution.

---

8 Klooster, *The Dutch Moment,* 81–83 and 160–164; Lou H. Roper, *Advancing Empire: English Interests and Overseas Expansion, 1613–1688* (New York: Cambridge University Press, 2017), 62–70 and 71–85.

9 Klooster, *The Dutch Moment,* 163; Roper, *Advancing Empire,* 79.

Despite the Crown's efforts, only a minority of traders participated in the official trade. Between 1651 and 1663, when the licensing system was operational, at least 15,147 enslaved Africans were transported to the Spanish Caribbean, primarily through smuggling and contraband.[10] At times, the unofficial trade surpassed the official trade by a factor of seven. For instance, between 1651 to 1654, the total number of slaves authorised by licences was approximately 910, while the actual number of disembarked captives reached 6,453.[11] Smuggling was not the only factor undermining royal revenues; licence holders themselves often violated regulations by exceeding their authorised quotas. In one instance, Juan Bautista Pluma, shipmaster of the *Nuestra Señora de Guadalupe*, received permission to transport 150 captives to "any port in the Indies".[12] However, when his ship reached Santo Domingo in 1656, it carried 259 captives.[13]

A critical factor in the rise of smuggling during this period was the Crown's limited capacity to enforce the official trade. Spanish American authorities were generally inclined to facilitate the activities of slave traders, whether they operated official licences or through unofficial channels. Ironically, the reopening of official markets appears to have boosted smuggling and contraband. The legalisation of the trade normalised the presence of enslaved individuals as commodities, making it easier to justify their presence aboard ships, even when those vessels lacked authorisation for slave trading. Following the dismantling of the traditional Portuguese system, new transatlantic and regional slave trade networks emerged during the 1650s to supply the Spanish Caribbean.

1 Changing the Rules of the Game: The 1662 *Asiento*

The Crown's efforts to revitalise the official slave trade during the 1650s proved unsuccessful. The immediate outcome was limited revenue from taxes and duties. Smuggling became more significant than ever, and the actors who had emerged during the unofficial circuits of the 1640s further consolidated

10 https://www.slavevoyages.org/voyages/cQoaSHfP, (accessed 29 March 2024)

11 Vila Vilar, "La sublevación de Portugal," 180.; https://www.slavevoyages.org/voyages/mtcmTkRg (accessed 29 March 2024).

12 Archivo General de Indias (henceforth AGI), Indiferente General (Henceforth IG), Leg. 2797, s.f., 1654. Licenses for Juan Bautista Pluma.

13 AGI, Escribanía, Leg. 6-A, s.f. 1657; https://www.slavevoyages.org/, voyage identification number 41463.

their positions. Meanwhile, the Crown's urgent need for revenue persisted. After the conclusion of the war with France in 1659, military deployment was redirected towards the ongoing conflict with Portugal. This period of chronic shortages saw various attempts to secure short-term funding and restructure the fiscal system.[14] It was within this context that a new a*siento* for the slave trade was negotiated.

The new *asiento,* signed in June 1662, represented an agreement between the *Consejo de Indias* and the Genoese firm of Domenico Grillo and Ambrosio Lomellino. This contract marked a turning point in the organization of the slave trade within the Spanish Empire. More importantly, it established a framework that would shape the trade until the mid-eighteenth century. The norms governing the operation of the trade changed, as did the role of the *asientista.*

Among the numerous innovations introduced by the 1662 *asiento,* four were particularly significant in reshaping the slave trade to Spanish America. First, this *asiento* established the monopolistic management of the trade, referred to by contemporaries as an *estanco.* This change granted a single entity exclusive rights to manage the African slave trade to Spanish America. Previously, the 'Portuguese *asientos*' had allowed multiple actors to participate by acquiring licences from the Crown, the *Casa de Contratación,* or companies farming out the licence market, colloquially known as *asentistas.* Until 1662, the system had permitted the official participation of multiple actors in the slave trade.

Second, the new *asiento* introduced the possibility of importing enslaved Africans from Caribbean outposts rather than directly from the West Coast of Africa. These Caribbean markets were beyond the territorial sovereignty of the Habsburg Crown and governed by rival states such as England and the Dutch Republic. In this context, the importation of enslaved Africans into Spanish America became inherently trans-imperial, with the political and operational choice of where this trade would occur assuming critical importance. Following the Peace of Münster (1648), the Spanish Empire officially recognised the Dutch presence in the Americas, but the *asiento* facilitated regular, substantial and legal exchanges between Curaçao and the Spanish American Main. Additionally, the English presence in the Caribbean was implicitly acknowledged

14 Rafael Valladares, *Banqueros y vasallos: Felipe IV y el medio general (1630–1670)* (Cuenca: Universidad de Castilla La Mancha, 2002); Xabier Lamikiz, "Fiscalidad y Fraude En La Reactivación de La Carrera de Indias, 1660–1700," in *Dinero Del Rey: Finanzas y Cambio Fiscal En La Monarquía Hispánica, Siglos XVI–XVII*, edited by Ramón Lanza García (Granada: Comares, 2021).

by the Spanish Empire through the *asiento*. Although Jamaica was captured by the English in 1655 and its sovereignty formally recognized by Madrid only in 1670, Jamaica had already begun supplying the *asiento* of Grillo and Lomellino with enslaved Africans. In sum, under this new operational framework, the *asiento* fostered the emergence of Curaçao and Jamaica as major trade hubs within the Dutch and the English empires, respectively.[15]

Third, the criteria for selecting suppliers for the *asiento* became increasingly tied with international politics rather than the complex social negotiations traditionally conducted between the Spanish Monarchy and some of its subjects. The contract stipulated that only subjects of monarchs and republics at peace with the Spanish Monarchy were eligible as suppliers. Consequently, during the administration of Grillo and Lomellino, Portuguese suppliers were excluded until 1668, and French suppliers were barred between 1667 and 1668, while Dutch and English suppliers were deemed eligible.

Finally, a fourth and significant change pertained to the institutional organisation of the slave trade within the Spanish Atlantic. Before 1662, the slave trade fell under the jurisdiction of the *Casa de la Contratación* and the Spanish American *audiencias*, similar to other transatlantic trades. The Grillo and Lomellino *asiento*, however, was placed under an autonomous legal framework overseen by the *Consejo de Indias*, the highest court for American affairs. This restructuring removed the *Casa de la Contratación* and the *audiencias* from their roles in overseeing the slave trade and the jurisdiction over the *asiento*. As a result, *asiento* operations were shielded from interference by Spanish American authorities, who had vested interests in the unofficial slave trade.

The Crown implemented these changes to bolster and secure fiscal revenues. The Genoese firm agreed to deliver 3,500 *piezas de Indias* annually for seven years (eventually extended to eleven years), paying 100 *pesos* for each *pieza* imported into Spanish America. The *pieza de Indias* standard was defined as a healthy enslaved adult, measuring seven *cuartas* in height and free from physical defects. By paying this fixed rate, Grillo and Lomellino were exempted from all other taxes or duties related to the slave trade. Conse-

15 Nuala Zahedieh, "The Merchants of Port Royal, Jamaica, and the Spanish Contraband Trade, 1655–1692," *The William and Mary Quarterly* 43, no. 4 (1986), 570–593; Wim Klooster, "Curaçao and the Caribbean," in *Riches from Atlantic Commerce: Dutch Transatlantic Trade and Shipping, 1585–1817*, edited by Johannes Postma and Victor Enthoven (Leiden and Boston: Brill, 2003), 203–218; Han Jordaan, "The Curaçao Slave Market. From the Asiento Trade to Free Trade, 1700–1730," in *Riches from Atlantic Commerce: Dutch Transatlantic Trade and Shipping, 1585–1817*, edited by Johannes Postma and Victor Enthoven (Leiden and Boston: Brill, 2003), 219–57.

quently, the Crown deprived Spanish American city councils of an important source of revenue.

The 1662 *asiento* was therefore conceived as a strategy to address one of the most pressing challenges faced by early modern global empires: the extraction of resources from specific geographical locations to be mobilised and expended elsewhere. In negotiating the *asiento,* Grillo and Lomellino offered a solution to this problem by promising to supply a significant number of warships to Spain in exchange for monopolistic control over the slave trade to Spanish America. Despite their lack of prior experience in the slave trade, transatlantic commerce, or shipbuilding, the Crown awarded the *asiento* to the firm, relying on its reputation as one of the most prominent international banking houses, with extensive experience in tax-farming in Spain.

The Crown's urgent need for ships gave Grillo and Lomellino considerable leverage in the *asiento* negotiations. However, the firm's primary interest lay not in shipbuilding but in gaining access to the *asiento de negros*. Consequently, Grillo and Lomellino sought to extricate themselves from their shipbuilding obligations as quickly as possible. After extensive petitioning, they persuaded the Crown's councils to cancel the construction of four ships in the Basque Country, substituting these with vessels imported from the Dutch Republic.[16] Of the six ships originally contracted, only four were ever completed.[17] To compensate the Crown, Grillo and Lomellino provided loans to fund the army in Flanders, which was under significant strain by 1667 during the War of Devolution (1667–1668). These loans aligned more closely with the firm's expertise as financiers and were less costly and logistically complex than direct involvement in shipbuilding in northern Spain.

For Grillo and Lomellino, the *asiento* represented a unique opportunity to gain access to Spanish America and its silver resources. This was particularly significant for Genoese entrepreneurs, who lacked the backing of their home state for overseas ventures. From the perspective of Genoese mercantile and financial networks, the *asiento* was a highly valuable asset, compensating for the disruption of traditional channels through which they accessed silver, primarily as bankers to the Spanish Crown. Although Portuguese financiers had dominated the Crown's banking sector in the 1620s, the Crown's 1648 bankruptcy severely undermined Portuguese solvency, creating opportunities for other financiers, such as Grillo and Lomellino.

16 AGI, Contaduría, Leg. 562, nº 1, fols. 1r-8r, 23-VII-1663.

17 Fernando Serrano Mangas, *Los Galeones de la Carrera de Indias 1650–1700* (Sevilla: EEHA-CSIC, 1985), 98–105.

Lending money to the Spanish Crown was less attractive in the late 1640s than it had been previously, as systematic payments in American silver, a common practice in the restitution of state loans, ceased in 1654.[18] Furthermore, starting in the mid-1650s and continuing through the 1660s, the Genoese faced a shifting set of financial demands from the Crown. These changes created new business opportunities for which the Genoese were less prepared compared to other competitors, particularly Spanish merchant-bankers. While the Genoese excelled in international finance, where silver circulated abundantly, the Crown primarily required copper coin (*vellón*) during this period to finance its war against Portugal (1640–1668) and France (1635–1659). Additionally, the Spanish Empire increasingly relied on diplomacy rather than military interventions in its European relations, further reducing the demand for international loans in silver. Despite consolidating their position as the leading international bankers to the Crown until the 1680s, Genoese merchant-bankers experienced a significant decline in returns from their assistance to the Spanish Empire after the 1660s.[19]

In response to these changes in international financial markets, the Genoese sought alternative economic niches that provided more secure and profitable access to silver. Some Genoese banking firms invested in public debt in Venice, the Austrian Habsburg Empire, or the Papal states.[20] Others turned their attention to provisioning the Spanish and Portuguese transatlantic trading systems. The openness of the Iberian empires to foreign merchants, combined with the Genoese's long-standing familiarity within Iberian societies, facilitated this shift. Nevertheless, the Genoese faced increasing competition from Dutch, French and English merchants in the main Iberian cities, as these groups redirected overseas trade from Lisbon and Cadiz towards Northern Europe. Consequently, Genoese merchant-bankers specialised in offering insurance and brokerage services to European investors in the trade with Spanish America and Brazil.[21] Grillo and Lomellino's entry into the *asiento* must therefore be

18 Carlos Álvarez-Nogal, *El crédito de la monarquía hispánica en el reinado de Felipe IV* (Valladolid: Junta de Castilla y León, 1997).

19 Carmen Sanz Ayán, *Los banqueros de Carlos II* (Valladolid: Universidad de Valladolid, 1988).

20 Giuseppe Felloni, *Gli investimenti finanziari genovesi in Europa tra il Seicento e la Restaurazione* (Milano: A. Giuffrè, 1971).

21 María Guadalupe Carrasco Gonzalez, *Comerciantes y casas de negocios en Cádiz, 1650–1700*, Cádiz, Universidad de Cádiz, 1997; Leonor Freire Costa, "Genoveses nas rotas do açucar: A intromissao em exclusivos coloniais portugueses (c. 1650)", in *Génova y la Monarquía Hispánica (1528–1713)*, vol. 2, edited by edited by Manuel Herrero Sánchez, Yasmina Rocío Ben Yessef Garfia, Carlo Bitossi and Dino Puncuh (Genova, Società Ligure

understood within this broader process of Genoese investment reallocation. However, their engagement with the *asiento* reflected varying degrees of interest across its different business opportunities. An analysis of their selective allocation of resources and personal involvement in specific aspects of the contract reveals the underlying strategic importance they attributed to the *asiento* as a whole.

2 Re-orchestrating the Trade

The organisational model for the *asiento* introduced in 1662 became a continuous template, used without interruption until mid-eighteenth century by various firms, partnerships and companies that contracted the *asiento*. While the privileges to each *asentista* evolved over time and were often expanded with each new *asiento*, the basic organisational principles established in 1662 remained largely unchanged. Operationally, the *asientistas* combined their roles as gatekeepers of the slave trade to Spanish America with their responsibilities as suppliers of enslaved Africans. When the *asentistas* delegated the African and transatlantic legs of the trade to third parties, as Grillo and Lomellino did, they both implicitly and explicitly coordinated diverse business organisations originating from different countries. These partnerships between *asientistas* and subcontractors managed multiple circuits for redistributing profits derived from the Atlantic world, which were ultimately enjoyed in Europe and sometimes beyond. Like Grillo and Lomellino, subsequent *asentistas* faced two major organisational challenges: (a) securing reliable suppliers of enslaved Africans with the capacity to transport them to the Caribbean on a regular basis; and (b) managing the importation of enslaved people from non-Spanish Caribbean hubs to Spanish American ports.

2.1 *Organising the* Asiento *from Europe*

The framework of the 1662 *asiento* compelled Grillo and Lomellino to structure their operations in an unprecedented manner. For them, the organisation of the transatlantic slave trade was primarily a European enterprise. Genoese captains frequently sailed to Africa to purchase captives, and the Genoese

di Storia Patria, 2011), 915–932; Nunziatella Alessandrini y Antonella Viola, "Genovesi e fiorentini in Portogallo: Reti commerciali e strategie politico-diplomatiche (1650–1700)", *Mediterranea. Ricerche storiche* 28 (2013), 295–322.

diaspora maintained a strong presence in the Iberian Atlantic.[22] However, the direct management of such a vast operation likely exceeded the capacity of a relatively small firm like Grillo and Lomellino. From the outset of the contract, therefore, the firm sought reliable and strategically positioned European partners capable of securing enslaved Africans in Africa and maintaining sufficient shipping capacity to deliver them to the Caribbean in consistent cycles.

Between 1662 to 1674, Grillo and Lomellino established partnerships with various international suppliers to ensure a steady flow of enslaved Africans to the Caribbean. These suppliers operated through diverse organisational forms, ranging from private partnerships to chartered and joint-stock companies. In September 1662, Grillo and Lomellino signed their first contract with the WIC for the delivery of 1,400 to 2,000 *piezas* under a single agreement. Soon after, negotiations began with the English Royal Adventurers into Africa (RA), although the activities of English privateers in the Spanish Caribbean led the Crown to undermine any potential agreement between the Genoese and the English company.

Following the initial contract with the WIC, a Dutch joint stock company, Grillo and Lomellino continued to engage with the Dutch market. In April 1663, they secured an agreement with two Dutch private traders, Karel Gijsberti and Volkert Gerritsz. Meanwhile, negotiations with the English resumed in 1664. By March and April of that year, Grillo and Lomellino reached an agreement with the RA for the delivery of 600 to 1,000 *piezas* initially, followed by an additional 3,000 *piezas* annually for the duration of their *asiento*.

The chartered nature of the RA and its compliance with the 1664 contract did not deter Grillo and Lomellino from returning to the Amsterdam market in 1666, where they contracted a group of private traders to secure deliveries of 700, and 400–450 *piezas*, respectively. However, from that year onwards, the WIC consolidated its dominance in the Dutch market, cracking down on its competitors. As a result, the WIC became the sole legal provider for the *asiento*. Between 1666 and 1672, at least four additional contracts were signed between Grillo and Lomellino and the WIC, securing the delivery of between 18,800 and 20,000 enslaved Africans.[23] In summary, Grillo and Lomellino

22 Maria Luísa Esteves, "Para o estudo do tráfico de escravos de Angola (1640–1668)," *Studia* 50 (1991), 29–60; Maria Luísa Esteves, "Para o estudo das relações comerciais de Angola com as Índias de Castela e Génova no período da Restauração (1640–1668)," *Studia* 51 (1992), 29–60.

23 See, respectively: AGI, Contaduría, Leg. 262, ramo 1, fols. 1r-6r; AGI, Contaduría, Leg. 262, ramo 1, fols. 7r-11r; AGI, IG, Leg. 2830, fols. 378r-85r; AHPM, 7356 Muñoz, s.f., 9-IV-1664; AGI, Contaduría, Leg. 262, ramo 8, fols. 30r-4v; AGI, Contaduría, Leg. 262, ramo 8, fols.

engaged firms, partnerships, chartered companies, and joint stock enterprises in Amsterdam, London, and Madrid, to transport between 51,950 to 52,500 African captives from West Africa to the Caribbean, all destined for further transport to Spanish America.

The contracts, or more accurately, subcontracts, signed by Grillo and Lomellino with slave-trading enterprises in Amsterdam and London effectively incorporated suppliers from diverse religious backgrounds into the fold of the Spanish Empire. These suppliers operated within business organisations that were inherently transnational, not only because of the international maritime labour forces manning the slaving ships, but also due to the socio-economic diversity and geographic origins of their investors. In the cases of chartered and joint-stock companies, a significant proportion of investments came from non-English and non-Dutch stakeholders, including members of the Portuguese Nations in Amsterdam and London, particularly in the RA and the WIC.[24]

Although the contracts between Grillo and Lomellino and the slave suppliers were negotiated and signed in Europe, the payment terms stipulated in the contracts required partial payments in Europe and partial payments in the Caribbean. Furthermore, the contracts specified gender and age ratios of the captives, as well as delivery schedules for their arrival in the Caribbean. Similar to the earlier licensing system under the Portuguese *asentistas,* these contracts included provisions for potential economic losses due to mortality rates during transport and expenses incurred for the sustenance of captives prior to their embarkation by Grillo and Lomellino's agents in Curaçao, Jamaica, or Barbados.

2.2 *The Trade from Africa*

Between 1651 and 1663, the Crown raised no objection to the acquisition of enslaved Africans directly from African markets. During this period, regulations permitted traders supplying the Spanish American markets to control purchases in Africa and deliveries to Spanish America. However, the 1662 *asiento* curtailed this practice, and Grillo and Lomellino were unable to maintain such control. During negotiations with the Crown, the firm did not articulate a clear position on whether it preferred to import enslaved people directly or indirectly from Africa. In contrast to their Portuguese predecessors, who

35r-9r; AGI, Contaduría, Leg. 262, ramo 8, fols. 42r-9v; Goslinga, *The Dutch in the Caribbean*, 514–17; GAA, NA, 3204, fols. 422r- 8v; AGI, IG, Leg. 2833, s.f. 30-X-1672.

24 Herbert I. Bloom, *The Economic Activities of the Jews of Amsterdam in the seventeenth and eighteenth centuries* (Williamsport: The Bayard Press, 1937), 39.

effectively combined the Portuguese *contratos* for importing captives from West Africa with *asientos* for delivering them to Spanish America, the Genoese displayed a pragmatic interest in sourcing as many captives as necessary to fulfil their contract, from whichever suppliers they could engage without specifying supply routes or origins. This ambiguity regarding suppliers and their role in the geographies of the inter-imperial slave trade may have been a deliberate strategy to manipulate the terms of the contract. Ultimately, the final version of the *asiento* prevented the firm from direct involvement on the West African coast, and it appears that Grillo and Lomellino were not particularly inclined to engage in the African and transatlantic legs of the trade.

An illustrative case occurred on 14 august 1663, when Grillo and Lomellino obtained permission to send the *San Juan Bautista* to Ardra to purchase slaves.[25] However, due to operational delays, likely stemming from lack of interest, the permit remained unused by April 1664, even though the ship was anchored in Cadiz and ready to sail. At that point, the firm petitioned the Crown for permission to redirect the ship to the Caribbean, where it would collect a cargo of enslaved Africans for delivery to Veracruz.[26] Despite occasional considerations of sending ships to Africa, Grillo and Lomellino ultimately refrained from doing so.

This decision can be interpreted in at least two ways. Initially, the firm may have been attracted by the potential profits from all legs of the transatlantic slave trade, including the African trade. However, after assuming their role as *asentistas,* they likely recognize the high risks and costs associated with accessing African markets, compounded by their lack of expertise in navigating these complexities. Alternatively, the permit to trade in Africa may have been a contingency plan to ensure a minimal flow of captives to Spanish America while negotiations with Dutch and English suppliers were still ongoing. Ultimately, the Genoese firm opted to bypass African markets altogether, focusing instead on intra-Caribbean exchanges. This approach, which involved subcontractors delivering captives from the Caribbean to Spanish American ports under the firm's name, demonstrates that their primary objectives lay in the intra-Caribbean trade rather than the broader trans-imperial transatlantic trade.

2.3 *The American Networks and the Colonial Markets*

In contrast to their limited involvement in the African trade and the Middle Passage, Grillo and Lomellino sought to tightly control the inter-imperial Caribbean slave trade and the distribution of captives in Spanish America.

---

25 AGI, IG, Leg. 2834, s.f. 9-IX-1663.

26 AGI, IG, Leg. 2834, s.f., 4-IV-1664.

This enhanced control over the Caribbean trade increased opportunities to maximise profits through diverse channels. The legal importation of enslaved Africans into Spanish American markets from the wider Caribbean was frequently accompanied by tax evasion, creating a perpetual cat-and-mouse game with royal officials. According to official records, Grillo and Lomellino transported approximately 21,234 captives from the Dutch and English Caribbean to Spanish America over an eleven-year period. This accounted for about 70% of the quota stipulated in their original contract. Furthermore, the firm used the trans-Caribbean trade as a cover for smuggling Spanish American commodities and European goods, leveraging the guise of the slave trade to facilitate illicit exchanges.

To manage their business in the Caribbean, encompassing the redistribution of enslaved Africans, tax evasion, and the smuggling of Spanish American commodities and European goods, Grillo and Lomellino deployed a network of official factors. These factors acted as key intermediaries connecting Curaçao, Jamaica, and Barbados with the three ports where the *asiento* was authorised to operate: Cartagena, Portobelo, and Veracruz. Cartagena and Veracruz regained their role as exclusive ports for channeling enslaved Africans into the regional Spanish American markets, though neither port ever recaptured the prominence they had achieved during the Portuguese *asientos*. Instead, Portobelo emerged as the primary gateway for the introduction of African captives to Spanish America in the decades that followed.[27]

In each of these ports, Grillo and Lomellino were entitled to appoint three representatives of their firm, who were permitted to travel to the Dutch and English Caribbean islands. As the number of Spanish American ports authorised to receive enslaved individuals expanded over time, the firm's network of factors grew to include locations such as Caracas, San Juan de Puerto Rico and Havana.

From an inter-imperial perspective, these factors coordinated voyages between the Dutch and English slave-supplying hubs in the Caribbean – primarily Curaçao, Jamaica, and Barbados – and Spanish American ports. Curaçao supplied 89,5% of the enslaved Africans, while the remaining captives were dispatched by the English from Barbados (5,5%) and Jamaica (5%).[28] These voyages were undertaken by fleets of five to seven ships hired by Grillo and Lomellino, while others were chartered from across Europe.[29]

27 García-Montón, "The Rise of Portobelo."

28 Marisa Vega Franco, *El tráfico de esclavos con América (asientos de Grillo y Lomelín, 1663–1674)* (Sevilla: EEHA-CSIC, 1984), 186–187, 194–202.

29 Vega Franco, *El trafico de esclavos*, 101–125.

In the intra-Caribbean transport, careful timing was critical to ensure that the enslaved were ready for transport from Curaçao and Jamaica. This aspect was pre-emptively addressed in the contracts between Grillo and Lomellino and their subcontractors, signed in Europe. To comply with contractual agreements, the factors also needed to manage substantial stocks of silver, whether in ingots or minted *pesos*, and commodities for payment and barter. The firm leveraged its access to regional markets for cochineal, cocoa, and indigo, commodities in high demand in European and Asian markets, the latter serviced by the Dutch and the English East India companies (VOC and EIC, respectively).

To execute these tasks, Grillo and Lomellino incorporated into their networks individuals with the expertise and experience necessary to operate within inter-imperial and Spanish American markets. The case of Francisco Hermans is illustrative. Born in Antwerp, Hermans possessed linguistic skills that proved invaluable in maintaining and strengthening relations with Dutch authorities and WIC shipmasters in Curaçao. After passing the scrutiny of the *Consejo de Indias* and demonstrating his status as a Catholic subject of the Spanish Crown, Hermans formally joined the *asiento* administration in May 1669.[30] With extensive experienced in Atlantic trade and smuggling, he brought valuable expertise to the firm. For example, in 1659 Hermans transported wine from the Canary Islands to Guinea, where he exchanged it for enslaved Africans, whom he then delivered to Buenos Aires. His associates in this venture included Benito and Manuel Almeida, Portuguese *vecinos* of Sanlúcar de Barrameda, and Mateo Domínguez from the Canary Islands.[31] By December 1669, Hermans was already in Cartagena, receiving the *San Fortunato* on her return from Curaçao, carrying 309 enslaved Africans and a significant quantity of contraband, including Asian cinnamon and black pepper, European cloth, and Italian silk.[32]

Similarly, Andalusians, Castilians, Creole, and Genoese individuals also joined the ranks of factors in the *asiento* networks. The factors oversaw the flow of enslaved Africans into three main ports, which concentrated 86,2% of the firm's documented trade. Approximately 11,400 captives were delivered to Portobelo, 4,800 to Cartagena, and 2,100 to Veracruz. The remaining 13,7% of enslaved individuals were disembarked at other ports, including Caracas,

30 AGI, IG, Leg. 2834, s.f., 23-III-1669 and 29-V-1669; AGI, Contratación, Leg. 5436, n.º 65, 11-V-1669.

31 García Fuentes, *El comercio español*, 144 and 157.

32 AGI, Contaduria, Leg. 1433, n.º 3.

Cumaná, La Guaira, San Juan de Puerto Rico, Santiago de Cuba, and Santo Domingo.[33]

Once the captives were introduced onto Spanish American soil, a new phase of the *asiento* began. While some enslaved individuals were sold at their ports of arrival, the majority were transported to other destinations for resale. For instance, from Portobelo, captives were transported across the Isthmus of Panama to Panama City. There, part of the group was sold, but most continued their journey to El Callao in Peru. After arrival in El Callao, the survivors were transported to Lima, where they were finally sold. Similarly, Veracruz served as both a port of entry and a transit hub. In September 1669, the *San Vicente* arrived from Curaçao with 501 enslaved. Approximately 200 were sold in Veracruz, while the remainder awaited redistribution. By December of that same year, one of the firm's factor oversaw the inland passage of these men, women and children, from Veracruz to Mexico City.[34]

The distribution of enslaved individuals required extensive logistical knowledge of routes and markets, which the factors alone did not possess. These operations also involved smuggling European and Asian commodities into inland markets and exporting Spanish American commodities in return. Reliable shipmasters and skilled crews were essential for navigating imperial borders in the Caribbean, while similar expertise was required to manage the Pacific coast routes from Panama to Peru. Surgeons, cooks, and guards were vital for ensuring the survival of the enslaved during the harsh marches through the inland passages, while muleteers and shipowners facilitated the transport of both enslaved individuals and contraband commodities.

Grillo and Lomellino engaged in fraud related to the importation of the enslaved and large-scale contraband. Cooperation with local authorities was therefore essential. The firm's factors played a crucial role in forging the necessary alliances at a local level. For example, Italian factors such as Giustiniano Giustiniani or Pedro Matias Cavalieri became deeply integrated in local society by marrying local women of high social standing and spending most of their lives in Spanish America.[35] The success of the 'Genoese' *asiento* heavily relied on the competence and local embeddedness of these factors, whether in

33 Vega Franco, *El tráfico de esclavos*, 186–187, 194–202.

34 Sierra Silva, "Portuguese 'Encomenderos'", 239–241.

35 Alejandro García Montón, "Esclavistas italianos, linajes Navarros y nueva nobleza Borbónica: Justiniano Justiniani, el Istmo de Panamá y el Marquesado de Peñaflorida (1630–1714)," in *Identità Nobiliare Tra Monarchia Ispanica e Italia. Lignaggi, Potere e Istituzioni (Secoli* XVI–XVIII), edited by Carmen Sanz Ayán et al. (Roma: Edizioni di storia e letteratura, 2019), 55–69.

dealing with local authorities, managing cross-American and Pacific transportation networks, or navigating local market for enslaved individuals and commodities.

In addition to mediating the interest of the *asentista* and managing transactions related to the *asiento,* the factors were also responsible for enforcing its clauses – a challenging and often hazardous task. As might be expected, the arrival of these factors in Spanish America was fraught with difficulties. While many local actors benefited from collaborating with the *asiento*, others did not. The *asiento* was partially intended to displace, or at least to compete with, the thriving merchant networks that operated within unofficial Spanish American markets, many of which maintained close ties with local authorities. A significant source of local opposition to the *asiento* arose from these authorities, who had previously profited from the unofficial slave trade. The Genoese firm frequently complained to the *Consejo de Indias* about the lack of support their agents received from Spanish American royal officials dispersed across the Caribbean.

It is difficult to precisely assess the extent, nature, and location of challenges to the *asiento* managed by Grillo and Lomellino. Nonetheless, the various lawsuits the firm initiated against smugglers, the numerous seizure operations conducted by their factors, and the reports submitted to the *Consejo de Indias* all serve as indicators of resistance to the *asiento*. At the same time, complaints filed by the firm provide valuable insights into the organisation of illegal trade. For instance, in January 1663, Domenico Grillo reported that in August 1662, the *San Vicente* and the *Águila Negra* called at Curaçao, aiming to transport approximately 250 *piezas* to Lima, Peru. Grillo claimed that the *San Vicente* was a Spanish ship, though its captain and crew were Portuguese, and included merchants from Cartagena. Similarly, the *Águila Negra,* a Dutch ship under contract to Lima-based merchants,[36] also carried merchants from Cartagena and Seville.

The investors behind the *Águila Negra* and the *San Vicente* were likely similar to individuals such as Gaspar Alfonso, a Panama-based merchant who specialised in shipping enslaved Africans from Cartagena to Portobelo during the 1650s. Alfonso was apprehended in 1664 by one of Grillo and Lomellino's factors, alongside local authorities in Portobelo, while attempting to disembark a cargo of fifty-nine *piezas*.[37] In cases like Alfonso's, Grillo and Lomellino occasionally incorporated such local smugglers into the *asiento*. However, it remains unclear what criteria governed the inclusion of some and the exclu-

36 AGI, IG, Leg. 2834, s.f., 14-I-1663.

37 AGI, Panamá, Leg. 24, R.2, N.54 ll-p.

sion of others. Regardless, it becomes evident that firms operating the *asiento* in a monopolistic fashion could not do so effectively without the tacit support and vested cooperation of local officials and merchant elites.

Grillo and Lomellino's factors also faced opposition from other quarters, notably local tax collectors. These individuals were typically prominent businessmen embedded within networks of alliances that connected them with royal officials and influential members of the colonial elite. As previously noted, one of the innovations of the 1662 *asiento* was the taxation structure it introduced: taxes on the slave trade were abolished, and all fiscal revenues were directly channelled to the royal treasury in Madrid. Implementing this change was contentious, as it disrupted local tax collection systems, diminished revenues, and undermined the social capital of those who held the rights to collect taxes locally. When Grillo and Lomellino's factors refused to pay taxes claimed by local tax farmers, disputes arose in cities such as Veracruz and Panama. The Crown and the *Consejo de Indias* maintained a firm stance on upholding the *asiento* privileges and tax exemptions, but local tax farmers escalated the conflict by petitioning the *Consejo de Hacienda* for revisions to their tax-farming contracts and discounts on previously agreed sums, straining relations between the *Consejo de Hacienda* and the *Consejo de Indias*.[38]

One of the most valuable tools available to Grillo and Lomellino for defending their interests overseas was the figure of the *juez conservador* (notorised magistrate). The *jueces conservadores* oversaw the enforcement of the *asiento*'s privileges and were the only officials authorised to intervene in cases where the *asiento*'s clauses were breached or challenged. However, the ability of *jueces conservadores* to implement their decisions was limited, as they were heavily reliant on local institutions and authorities. Nonetheless, the jurisdictional powers granted to them insulated *asiento*-related matters from interference by other local authorities or courts. The critical importance of the *jueces conservadores* was well recognised by detractors of the *asiento*. For instance, the guild of transatlantic merchants of Seville (*consulado*) attributed the Genoese firm's power to its dual monopoly on the importation of enslaved Africans and jurisdiction over all matters related to the *asiento*.[39] This concentration of authority represented a significant departure from the Portuguese *asientos,* establishing a new jurisdictional framework that would sustain the trade into the eighteenth century.

38 AGI, Escribanía, Leg. 292-A, Lawsuit between alcabala tax collectors and Grillo and Lomellino, 1665.

39 AGI, IG, Leg. 2834, s.f., 19-III-1669.

During the eleven years of the 'Genoese' *asiento*, Grillo and Lomellino proposed the appointment of at least forty-one *jueces conservadores*. Thirty-seven were assigned to Spanish America, spanning locations from México City to Buenos Aires, while the remaining four served in Castile. Notably, these appointments were not limited to the ports officially designated for the *asiento* trade, but extended to regions where Grillo and Lomellino alleged that their monopoly was being violated. This strategy allowed the firm to enforce its jurisdiction across all Spanish American constituencies.

The appointments were made in Madrid, where Grillo and Lomellino submitted their nominees to the *Consejo de Indias* for approval. The candidates were selected for their technical knowledge of conflict resolution, legal procedures, and litigation. These candidates fell into two categories. The first comprised individuals drawn from the local communities where they would serve, chosen for their familiarity with local smuggling networks, understanding of regional power dynamics, and ability to identify potential collaborators. Many of these individuals held positions as governors or royal officials, which provided them with the executive authority necessary to enforce their decisions as *juez conservador*. However, integrating these individuals into the *asiento*'s sphere of influence often required dislodging them from local interests that conflicted with the monopoly.

The second group of *jueces conservadores* comprised men recently appointed by the King to serve as high-ranking royal officials in Spanish America. Through their networks of contacts at court and in various councils, Grillo and Lomellino were able to gather information about these new appointees. They shortlisted some of these individuals and subsequently proposed their names as *jueces conservadores* of the *asiento*. The primary advantage of integrating this group of newly appointed colonial officials into the *asiento* was the opportunity to co-opt them while they were still in Spain, before their departure to the Americas. Equally significant was the fact that these men were not yet embedded within local elites, making them more amenable to overseeing the *asiento* in their respective jurisdictions.[40]

The appointment of *jueces conservadores* by Grillo and Lomellino does not necessarily imply that these individuals always acted in the firm's interest or supported its factors in Spanish America. While some *jueces conservadores* benefitted from aligning themselves with Grillo and Lomellino, others prioritised their personal gain or even opposed the firm. For instance, Don Diego Ortíz de Largacha, governor and *alférez mayor* (lieutenant major) of Veracruz

40 Alejandro García-Montón, "Corona, Hombres de Negocios y Jueces Conservadores. Un Acercamiento En Escala Transatlántica (s. XVII)," *Jerónimo Zurita* 90 (2015), 75–112.

and *juez conservador* of the *asiento*, became one of the most influential figures in Veracruz in 1667. His wealth included real estate, livestock, jewelry, and African slaves.[41] In 1665, Ortíz de Largacha had supported the *asiento* factors in a contentious lawsuit against local tax farmers, which also implicated other high-ranking officials in Veracruz.[42] Despite the risk of alienating his peers, Ortíz de Largacha's ruling upheld the *asiento's* privileges, leading to a significant financial loss for the tax farmers. Collaboration with Grillo and Lomellino's factors allowed him to further enhance his personal fortune.

In contrast, Andrés Robles, the *juez conservador* in Buenos Aires, also amassed personal wealth through the *asiento*, but at the expense of Grillo and Lomellino. Robles never remitted the 60,000 *pesos* or the cloth seized from two slave ships attempting to call at Buenos Aires to smuggle goods, keeping the profits for himself.[43]

Some *jueces conservadores* served the private interests of the *asentistas*, while others prioritised their own wealth or aligned with local opponents of the *asiento*. However, their role was not necessarily a binary choice between these sides. In 1672, Grillo and Lomellino's factors in Lima expressed outrage at the decisions made by Don Álvaro de Ocampo, the *juez conservador* in the region. Ocampo adhered strictly to his judicial responsibilities, refusing to take sides in disputes involving the *asiento* factors, the Viceroy of Peru, and the Lima merchant guild. His impartiality displeased the factors, who resented his refusal to accept a salary for fulfilling his duties as magistrate.

3 Conclusion

Following a decade during which the official African slave trade to Spanish America was effectively suspended by the Crown and another ten years during which it operated beyond its control, the *asiento* of Grillo and Lomellino reorganised the foundations of the contract and the trade itself. Institutionally, the 'Genoese' *asiento* marked a decisive break from the 'Portuguese' *asiento* system. From 1662 until the 1740s, firms and companies engaged in the *asiento de negros* operated as monopolistic players within an exclusive

41 Michel Bertrand, *Grandeza y miseria del oficio: Los oficiales de la Real Hacienda de la Nueva España, siglos XVII y XVIII* (México D.F.: Fondo de Cultura Economica, 2013), 460–61.

42 AGI, Escribanía, Leg. 292-A Lawsuit between alcabala tax collectors and Grillo and Lomellino, 1665.

43 AGI, IG, Leg. 2835, s.f., 27-V-1673; AGI, Buenos Aires, Leg. 3, Lib. 9, fols. 237v-40v.

and differentiated jurisdictional space in the Spanish Empire's framework. The fiscal system governing the trade in enslaved Africans was also transformed: instead of revenues being collected locally in Spanish America, all income was now channelled directly to the royal treasury in Madrid, to the detriment of Spanish American town councils.

The geography of the trade also shifted. The primacy of Cartagena and Veracruz as leading slaving hubs declined, and official slave trade operations gradually expanded to multiple ports. The trans-imperial intra-Caribbean routes became the primary source of enslaved Africans for Spanish America. Consequently, the business of slavery grew increasingly fragmented and specialised, with transatlantic operators and intra-Caribbean slave traders flourishing, at the devastating cost of the lives and suffering of enslaved Africans.[44]

The profile of merchants involved in the trade also evolved significantly compared to the pre-1640 period. Although Grillo and Lomellino were the public faces of the *asiento*, it is incorrect to characterise the post-1662 *asiento* as an exclusive Genoese enterprise. Under the Genoese firm's aegis, Dutch and English, previously excluded from Spanish America due to their religious beliefs or hostile relations with Spain, entered the trade and aligned their interests with the *asentistas*. These newcomers were often companies that emerged from transnational investment networks.

The post-1662 *asiento* also opened the door to further internationalisation of the slave trade to Spanish America. While the RA and the WIC were prominent newcomers, Italians, Spanish, and Creoles continued to participate and benefit from the new *asiento* system. Over time, Portuguese actors also re-entered the trade, underscoring the broad and diverse participation in this evolving system.

---

44 Gregory E. O'Malley, *Final Passages: The Intercolonial Slave Trade of British America, 1619–1807* (Chapel Hill: University of North Carolina Press, 2014); Borucki, Eltis and Wheat, "Atlantic History", 433–461.

CHAPTER 3

Outsourcing: A Chartered Privileged Approach to the *Asiento*

The 1660s proved to be an eventful decade in English history. In 1660, the Stuart Monarchy under king Charles II was restored following the country's retreat from republicanism after a brutal civil war. From 1665 to 1667, the Anglo-Dutch War raged in the Atlantic, and 1666 saw both a major plague epidemic and the Great Fire of London devastate the capital.

Since the early seventeenth century, the Atlantic region had become increasingly significant for English traders, and by the 1650s, it had assumed an important role in the English economy. The Stuart kings demonstrated a keen interest in overseas trade, strengthening the Caribbean colonies, and controlling their economic output. This royal focus, as will be seen below, was not always welcome by the communities of planters and colonial producers across the Atlantic, who sought greater freedom to trade and a more open Atlantic policy. Dissatisfaction was exacerbated by the increasing taxation and duties imposed on production and trade by the metropole.

No trade attracted greater royal attention than that to Africa's western coast. As colonial production expanded and reliance on the commodification of cash crops grew, so too did the need to secure a steady supply of labour. The growing importance of enslaved African labour meant that English trade to Africa was, from the early seventeenth century, protected by a monopoly granted to charted companies, most importantly the Guinea Company. Royal charters for trading companies in England often emerged after protracted periods of petitioning and lobbying to Parliament and various royal councils. Such charters frequently privileged the few individuals who had driven the petitioning process.

During the period of republican rule, however, Atlantic trade was opened, albeit with some caveats, to all Englishmen. This policy aimed to weaken the growing power of exclusive chartered groups within society. The liberalisation of trade during the Commonwealth period allowed the Caribbean colonies to be consistently supplied with European and Asian commodities, as well as enslaved labour. It also enabled colonial production to be exported reliably to the metropole without much delays, as trade agreements were negotiated directly between metropolitan merchants, ship captains, and colonial planters, bypassing the perceived inefficiencies of chartered institutions.

It was therefore a source of considerable frustration for traders and planters when the restoration of the monarchy reinstated a restrictive monopoly, enshrined in a charter and granted to an exclusive group of men, this time with minimal commercial experience and direct ties to the Crown. In 1660, the feared monopoly was granted to the Company of Royal Adventurers into Africa (RA), which was launched as a distinctly royal enterprise with the Duke of York (the future King James II) serving as its governor. Despite extensive privileges and aristocratic membership, the RA's lack of experience and inadequate planning for sustained capital influx, combined with unfulfilled hopes of discovering sources of African gold, nearly bankrupted the Company soon after its creation. This experiment with royal involvement in a chartered trading company was novel, although it foreshadowed similar endeavours later in the century, as discussed in Chapter 7.

The RA's royal and aristocratic composition and its initial focus on pursuing gold in Africa, rather than engaging in the transatlantic (slave) trade, resulted in significant financial losses. Consequently, the monopoly had to be restructured in 1663. This relaunch incorporated a substantial number of non-aristocratic Atlantic traders, who brought expertise, extensive networks, and a structured understanding of the complex circuits of trade in the Atlantic. These traders were drawn to the RA by the prospect of accessing the Company's privileges, playing a pivotal role in the labour supply chain to English colonies, and potentially accessing the Spanish Empire, whether through illegal smuggling or legally via the *asiento* contract.

This chapter explores England's initial engagement with the Spanish *asiento*, an arrangement that would re-emerge in the eighteenth century when British chartered and joint-stock companies operated as direct *asentistas* under the Bourbon Monarchy. While historiography has extensively addressed British participation in these later *asientos*, the RA's subcontracting role in the Spanish *asiento* during the 1660s has received little scholarly attention. This neglect may partly stem from the tendency to dismiss the RA as an unsuccessful enterprise and to view its decision to contract with *asentistas* for such a significant endeavour as an example of its members' folly. This chapter seeks to illuminate the processes and motivations behind the RA's decision to contract part of the *asiento* with *asentistas* Grillo and Lomelilino, as well as the arguments of its opponents who sought to challenge it.

The initial contract between the Company and the Genoese *asentistas* was secured with the assistance of an influential Atlantic trader and member of the Company, Sir Martin Noell. Noell utilised both the resources of the Company and his extensive private network to negotiate what became the first of two contracts involving the RA. This agreement was signed in 1663, following extensive negotiations during 1662.[1] A subsequent contract was negotiated directly between the *asentistas* and the Company one year later. The decision to engage in a contract to support the empire of another state, while simultaneously holding an exclusive monopoly within the English realm, was, as will be discussed below, deeply unpopular among English traders and planter communities. This decision arguably inflicted irreparable longer-term damage to the relationship between London and English Caribbean societies.

1 A Smoking Screen: Sir Martin Noell and the Negotiations with the *Asiento*

A range of motivating factors persuaded the Company's management, and by extension English authorities, that the opportunity to engage with Spain through the *asiento*, despite being fraught with challenges both domestically and abroad, was worth pursuing. Of these, the most compelling was the potential access to the closed Spanish Empire, with its extensive and lucrative colonial markets for commodities and bullion.

The contracts established between the RA and the *asentistas* positioned the Company as a subcontractor to the *asiento*. The agreements, formalised in Europe, specified quotas, gender composition, and pricing for enslaved individuals purchased in West Africa and delivered to Barbados or Jamaica. From there, the enslaved were transported in *asiento* ships, to Spanish America. Half of the payment was provided upfront upon signing the contract. This mechanism, which the *asentistas* also employed with the WIC as detailed in Chapter 4, was essential for ensuring sufficient capital for both the RA and the WIC to fulfil their contractual obligations, particularly given the dire financial circumstances both companies faced. The advance payment system also represented a significant advantage for the RA, eliminating the uncertainties and delays associated with negotiating payments on-site in the Caribbean. This region was characterised by scarce monetary resources, with transactions often reliant on silver or colonial commodities for bartering, a situation that incentivised illicit trade and inflationary cycles throughout the colonial Caribbean.

Negotiating payments in Barbados or Jamaica carried significant risks, including protracted delays that could result in the detention of ships, crews, and enslaved. This, in turn, necessitated extensions of credit for mariners'

1 Vega Franco, *El trafico de Esclavos*, 42–43.

wages and the upkeep of the enslaved. Pre-agreed conditions and partial payments mitigated the likelihood of disputes, while ready cash enhanced liquidity and fostered trust between parties. Furthermore, advanced payments and participation in the *asiento* provided a compelling justification for renewing the Company's patent and extending its privileges, while simultaneously pre-empting rival European states, such as the Dutch Republic or France, from seizing the opportunity.

When initially approached regarding potential participation, the Company responded favourably to the proposal to act as supplier to the *asiento*. However, a raid conducted by Christopher Myngs, an Englishman, on Santiago de Cuba during the sensitive negotiations prompted Spanish authorities to reconsider the involvement of an English company as a subcontractor. Their concerns were heightened by the prominent role of James, Duke of York, the brother of the English king, as governor of the Company. Madrid feared inter-state escalation, with James and his Company being held accountable for potential English violence in the Caribbean.[2] To avoid such risks, the RA was excluded from the negotiations, leaving the *asentistas* and the Spanish Monarchy to engage with Sir Martin Noell, a longstanding Atlantic trader and members of the Company, who agreed to undertake the contract in a private capacity.

Interestingly, the private negotiations between Noell and the *asentistas* were openly discussed with the Company. This suggests that Sir Martin Noell was representing the broader interests of the Company while ensuring acceptance by the Spanish authorities. Although primary sources documenting communications between Noell and the RA outside official meetings are scarce, there is no evidence to suggest that Noell and the RA considered a system under which the former might obtain licences from the RA to fulfil the contract with the *asentistas*. The RA had ceased issuing licences for private trade at the time of the negotiations between Noell and Grillo and Lomellino. Drafts of the proposed new patent further indicate that the Company was firmly committed to prohibiting private trade by its members.

While Noell negotiated with the *asentistas,* discussions in England regarding the extension of the Company's trading patent were finalised. Support for broadening the existing patent, likely encouraged by the knowledge of the contract signed between the holders of the *asiento* and the WIC on 15 Septem-

2 W. N. Sainsbury, ed., "America and West Indies: May 1664," in *Calendar of State Papers Colonial, America and West Indies: Volume 5, 1661–1668*, (London: Her Majesty's Stationery Office, 1880), 205–212. *British History Online* (BHO), accessed November 29, 2017, http://www.british-history.ac.uk/cal-state-papers/colonial/america-west-indies/vol5/pp205-212.

ber 1662, helped ensure the Company's continued privileged access to the West African coast on behalf of England. As English Company members had realised decades earlier, the threat of Dutch hegemony provided a powerful and persuasive argument for the Company's continued existence and privileged position.

Martin Noell (1615–1665) played a key role in negotiating and securing the contracts with Grillo and Lomellino. Noell had been heavily involved in the official Africa trade since the Interregnum (1649–1660), during which he became a member of the English East India Company (EIC) as it gained access to the Guinea trade.[3] As a long-time supplier of indentured European labour to the English American colonies, he had extensive experience in meeting the labour needs of the Caribbean markets and considerable expertise in shipping human cargo. Like many London merchants engaged in Atlantic provisioning and the tobacco trade, Noell owned land in both Barbados and Jamaica.[4]

During the 1640s, Noell observed the shift from small-scale tobacco production to large-scale sugar production, which accelerated reliance on enslaved labour as cultivation practices changed. Sugar production demanded intensive labour, and the plantation model concentrated land ownership into fewer hands over time. The promise of land had long motivated indentured European servants to cross the Atlantic, but as land became scarcer and tobacco gave way to sugar, interest in indenture contracts declined. This combination of labour-intensive sugar production and a reduction in available indentured contract labourers led to an increasing reliance on enslaved labour.

In March 1663, Noell, along with fellow RA member Alexander Bence, travelled to Amsterdam to meet with Grillo and Lomellino's correspondent, Francesco Feroni, to negotiate what became the first contract with the *asiento*. At the same time, Feroni continued his negotiations and contracting with the WIC. Alexander Bence brought significant experience to the negotiations. In

3 Julie M. Svalastog, "Challenging Porous Frontiers: Atlantic Merchants and the Potential of the Indian Ocean, 1640–1650," *Journal of Early American History* 9, no. 2–3 (2019), 145–62; Julie M. Svalastog, *Mastering the Worst of Trades: England's Early Africa Companies and Their Traders, 1618–1672* (Leiden: Brill, 2021).

4 David Armitage and Michale Braddick, *The British Atlantic World, 1500–1800* (Basingstoke: Palgrave Macmillan, 2002), 53; Nuala Zahedieh, *The Capital and the Colonies: London and the Atlantic Economy 1660–1700* (Cambridge: Cambridge University Press, 2010); Nuala Zahedieh, "Making Mercantilism Work: London Merchants and Atlantic Trade in the Seventeenth Century," *Transactions of the Royal Historical Society* 9 (1999): 143–158; Bernard Bailyn, "Communications and Trade: The Atlantic in the Seventeenth Century," *The Journal of Economic History* 13, no. 4 (1953), 381.

addition to his involvement with the EIC and the short-lived Morocco Company (established in 1661), Bence had a well-established trade network in Spain, where his son, Alexander Bence jr., had served as the family firm's representative in Alicante for several years before the *asiento* negotiations began.[5] Bence sr. also spent considerable time in Cadiz and at the court in Madrid.

Bence jr. reportedly travelled to Madrid during this period, where, according to the correspondence with RA member William Coventry, he attempted to secure not only a deal for the RA to supply enslaved people to the Spanish West Indies but also the possibility to transport enslaved people directly into Spain, a circuit not included in the remit of the *asiento de negros*. Unfortunately, little is known about this latter endeavour, as primary sources remain silent regarding the negotiations and their outcomes. There is scant evidence in the Company's records to suggest this initiative ever materialised.

In a letter to Richard Fanshawe, then England's diplomat to the Spanish court, Coventry introduced Alexander Bence jr. and described his mission, which centred on ensuring fair, if not favourable, treatment for the Company during the Amsterdam negotiations conducted by Francesco Feroni:

> I Am commanded by his Royal Highness [James Stuart, Duke of York] to recommend to your favour this Gentleman Mr. Alexander Bence, who is employed by his Royal Highness direction on behalf of the Company of R. Adventurers Trading into Africa; the occasions on which he is employed are chiefly two; the one to follow the Companies concerns about a Licence to Import Negroes into Spain (…) The other is to negotiate with the Seigniors Grilloe & Lomeline, concerning the delivering Blacks in the West-Indies, and concerning which they have a treaty depending in Holland (…) but because it may probably happen that the Person treating in Holland [Feroni], will reserve much to Seign. Grilloe, and Lomeline for their own determination, and that perhaps he (dwelling in Holland) may not be so equal to our Company, as we hope Seign. Grilloe and Lomeline are. His Highnes hath judged it best to have a Person at Madrid, who being fully instructed in all the concerns of the Company, may be ready on all occasions to promote their Interest

5 Marine Lives: Will of Alexander Bence (the Elder): http://www.marinelives.org/wiki/MRP:_Alexander_Bence_the_elder_will (accessed on 03.05.2024), Will of Alexander Bence the Younger (RA investor): http://www.marinelives.org/wiki/MRP:_Sir_Alexander_Bence_will (accessed on 03.05.2024)

> (…). It is a Trade which his Royal Highness hath been pleased in a most peculiar manner to support, both with his countenance and care (…).[6]

Fearing that Feroni might 'reserve too much' for the *asentistas*, the Duke of York, to whom Coventry served as a private secretary, sought to ensure the Company had a capable representative in Madrid. The aim was that direct dealings with Grillo and Lomellino would yield more favourable terms. While in Madrid, Bence jr. collaborated with other Englishmen engaged in similar missions, such as John Reid, who was appointed sub-commissioner of prizes at Barbados and served as the RA's factor there, and Henry Rumbold, who acted as England's consul to the Spanish court and presented Martin Noell's interests.[7]

Rumbold, who had previously served as consul in Cadiz, Seville, and Sanlúcar de Barrameda, as well as in the Prize Office in the mid-1660s, was well versed in the complexities of overseas trade, particularly in the Atlantic. His familiarity with Reid, derived from their shared roles in managing prize affairs in Barbados, facilitated coordination in advancing the RA's interests during the Madrid negotiations.

2 Martin Noell and Alexander Bence in Amsterdam

The Amsterdam City Archives contains a reference to a notarial deed indicating that Sir Martin Noell and Alexander Bence sr. were present in Amsterdam specifically to meet Francesco Feroni as part of negotiations over servicing the *asiento*.[8] According to this first notarised agreement, the Englishmen committed to supplying 600 to 1000 enslaved individuals, referred to as "indische negros of mooren". Some of these individuals were reportedly already in Barbados and available for transportation on the *asiento* ships of Grillo and Lomellino. The remainder were to be shipped from West Africa to Barbados

6 William Coventry, from Madrid, 9 April 1664. From Richard Fanshawe, *Original letters of His Excellency Sir Richard Fanshaw: during his embassies in Spain and Portugal* (London: A. Roper and the Black Boy, and R. Basset at the Mitre in Fleetstreet; and W. Turner, at the Angel at Lincolns-Inn Back Gate, 1702), pp. 59–60.

7 The National Archives (TNA): T 70/75, p. 19–20 for more on the sending of John Reid to the colonies.

8 Stadsarchief Amsterdam (SAA): Notarieel Archief (NA): 1148, fol.205, 03.12.1664 (written *1664-03-12*)

and handed over to the Genoese agents for further transport to the Spanish West Indies.[9]

The ship *St. Jean Baptist* was expected to depart from Cadiz for the Spanish West Indies, calling at Barbados. On board this ship were agents representing the *asentistas* as well as Mr. Giles Lytcott, representing Noell and Bence. Half of the cargo was paid for upfront in Europe upon signing the contract, while the second half was to be settled using silver and commodities loaded on board after the sale and prior to departure from Spanish territories. The expenses for freight and travel arrangements were borne by Grillo and Lomellino.

The deed refers to "indische negros of mooren". In English primary sources, the term "moors' typically refers to people from Northern Africa, differing from the broader Iberian usage, which could encompass individuals from North Africa and sub-Saharan Muslims. This is the only known mention of North Africa as a potential source for enslaved individuals under the *asiento*. A letter from that same year, drafted on behalf of the English king, specifically mentions Tangier as a possible location for trafficking enslaved individuals to supply the *asiento*. Tangier had recently been added to England's overseas possessions as part of the dowry of Catherine of Braganza, the Portuguese princess and wife of King Charles II.

Using Tangier as a foothold, Noell, Bence and the Duke of York expressed interest in the Moroccan coast. This interest is unsurprising given the Bence family's prior involvement in the Morocco Company, alongside the Duke of York, which had held a monopoly on trade with the Moroccan Coast.[10] Henry Rumbold was also involved in managing Tangier in his role with the Navy, while his son, Henry Rumbold jr., served as storekeeper in the town.[11] Despite this contemporaneous interest, there is little evidence that the Morocco Company or Tangier played any significant role in the *asiento* or the English slave trade more broadly.

9 TNA: CO 1/17, 106 and 107

10 Marine Lives: Will of Alexander Bence (the Elder): "*Sept. 11. (1661) 170. Grant to the Duke of York, Lord Willoughby of Parham, Col. Wm. Legg, and Tho. Culling, Alexander Bence, Robert Starre, John Lewis, and Philip Payne, of London, merchants, of all regions, countries, and territories from Cape Blanco, situate in 20° N. lat., on the continent of Africa, unto 2 leagues to the northwards of Sallee, lying in 34° N. lat., on the north part of Africa, bordering on the Atlantic Sea, and of the free trade thereof for 31 years...*".

11 Tristan Stein, "Tangier in the Restoration Empire," *The Historical Journal* 54, no. 4 (2011), 985–1011.

3 The Terms of the First Contract and the Deployment of the *Asiento*

Upon conclusion of the first contract, detailed clauses granted the *asentistas'* agents permission to settle in Barbados and Jamaica to oversee the trade. This was a slightly more intrusive arrangement than what the WIC had negotiate for Curaçao, where *asiento* agents were limited to accounting for the enslaved, organising transport to Spanish America, and handling payments to the WIC in cases of delayed transport (see Chapter 4). The RA also stationed its own agents on the island to perform comparable duties. While English sources do not specify the names of the agents representing the *asentistas* in Barbados, the RA was represented at various times by Giles Lydcott, John Reid, and prominent figures in the early modern English Caribbean, such as the Colleton and the Modyford families.

According to the agreement, the RA purchased enslaved individuals in Africa, transported them to Barbados and Jamaica, and transferred them to the *asentistas'* ships. This arrangement was similar to the system the *asentistas* had negotiated with the WIC. The RA, however, enjoyed a privilege not granted to the WIC: the placement of a Company factor "was to be placed aboard such ships", a clause documented by G.F. Zook.[12]

Grillo and Lomellino also requested that the English freight two ships in Spain for use in the transatlantic slave trade outside the *asiento*. To conceal the involvement of the *asentistas* and avoid scrutiny from Spanish authorities, the ships had to be chartered by a Spanish merchant acting on behalf of the English. This arrangement was agreed upon by Alexander Bence, John Reid, and a Mr. John Allen.[13] Despite careful planning, this arrangement encountered significant problems. In a 1667 letter to fellow RA member Henry Bennet, Earl of Arlington, John Allen explained:

> in respect it was dangerous for the Grillos that the Court of Spain should know the ships' contracts were made with English, the freight was to be paid to a Spaniard, who instantly assigns it to George Wallis, of Cadiz, for the use of the contractors in England.[14]

12 G. F. Zook, *The Company of Royal Adventurers Trading into Africa* (Cornell University: Lancaster, Pa., Press of the New Era Printing Co., 1919), p. 93.

13 As far as can be ascertained, Allen was not a member of the company himself, but a near relative – Thomas Allen, served as an RA factor on the African coast. Thomas was accused of conducting private trade, and we find John writing to the RA in his relative's defense – TNA: CO 1/17, no. 103 – 18.12.1663.

14 BHO: Calendar of State Papers Colonial (Cal. S.P. Col), Vol 5, no. 1481, May 14, 1663.

The secrete agreement stipulated that Grillo and Lomellino would cover the cost of freighting the ships via an RA agent in Cadiz. Payments were to be made in instalments of 5,000 pieces of eight per ship every four months to avoid suspicion. However, these instalments were never paid. This failure coincided with Gillo and Lomellino's default on a payment to the Spanish Monarchy under the *asiento*, suggesting potential liquidity issues. By the time Allen wrote his letter, two years of freight costs had accumulated, amounting to 80,000 pieces of eight. Allen explained that, despite assurances from the Genoese that their agents in Jamaica and Barbados had been instructed to settle the dues, payments remained outstanding. Therefore, John Allen

> begs a letter to the Ambassador at Madrid to countenance his agents in fair demanding of the money from the Grillos, and, if they refuse then to pay it, that by a letter from his Majesty the matter may be presented by his Excellency to the Queen Regent of Spain.[15]

It is unclear how this dispute was ultimately resolved. According to Alejandro García-Montón's research, Martin Noell remained dissatisfied with the outcome of the agreement and this first *asiento* contract overall. In his final will, written before his death during the plague of 1666, Noell claimed that the Genoese merchants owed him significant sums.[16] Despite his frustration, the outcome for the RA appears to have been favourable, as the Company signed a second contract with Grillo and Lomellino at the earliest opportunity. By the end of June 1664, the second (direct) contract was ratified, and the RA operated as an *asiento* contractor in its own right until 1667.[17]

15 *Ibid.* TNA : T 70/75, p. 52. E. Donnan, *Documents Illustrative of the History of the Slave Trade to America*, vol. 1, 1441–1700 (Washington D.C.: Carnegie Institution of Washington, 1930), fn. 171.

16 Alejandro García-Montón, "Seducing Smugglers: The Spanish Empire's Incentives for Inter-Imperial Official Slave Trade, 1640–1670", unpublished paper presented at workshop: *Slavery, Trade, Law, and Empires in the Early Modern Atlantic,* Austin: University of Texas at Austin, 11 April 2019, 22–25. TNA: CO 1/17, p. 105, undated. 1663 can be too early but the document itself is undated and bound with material relating to matters about the colonies from the summer of 1663. Lytcott's name is spelled in numerous ways: Lidcot/Lydcott/Lydcote. By 1663 Lytcott had already been frequenting the English Caribbean for a decade, after the subcontract expired, he directed his attention to attacking Spanish shipping.

17 TNA: T 70/75, p. 16. June 16, 1664. Scelle, *La traite négrière,* vol. 1, 524.

4 Contracting the Company of Royal Adventurers into Africa

The year 1664 opened a new chapter in the relationship between English slave traders and the *asiento*. The new contract signed with the *asentistas* was not with individual members of the Company, such as Noell or Bence, but rather with the RA itself. As outlined in a petition submitted by the Company to the English king, the RA committed to transporting a higher number of enslaved Africans than under Noell's contract, amounting to 3,500 annually. The destination of the Company's slaving ships was Barbados, where the agents of the *asentistas* guarantee a price of £20 for each *pieza de Indias*.[18] According to the Company, the contract had the potential to generate a total of 85,000 Spanish pieces of eight annually in Spanish silver.[19]

In addition to the £20 price per enslaved, the English king had, since early 1663, levied a duty of 10 pieces of eight for each enslaved person sold to Spanish slave traders. However, this duty was waived in the case of trade conducted by the RA under the *asiento*, indicating that the English monarch sought to penalise smuggling and illicit trade while respecting Spain's political economy of empire. As we argue below, this selective enforcement of trade regulations diverged from the strict rules imposed on English colonial settlers and became only one of many reasons why contracting the *asiento* proved to be a highly contentious decision, with unforeseen and long-lasting effects on the shape of the English Atlantic.

The importance of England's Caribbean colonies to its economy steadily increased from the early seventeenth century. Tobacco, the first major cash crop, experienced a price boom in the 1630s, leading to a surge in transatlantic migration. However, by the early 1640s, the tobacco market had become saturated.[20] In the Caribbean, tobacco was gradually replaced by sugar. By the later 1640s and early 1650s, the potential of sugar and other colonial products

18 Relying on the National Archives Currency Converter for the decade 1660, £20 would be equal to £2100 (2017), *Currency converter: 1270–2017*, https://www.nationalarchives.gov.uk/currency-converter, accessed 03.05.2021. TNA: State Papers (SP) Spain, 94/46, p. 3. A. P. Thornton, "Spanish Slave-Ships in the English West Indies, 1660–85," *The Hispanic American Historical Review* 35, no. 3 (1955), 379; A. P. Thornton, "The Organization of the Slave Trade in the English West Indies, 1660–1685," *The William and Mary Quarterly* 12, no. 3 (1955), 399–409.

19 Spanish pieces of eight were, according to Zook, accepted at four shillings each. Zook, *Ibid.*, p. 74, fn6; TNA: Colonial Office (CO) 1/19, P. 5–7. T 70/75, p. 16.

20 Menard, R.R., *Sweet Negotiations: Sugar, Slavery, and Plantation Agriculture in Early Barbados* (Charlottesville: University of Virginia Press, 2006), 16 and 19–21.

was increasingly recognised by political administrators, influenced by prominent Atlantic merchants-turned-politicians, including Martin Noell.

This growing recognition also led to rising tensions between the colonies and the colonial administration in England, as sentiments in the metropole shifted towards stricter colonial management. The colonies were expected to prioritise the economic interests of the mother country, and their output was to be protected and regulated.[21] As early as 1651, the first of several Navigation Acts was enacted, banning all trade between the colonies and non-English merchants. These regulations contributed to the outbreak of the First Anglo-Dutch War (1652–1654). The war ended in a near-stalemate between two nations that had been allies for much of the preceding decades, but it underscored the Caribbean colonial communities the inequity of their subordinate role in England's economy.[22]

Concerns about colonial rights to trade freely were evident in correspondence from Barbadian governor Sir Francis, Lord Willoughby, to state officials in London. In letters addressing early conflicts between planters and the metropole, the governor emphasised that if the island were denied trade with foreign merchants and forced to rely solely on English shipping, the colonists requested in return:

> To have as great freedom of trade as ever, no companies to be placed over them, and no commodities engrossed into private men's hands.[23]

This request fell on deaf ears. By the time the contracts with the *asentistas* were signed, the Navigation Acts, combined with the RA's expanded privileges in 1663, ensured the Company exclusive access to the West African coast on behalf of England. These restrictions left colonists with no alternative legal means to access enslaved labour. This situation further aggravated English colonists in the Caribbean as well as Dutch traders across the Atlantic. Unsurprisingly, tensions escalated, leading to increase complaints and petitions from the English Caribbean and contributing to the outbreak of the Second Anglo-Dutch War (1665–1667).

21 Armitage and Braddick, *The British Atlantic*, 53; Zahedieh, *The Capital and the Colonies*; Zahedieh, "Making Mercantilism Work", 149.

22 TNA: CO 1/11, CO 1/12, J. E. Farnell, "The Navigation Act of 1651, the First Dutch War, and the London Merchant Community," *The Economic History Review* 16, no. 3 (1964), 439–454.

23 BHO: Calendar of State Papers Colonial (Cal. S.P. Col), Vol 9, pp. 85–87, http://www.british-history.ac.uk/cal-state-papers/colonial/america-west-indies/vol9/pp85-87. Accessed 21.11.2017.

5 Competing for Enslaved Labour: A View from the English Caribbean

The combination of the Navigation Acts and the RA's renewed patent rendered the colonists entirely dependent on the Company for enslaved labourers and the credit needed to purchase them. The only alternative was the risk of engaging in illegal trade. The contracts between the RA and the *asentista* became a major point of contention between the Company and the English planter community in the Caribbean. This was a problem the WIC did not face, as it lacked significant plantation colonies by the 1660s, having lost northeastern Brazil in 1654 and with Suriname still in its infancy as a plantation economy.

Interactions between the RA and the English colonies were fraught and rarely successful. The Company's agreement to supply the Spanish American markets with large numbers of enslaved individuals via Barbados and Jamaica further strained relations with the colonists, who themselves required enslaved labour. Colonists were also expected to refrain from trading with foreign merchants, even though Dutch private traders and French merchants from Nantes offered viable alternatives for importing enslaved labourers. These foreign traders operated outside the purview of the WIC, making them attractive options for planters frustrated by the constraints imposed by the RA and English regulations.

The Company's second patent effectively restricted the English slave trade to its exclusive control. Planters and colonists could legally purchase labour only from fellow Englishmen, and the only Englishmen permitted on the coast of Africa were representatives of the RA. The colonists, already frustrated by the closure of a trade that had been open for all for the preceding decade, now doubted the Company's capacity to meet its obligations both to them and to the *asiento*. They were justifiably concerned that they would lose access to enslaved labourers in favour of traders offering Spanish bullion, while the colonists themselves could only afford to pay the Company in commodities, bills of exchange, or promissory notes redeemable in London.

Deliveries under the *asiento* were made in Barbados and Jamaica, the two largest English Caribbean colonies. The market was divided between English planters offering sugar and other colonial commodities (primarily sugar and some tobacco), often on credit, in exchange for enslaved labourers, and the *asiento* agents offering Spanish American commodities (such as indigo, cochineal, and cacao) or bullion. During the early 1660s, English colonists were grappling with market saturation and declining sugar prices, which further reduced the bartering value of sugar. The purchasing power of planters exchanging sugar for enslaved labour plummeted, as legal colonial exports were restricted to a one-directional trade funnelled exclusively to the English domestic market. Planters were barred from accessing other consumption markets in Europe or elsewhere, compounding their economic challenges.

The Company's announcement in the summer of 1664 that it had reached an agreement with Grillo and Lomellino triggered a surge of petitions from the English Caribbean community. These petitions demanded that the English trade to West Africa be opened to all Englishmen and called for a cap on the prices the Company could charge for enslaved Africans sold in the colonies, prices they argued should be lower than those offered to the *asentistas*. A joint petition presented by Paul Painter on behalf of a group of Caribbean planters summarised the concerns of the colonial community in the early 1660s:[24]

> there is of late a new erected Company of Adventurers Trading into Africa, who claiming to themselves the sole and only Trade of Negroes on the coast of Guiney, have totally obstructed the former free Trade of all Adventurers thither; and having contracted with Forreiners for supply of the Spanish Plantations with Negroes, do leave the English Plantations in America, which produce the same Commodities with the Spanish, either ill supplied, and at excessive prices, or not at all supplied; by reason whereof, and of the obstruction of the freedom of Trade in Negroes as aforesaid, all His Majesties Plantations in America be provided, will speedily be brought to the inevitable destruction.[25]

For the planters, the *asiento* contract clearly violated key provisions of the Navigation Acts, as it allowed agents of the *asentistas* to establish themselves in Barbados and Jamaica and operate there as traders. The planters cited the 1660 version of the Act, which included a clause explicitly barring non-English subjects from conducting trade in the colonies:

---

24 British Library (BL): Petition titled *An Answer of the Company of Royal Adventurers of England Trading into Africa to the Petition and Paper if certain Heads and Particulars thereonto relating and annexed, exhibited to the Honourable House of Commons by Sir Paul Painter, Ferdinando Gorges, Henry Bateson, Benjamin Skutt and Thomas Knight, on the behalf of Themselves and Others concerned in His Majesties Plantations in America.* Anno Dom. 1667. Zook, *The Company of Royal Adventurers*, chapter IV.

25 Printed petition, '*The Humble Petition of Sir Paul Painter Knight, Ferdinando Gorges, Henry Bateson, Gentlemen, and Benjamin Skutt and Thomas Knights Merchants, on behalf of themselves and others concerned in His Majesties Plantations in America*'. Copy dated 15 Nov 1667.

> That no alien or person not born within the allegiance of our sovereign lord the King, his heirs and successors … shall from and after (…) exercise the trade of a merchant or factor in any of the said places (the English colonies); upon the pain of forfeiture and loss of all his goods and chattels.[26]

Despite all pleas and arguments, such a permission was granted to the Company by King Charles II, likely at the behest of his brother, as early as 1663, and used as a concession during negotiations with the *asentistas*. Noell's first agreement with the Genoese arranged for the ship *St. Jean Baptist* to sail from Cadiz for the Spanish West Indies, carrying agents of the Genoese alongside Mr. Giles Lytcott, who represented the Company. The ship was also laden with a '*parcell of negroes*' supplied by the RA. The cargo was to be paid for with silver and commodities from the Spanish colonies.

Although confirming the outcome of the *St. Jean Baptiste*'s voyage has proved challenging, the arrangement that allowed the RA to sell its cargoes of enslaved Africans to *asentista* agents settled in the English colonies, and to be paid in Spanish American commodities, contradicted several clauses of the Navigation Acts. Moreover, it undermined the very purpose of these Acts as instruments for defining the boundaries of England's political economy of empire.

The rising frustration these developments caused among the Caribbean planters, as well as among English colonial and metropolitans traders unaffiliated with the privileged Company, had long-term effects on colonial relations in the English Atlantic. The mismanagement of trade by various companies, which the *asiento* contract being but one unpopular decision, further solidified the negative view held by English colonial subjects towards monopolies.

The Company's own records reveal its struggles from the outset to meet the contractual obligations for delivering enslaved Africans to the *asentistas*. The only surviving records of the Company's transports to the West Indies pertain to Barbados during the winter season of 1663/1664, approximately six months before the contract with Grillo and Lomellino was signed. In that period, the Company transported just over 3,000 enslaved Africans, a comparably high number that likely contributed to the perception, both within and outside

26 'Charles II, 1660: An Act for the Encourageing and increasing of Shipping and Navigation.', in *Statutes of the Realm: Volume 5, 1628–80*, ed. John Raithby (s.l, 1819), pp. 246–250. *British History Online* http://www.british-history.ac.uk/statutes-realm/vol5/pp246-250 [accessed 3 May 2024].

the Company, that it could handle the contract with the *asiento*.[27] In the agreement with Grillo and Lomellino, however, the Company promised to double this number, committing to deliver 3,500 enslaved from the Calabar coast to Barbados and Jamaica annually under the contract.[28]

Johannes Postma's research indicates that the Dutch imports under the *asiento* through Curacao during the same period totalled around 3,600 enslaved between 1663 and 1667. Comparing the Company's commitments to these figures, the contract appears overly ambitious. The outbreak of war between England and the Dutch Republic in March 1665 was particularly ill-timed for the Company, as the contract to supply the Spanish Americas had been signed less than a year earlier. The war severely disrupted Atlantic trade, increasing risks and costs for the Company's slave traders operating between West Africa and the Caribbean.

Some arguments can be made to explain the reasoning behind the *asiento* contract from the Company's perspective. Firstly, the contract was negotiated during a period of peace and relative prosperity compared to the years of escalating Anglo-Dutch rivalry that followed. Additionally, the Company believed it could service both the *asentistas* and English planters, because on the potential of trading in New Calabar (in present-day Nigeria).[29] Data from voyages undertaken under English flag during the *asiento* period suggest that Calabar was the most frequented port of purchase, accounting for 27% of the enslaved Africans acquired by the Company (see Tables 3.1 and 3.2). For 40% of the voyages, the region of purchase is unknown, but many likely also originated from the Calabar coast.[30]

Although Postma's numbers suggest that fulfilling the contract was improbable, the RA's imports during the winter of 1663/1664, totalling 3,000 enslaved individuals, represented an exceptional trading season. This figure nearly matched the total number imported via Dutch Curacao over five years of *asiento* trade. It is therefore plausible that the RA assessed its capabilities based on this anomalously successful trading year.

27 TNA: T 70/646.The only surviving ledger of the RA for their slave imports in the Caribbean referred to Barbados and stated that in the period stretching from August 11, 1663 to March 17, 1664 the company imported a total of 3,075. Zook, *The Company of Royal Adventurers*, 82.

28 TNA: CO 1/19, no.5–7.

29 Donnan, *Documents Illustrative of the History*, p. 108.

30 TNA: T 70/75, p. 16.

TABLE 3.1 African ports of slave purchases under English flag during the contracts with the *asiento*, 1664–1667

Places of trade in Africa	1664	1665	1666	1667	Total
Ardra	5	7		3	15
Calabar	8	8	9		25
Gambia	4	1			5
Kormantine	3	4	1		8
Madagascar	2				2
Port of trade unknown	18	7	5	6	36
Total	**40**	**27**	**15**	**9**	**91**

SOURCE: TSTD, HTTP://SLAVEVOYAGES.ORG. (ACCESSED: 27.09.2024). PART OF THIS INFORMATION ALSO AVAILABLE IN JULIE SVALASTOG, *MASTERING THE WORST OF TRADES: ENGLAND'S EARLY AFRICA COMPANIES AND THEIR TRADERS, 1618–1672* (LEIDEN: BRILL, 2021).

TABLE 3.2 African regions of slave purchases under English flag during the contracts with the *asiento*, 1664

RA ships reportedly lost to the Dutch – no port recorded	6
West Central Africa and St. Helena, incl. Angola	1
Bight of Biafra and Gulf of Guinea islands, incl. the Calabar coast	11
Bight of Benin	2
Gold Coast	2
Other Africa	14
Total	36

SOURCE: TSTD, HTTP://SLAVEVOYAGES.ORG. (ACCESSED: 27.09.2024). PART OF THIS INFORMATION ALSO AVAILABLE IN SVALASTOG, *MASTERING THE WORST OF TRADES: ENGLAND'S EARLY AFRICA COMPANIES AND THEIR TRADERS, 1618–1672* (LEIDEN: BRILL, 2021).

6 Conclusion

The fears expressed by colonial planters, coupled with the suboptimal outcome and eventual abandonment of the *asiento* contract, have led many to view the RA's confidence in fulfilling its obligations to Grillo and Lomellino as hubristic. This perception is reinforced by the broader difficulties the RA faced by the late 1660s, including prolonged warfare, insufficient returns, liquidity shortages, and mounting colonial debts. These issues culminated in the Company's bankruptcy and the establishment of its successor, the Royal African Company (RAC), in 1672, a trajectory mirrored by the fate of the First WIC.

However, Company records suggest that the RA was at its peak during the early summer of 1664, when negotiations with Grillo and Lomellino were concluded. Unaware of the troubles to come, the Company had just experienced its highest returns during the preceding winter. The potential for the *asiento* contract motivated merchants with Atlantic expertise to join the Company during the period between its first and second patents, likely influencing the decision to place the English slave trade under a patent of privilege in January 1662.

From the perspective of these experienced merchants, relying solely on the elongated and volatile debt cycles of the English Caribbean, compounded by dependence on the personal credit of selected members, was unsustainable. The *asiento* offered an opportunity to introduce bullion into the Company's trade, alleviate its debts, and improve liquidity. On paper, the arrangement appeared optimal: the RA assumed the risks of the African trade and the transatlantic crossing, while Grillo and Lomellino shouldered the responsibility of transporting the cargoes from the English colonies to the Spanish American markets and ensuring payment in cash.

Sir Ellis Leighton, the Company secretary, expressed frustration when the RA was accused of prioritizing Spanish traders over English planters. Responding to complaints from Paul Painter, Leighton asserted that only 1,200 enslaved Africans had been sold to Spanish traders and blamed the outbreak of the Anglo-Dutch War for the planters difficulties.[31] He argued that the planters' inability to pay for the enslaved had instead endangered the Company. Leighton concluded by noting that while free trade might suit the needs of individual colonies, the king and the Company had to consider the broader interests of England's trade.[32]

Regardless of projections, price fluctuations, and supply challenges, the *asiento* had a lasting impact on the English Atlantic. By breaching the contentious Navigation Acts, it became another symbol of royal favouritism and metropolitan *adhocracy* to the English Caribbean community. The contract reinforced alliances among private traders excluded from the African-Caribbean

31 Printed pamphlet, *Answer of the Company of Royal Adventurers to Sir Paul Painter et. al.* See pamphlet, the duke offered either £17 or 2,500 pounds of muscovado sugar pr. slave

32 *Ibid.*

trade monopoly and planters chafing under its restrictions. These alliances ultimately succeeded in dismantling the monopoly on Atlantic trade by the end of the century, following the fall of the Stuart monarchy. However, as William Pettigrew's noted in *Freedom's Debt*, the dismantling of monopolised slave trade paradoxically resulted in an appalling increase in the trade of enslaved Africans, as free trade in human beings boomed.[33] The colonial communities' rights to trade freely came at a devastating cost to thousands of unfree Africans.

Despite the RA's failures, its successor, the RAC, continued the same practices. The RAC maintained its trade monopoly at a loss and took on later *asiento* contracts, including agreements with Barrosso and Porcio, as well as Balthasar Coymans. By the early eighteenth century, yet another English company, the South Sea Company, became the first and only English holder of the *asiento* itself. As *asentista* after 1717, the South Sea Company subcontracted the deteriorating RAC. The South Sea Company's infamous bubble in 1720, where the Spanish *asiento* played a significant role, would go down in history as another cautionary tale of monopolistic ambitions in the Atlantic trade.

33 William Pettigrew, *Freedom's Debt: The Royal African Company and the Politics of the Atlantic Slave Trade, 1672–1752* (Chapel Hill: University of North Carolina Press, 2013.

CHAPTER 4

Outsourcing: A Joint-Stock Approach to the *Asiento*

In 1657, the Dutch governor in Curaçao ordered a ship to call at Caracas to deliver a letter to the local governor, inviting the inhabitants of the Spanish Main to come to the island to engage in trade. The recipient was reportedly inclined to accept the invitation but "did not dare show the same publicly".[1] Direct trade between the Spanish Americas and the Dutch Caribbean was explicitly forbidden under the Peace of Münster (1648).[2] Nevertheless, in the Caribbean, Dutch and Spanish American merchants frequently engaged in illicit trade. One such merchant promised to equip a ship to fish for turtles in the near Curaçao, thus creating an opportunity to send an agent to the Dutch island to establish trading contacts.[3]

The 1650s witnessed a surge of trade generally, and in the slave trade specifically, via Curaçao, as the Dutch entrepôt became increasingly significant for Dutch merchants seeking access to the Spanish American colonies. However, it was the contract that the WIC, the Dutch joint stock company holding a charter issued by the States General – the highest authority in the Dutch Republic – signed with the 1662 *asentistas* that shaped Curaçao's development into a major hub for the trade and distribution of enslaved Africans, Spanish American commodities, and Euro-Asian goods in the Caribbean.

The commercial significance and growth of Curaçao are directly linked to Dutch involvement in the 1662 *asiento*, when the WIC played a pivotal role as supplier of a substantial number of enslaved people to the *asentistas* Grillo and Lomellino. However, during the 1660s and early 1670s, the Company faced severe financial difficulties, ultimately succumbing to bankruptcy in 1674 when it was dissolved.[4] The apparent contradiction between the WIC's

1 Charles T. Gehring and J.A. Schiltkamp, *Curaçao Papers, 1640–1665* (Interlaken, NY, 1987), 93.

2 Article VI of said treaty stated that subjects of the States-General were forbidden to trade in the Spanish possessions in the West-Indies (and vice versa). Lieuwe van Aitzema, *Saken van Staet en Oorlogh in, ende omtrent de Vereenigde Nederlanden*, vol. III (The Hague: Johan Veelt, Johan Tongerloo, ende Jasper Doll – Boeck-verkoopers, 1669), 260.

3 Gehring and Schiltkamp, *Curaçao Papers*, 94.

4 Odegard, "Recapitalization or Reform?", 102.

importance as a subcontractor for the *asiento* and its dire financial state is explored next.

1 The WIC: A Joint Stock Company

Established in 1621, the WIC received an official charter granting it exclusive rights to trade and establish colonies in West Africa and the Americas on behalf of the States General.[5] Its organisation mirrored the decentralised structure of the Dutch Republic, consisting of five regional Chambers. This structure was intended to ensure a fair division of economic activity among participating Dutch cities and regions. An overarching board of delegated directors, the *Heren XIX*, coordinated Company's activities and managed its consolidated accounts. From its inception, the WIC operated as a publicly traded joint-stock company, with shares that were transferable and sellable.

Between 1621 and 1623, the five Chambers raised capital independently, collectively amassing approximately 7.1 million guilders.[6] The appeal for investors lay in the lucrative Atlantic trade network pioneered by Portugal and Spain, which encompassed overseas colonies extracting silver and producing tradable commodities such as sugar, indigo, cochineal, and cacao. Investors anticipated that if the WIC succeeded in challenging Iberian dominance in the Atlantic, they would benefit from significant profits. With this ambition, the *Heren XIX* developed a 'Grand Design' aimed at dislodging the Portuguese from Angola and Brazil. Following another round of capital acquisition in 1624, the WIC launched multiple assaults on Portuguese Atlantic possessions. While these efforts largely failed, the Company resorted to preying on Spanish Caribbean shipping – a lucrative enterprise combining privateering with the acquisition of Atlantic commodities.

This business model, although unsustainable in the long term, proved effective during the 1620s and the 1630s. The Company's most notable achievement during this period was the capture of part of the Spanish silver fleet near Cuba in 1628, an event that delighted Dutch investors and politicians. Dutch imperial ambitions in the Atlantic persisted, and the WIC successfully captured parts of northeastern Brazil in 1630. Subsequently, the Company ousted

5 See for the history of the WIC Henk den Heijer, "The Dutch West India Company, 1621–1791", in *Riches from Atlantic Commerce. Dutch Transatlantic Trade and Shipping, 1585–1817*, edited by Johannes Postma and Victor Enthoven (Brill: Leiden 2003), 49–46.

6 Henk den Heijer, *De geoctrooieerde compagnie* (Deventer: Wolters Kluwer, 2005), 37–68.

the Portuguese from the West African Gold Coast (rebranding the Portuguese *Castelo da Mina* as Dutch Elmina) and captured Luanda in 1641. By the early 1640s, the WIC had established an Atlantic empire, comprising a significant sugar colony (northeastern Brazil) and African trading posts (São Tomé, Elmina, and Luanda), which provided sources of enslaved labour and gold.

Transitioning from empire-building to profitability proved more challenging than anticipated. The costly conquests required monopolisation and regulation of colonial access, which was difficult to achieve. Private Dutch merchants criticised the WIC for failing to supply sufficient goods to the colonies, while the Company simultaneously contended with expensive wars and uprisings. In the 1630s, the WIC raised additional capital, reaching 17 million guilders in 1639.[7] Thereafter, the Company relied on loans and the freighting of third-party ships to address operational shortcomings. Many directors and shareholders capitalised on this by renting ships to the Company, sometimes simultaneously acting as both shareholders and creditors.

The 1645 revolt by the Portuguese planters in Dutch Brazil eventually led to the loss of that colony to Portugal in 1654. A similar fate befell the WIC's Angolan possessions six years earlier. Overwhelmed by debt and without a viable empire, the Company saw its stock prices plummet. By the mid-1650s, the WIC retained New Amsterdam in North America and a few minor Caribbean islands, which had primarily served as bases for privateering. Among these was Curaçao, described by one contemporary Englishman as a "cursed little barren island".[8] Despite its barrenness, Curaçao offered a significant advantage: its location outside of the Caribbean hurricane zone and proximity to the Spanish Main.[9]

While the WIC was engaged in the costly defence of Dutch Brazil, the Amsterdam merchant community increasingly shifted its focus to the Caribbean. English and French colonists in the region required little persuasion to purchase enslaved people and supplies from Dutch fleets. Traditional historiography maintains that it was the Dutch who were responsible for the Caribbean sugar boom, allegedly encouraging sugarcane cultivation, providing cap-

7 Den Heijer, *De geoctrooieerde compagnie*, 63.

8 Donnan, *Documents Illustrative of the History*, Vol. 1 (Washington D. C.: Carnegie Institution of Washington 1930), 111.

9 See also Jan de Vries, "The Dutch Atlantic Economies", in *The Atlantic Economy during the Seventeenth and Eighteenth Centuries*, edited by Peter A. Coclanis (Columbia, SC: University of South Carolina Press, 2005), 1–29. De Vries argues that the collapse of the Dutch Atlantic Empire was followed by a "second Dutch Atlantic economy", based primarily on trade with foreign colonies.

ital, and consistently underselling competitors.[10] Recent research, however, has demonstrated that this claim is greatly exaggerated. Nonetheless, Dutch trade in the Caribbean flourished during the 1650s. In addition to English and French colonists, inhabitants of the Spanish America were enthusiastic customers of Dutch merchants.

The island of Curaçao was ideally situated to supply the Spanish colonies in South America with European and Asian goods, as well as enslaved labourers, either legally or illegally, depending on the political economy of the Dutch and Spanish empires and the stipulations of international treaties. Yet, the indebted and struggling WIC was unable to fully capitalise on this advantageous position. With share prices low, raising new capital was not an option, forcing the Company to seek alternative means of financing its operations. Independent merchants were thus allowed to trade in the Caribbean upon payment of a fee to the Company, and from the 1650s onwards, the WIC also subcontracted the services of private merchants in the slave trade.

Private slave traders contracting with the WIC financed their voyages through bottomry loans, which enabled borrowers to secure funds for a specific voyage, while also absorbing the "risks of the sea", such as shipwrecks and pirate attacks.[11] When bottomry loans proved insufficient to cover the risks of the voyage and the fees owed to the Company, the WIC adopted a model akin to the Spanish practice of the early seventeenth century. It began issuing licences to individual merchants, granting them the right to trade in enslaved people within the Company's jurisdiction.[12] However, licensing the trade did not signify the relinquishment of the WIC's monopoly on the Dutch slave trade. The Company insisted that the permissions granted to private merchants to trade with and within Africa were merely "provisional".[13]

In this respect, the WIC's relationship with licensed slave traders resembled that of the Portuguese *asentistas* during the first half of the century. The primary difference lay in the purpose: while the WIC used licensing to offset its operational shortcomings, the Portuguese *asentistas* employed it as an extension of a longstanding practice. Licensing the slave trade had been the default

10 See for instance Herbert Klein, *The Atlantic Slave Trade* (Cambridge: Cambridge University Press, 1990). See for a critical appraisal of this reading of the history, Christian Koot, *Empire at the Periphery. British Colonists, Anglo-Dutch Trade, and the Development of the British Atlantic, 1621–1713* (New York: New York University Press, 2011).

11 Den Heijer, *De geoctrooieerde compagnie*, 137.

12 Henk den Heijer, *Goud, ivoor en slaven. Scheepvaart en handel van de Tweede Westindische Compagnie op Afrika, 1674–1740* (Zutphen: Walburg Pers, 1997), 26–30.

13 NL-HaNA (Dutch National Archives, The Hague), WIC (Archive of the first WIC) 17, minutes of the meetings of main shareholders, 27 October 1665.

system of the Spanish Monarchy since its early days, a system sustained whenever the importation of enslaved Africans to Spanish America was directly managed by the Crown, as was the case in the 1650s. Furthermore, and contrary to the Monarchy and its Portuguese *asentistas*, the WIC was unable to market the licences in secondary markets and profit from this instrument in a meaningful financial manner.

2 The WIC: The Provisions of the *Asiento* and Curaçao

Georges Scelle argues that the 1662 *asiento* was primarily an instrument for financing the Spanish Monarchy, rather than a mechanism to ensure a reliable supply of enslaved labour to Spanish American colonies.[14] This claim aligns with a longstanding scholarly tradition conceptualising the Spanish *asientos* as fiscal, logistical, and allocative mechanisms that enabled the Monarchy to distribute wealth and social capital to elites aligned with the Crown. Simultaneously, they increased the state's efficiency in collecting tax revenue and reduced administrative costs. Despite this, Grillo and Lomellino committed to delivering 24,500 enslaved people to the Americas over seven years, with a preferred annual shipment of 3,500 individuals.[15] For each *pieza de india* sold in the Spanish American ports, they were required to pay a fixed fee of 100 *pesos*. Discounts applied for younger individuals, while older or unhealthy enslaved people were classified as "undeliverable" and excluded from the total.

Crucially, and in contrast to pre-1640 'Portuguese' *asientos*, Grillo and Lomellino were expected to organise the trade themselves, rather than issuing licences to third-party traders. To this end, they were permitted to introduce enslaved people into Spanish American ports using a fleet of five 500-ton ships. To facilitate these transactions, the firm was authorised to appoint agents and *jueces* to oversee the operations, provided these officials were subjects of the Spanish Crown.

Foreign involvement in procuring enslaved Africans was inevitable, as Spain lacked any establishments on the African coast. The *asiento* clearly anticipated that Grillo and Lomellino would engage with non-Spanish traders to meet their obligations. They were authorised to purchase enslaved individuals from any nation at peace with Spain, which excluded Portugal and France. The remaining viable candidates with access to the African markets were the English and the Dutch. Since the Genoese were uninterested in man-

14 Scelle, *La Traite Négrière*, vol. 1 502–503.

15 For the text of the 1662 *asiento*, see Vega Franco, *El Trafico de Esclavos*, 203–217.

aging the transatlantic trade themselves, preferring instead to focus on inter-Caribbean commerce, the English and Dutch Caribbean ports emerged as logical hubs for exchange. This arrangement was facilitated by the fact that, prior to the 1662 *asiento,* Barbados, Jamaica and Curaçao had already established themselves as centres for trade in Caribbean commodities and enslaved people, often operating in defiance of legal boundaries and redefining spaces of illegality.[16]

These Caribbean islands thus emerged as preferred intermediaries between the transatlantic slave traders – the WIC and the RA – and the ships of the *asentistas,* facilitating the supply of enslaved people to the Spanish colonies. The use of Caribbean hubs for distributing transatlantic shipments of enslaved Africans aligned with the exclusive and monopolistic ambitions of the Spanish, English and Dutch empires. Both the WIC and the RA held government-issued charters (or patents) granting them the exclusive right to participate in the Atlantic slave trade on behalf of their respective sovereigns, as did the *asentistas* under their contract with the Spanish Monarchy. Importing enslaved Africans destined for Spanish America via Barbados, Jamaica, and Curaçao allowed all parties to adhere to the political economies of their respective empires, as defined by the Habsburgs in Madrid, the Stuarts in London and the States General in The Hague. The Caribbean appeared to be transitioning from a sphere of illegality and smuggling in the slave trade to one of regulated and ostensibly legal exchanges among monopolistic partners.

3 Outsourcing the Slave Trade to a Joint-Stock Company

Even before the signing of their *asiento* contract, Grillo and Lomellino contracted the RA in February 1662 to deliver 3,500 enslaved people annually for two years (a total of 7,000 individuals) to Barbados and Jamaica.[17] As discussed in the previous chapter, the English failed to meet the agreed delivery numbers, and by 1663, pressures in Madrid sought to annul the contract for political reasons. Nevertheless, a new agreement was negotiated in 1664, stipulating a delivery of 3,000–4,000 enslaved people within a year.[18] However, by 1664, the English company was on the brink of collapse due to the Second

16 Cátia Antunes, Rob Post and João Paulo Salvado, "Het omzeilen van monopoliehandel. Smokkel en belastingontduiking bij de handel in brazielhout, 1500–1674", TSEG – The Low Countries Journal of Social and Economic History 13, no. 1 (2016), 23–52.

17 Vega Franco, *El trafico de Esclavos,* 42–43.

18 Vega Franco, *El trafico de Esclavos,* 43–45.

Anglo-Dutch War, which particularly devastated English holdings in West Africa. The inability of the English to fulfil their initial contract left Grillo and Lomellino seeking a new partner to manage their transatlantic slave deliveries. With the Portuguese and French ruled out, the Dutch were the only viable option.

In 1662, the WIC remained the monopolist of the Dutch slave trade. Financially strained and depleted of capital, resources, and manpower, the opportunity to subcontract part, if not all, of the *asiento* must have appeared promising. The subcontract with the *asentistas* offered the possibility of accruing Spanish silver into its Caribbean coffers and potentially revitalising the Company's overall finances. Curaçao, falling under the administrative jurisdiction of the Amsterdam Chamber, became central to these negotiations. Grillo and Lomellino authorised their agent, Alejandro Bosco, to initiate discussions with the Amsterdam Chamber in the summer of 1662. These negotiations culminated in a contract signed on 15 September 1662,[19] under which the WIC committed to delivering between 1,000 and 1,400 enslaved Africans to Curaçao in the first half of the following year, with an additional 700–1000 individuals to follow in the latter half of 1663.

While the RA had originally been contracted to deliver 3,500 people, the WIC was tasked with supplying 2,000. This difference did not necessarily reflect contrasting perceptions of Dutch and English capabilities in the slave trade but rather indicated that the *asentistas* regarded the WIC as a reliable partner to complement what the English had failed to deliver. In other words, the WIC was perceived as complementary to rather than an alternative for the RA.

Grillo and Lomellino's trust in the Dutch grew after the 1662 contract, despite some difficulties in meeting its terms.[20] The *asentistas* subsequently offered the WIC new contracts: in 1667 (for 4,000 enslaved people to be delivered to Curaçao the following year), in 1668 (again for 4,000), in 1670 (for 3,000), in 1671 (for 4,000–4,500 slaves), and in 1672 (for 3,000).[21] These short-term contracts provided Grillo and Lomellino with the flexibility to adjust their choice of trading partner to the political volatility of the 1660s

19 See for a printed copy of the contract, S. van Brakel, "Bescheiden over den slavenhandel der West-Indische Compagnie", *Economisch-Historisch Jaarboek*, IV (1918), 61–66.

20 NL-AsdSAA (Amsterdam City Archives), NA (Notarial Archives) 2724 (notary Vincent Swanenburgh), 15 September 1664. The WIC failed to deliver the slaves for the September 1662 contract on time in Curaçao.

21 See for a copy of the 1667 contract, Postma, *The Dutch in the Atlantic Slave Trade*, appendix 3, 349–353. For a copy of the 1672 contract, see A. Eekhof, "Twee documenten betreffende den slavenhandel in de 17e eeuw", *Nederlands Archief voor kerkgeschiedenis* XI (1914), 281–294.

and to renegotiate terms as necessary. Similarly, the WIC initiated renegotiations as it gained experienced in managing the slave trade under the *asiento*. For example, after the first contract, agreements included more cautiously worded commitments regarding the number of enslaved people to be delivered, thereby reducing the likelihood of the Company being blamed for supply shortfalls.[22]

For the *asentistas*, negotiating short-term and regular contracts allowed them to continually assess alternative partners and respond to volatile conditions in African supply markets as well as fluctuations in the Caribbean and intra-American markets. This flexibility enhanced adaptability, which in turn increased the potential for improved economic outcomes.

While the repeated renewals of the *asiento* contracts might suggest a mutually satisfactory partnership between the Genoese firm and the WIC, this was not entirely the case. The WIC consistently failed to deliver the full number of enslaved Africans stipulated in its contracts. Between 1663 and 1674, the Company managed to supply about 70% of the promised number of enslaved people to the Caribbean agents of the *asentistas* in Curaçao (see Table 4.1). In the meantime, the *asentistas* faced difficulties with the Spanish Crown, primarily due to arrears in their annual payments. The precise reasons for these delays have been discussed earlier. However, it is important to note that Grillo (following the death of his partner) secured an extension of the *asiento* from the Queen Regent in 1668, with modified terms lasting until 1674.[23] As was customary, the Monarchy granted the *asentistas* a second opportunity to fulfil the clauses of the initial *asiento*. This decision recognised the long-standing relationship between the two parties, ensured the continued supply of the American markets to avoid local unrest, and aimed to recover the potential fiscal revenues associated with the trade.

4 The WIC and the *Asiento*

For the WIC, participating in the *asiento*, even as subcontractor, offered virtually guaranteed sales for a significant number of enslaved Africans. The Company's involvement in the slave trade had been in serious decline due to a crippling lack of working capital. Private merchants had captured a significant share of the market for delivering enslaved people to non-Dutch buyers in the

22 Cornelis Goslinga, *The Dutch in the Caribbean and on the Wild Coast, 1580–1680* (Assen: Van Gorcum, 1971), 365.

23 Scelle, *La traite Négrière*, vol. 1, 534–536.

TABLE 4.1 Deliveries of *piezas de Indias* on Curaçao by WIC for Grillo and Lomelin, 1663–1674 (the figures for *piezas de Indias* have been rounded to whole numbers)

Year	Contracted	Delivered
1663	1400	1136
1664	700	770
1665		110
1666		0
1667		300
1668	4000	901
1669	4000	3031
1670		1330
1671	3000	2618
1672	4500	2060
1673	3000	1759
1674		616
	20,600	14,631

SOURCES: THE VARIOUS *ASIENTO* SUBCONTRACTS (SEE TEXT) AND SAA, NA 3226 (NOTARY HENDRICK OUTGERS), 9 NOVEMBER 1676.

Caribbean. Furthermore, the Dutch colonial sphere lacked a substantial Atlantic plantation colony in the 1660s. While Brazil had been a natural focal point for slave deliveries prior to 1645, new Dutch plantation colonies only began to emerge in the 1670s.

This absence of competing plantation interests positively influenced the WIC's negotiating position. Unlike the RA, the Dutch Company did not face opposition from planter groups concerned about competition for their supply of enslaved labour. Grillo and Lomellino offered to pay 107.5 *pesos* for each *pieza de indias* delivered to their factor in Curaçao, an amount that remained constant throughout their contracts.[24] Payments were preferably made in Spanish silver pieces of eight in Curaçao, although it is likely that the WIC also accepted payments in kind, given the increasing importation of Spanish

24 For a sense of scale: an earlier (non-asiento related) contract with a private party for the delivery of slaves to the Spanish Main via Curaçao dating from 1659 mentioned a price of 125 *pesos* per slave. Klooster, "Slavenvaart op Spaanse kusten", 124.

American commodities into the island.[25] To further enhance its appeal to the *asentistas,* the WIC agreed to waive all additional tariffs typically imposed on slave sales in Curaçao.

As soon as the WIC signed the *asiento* subcontract in 1662, it began scrambling to gather sufficient resources to fulfil its obligations. Although the directors may have preferred to organise the slaving voyages themselves, rather than relying on private merchants under the system of 'recognition payments' (licences), the chronic lack of working capital remained unresolved. From the outset, it was clear that the WIC would need to charter third-party ships and rely on expensive bottomry loans to meet its contractual commitments. Grillo and Lomellino agreed to provide two advances of 50,000 guilders, payable in Amsterdam in two instalments.[26] However, part of this advance was not forthcoming. Francesco Feroni, who succeeded Alejandro Bosco as their agent, had to be summoned in 1663 to make the payment. Feroni, aware of the WIC's financial difficulties, refused to proceed without sufficient guarantees.[27]

The WIC's organisation structure also complicated the execution of the *asiento.* Although the Amsterdam Chamber, which controlled Curaçao, took the lead in matters related to the contract, its directors consulted their counterparts in other Chambers. For instance, the Zealand Chamber was immediately invited in 1662 to equip a slave ship for the initial contract. Subsequent subcontracts involved the overarching body of the WIC, the *Heren XIX*. To meet the requirements of the 1667 subcontract, the *Heren XIX* instructed multiple Chambers to dispatch slave ships to Curaçao. These subcontracts were also discussed at meetings of the main participants (largest shareholders).

One contentious issue in many WIC meetings was the terms under which third parties were enlisted for voyages under the *asiento*. The Chambers attempted to coordinate these terms to ensure a level playing field for all third parties, regardless of their port of departure within the Republic. Third-party involvement often required substantial loans to the WIC through bottomries, one of the few remaining financing mechanisms available to the Company. While these loans provided security to lenders (as they were voided in cases of shipwreck or irreparable damage), they came with exorbitant interest rates. Upon the successful return of a ship, the WIC was obliged to repay

25 Payments in produce (like cochineal, cacao or hides) were likely accepted as well. Klooster, *Illicit Riches*, 110.

26 Van Brakel, 'Bescheiden over den slavenhandel', 64.

27 NL-AsdSAA, NA 3177 (notary Arnout van Zurck), 26 May 1663. See also ibid, NA 2724 (notary Van Swanenburg), 15 September 1664.

the principal and a significant risk premium, which placed further strain on its finances.

In addition to bottomry loans, the WIC offered profit-sharing arrangements to private shipowners. However, these arrangements proved financially disappointing for the Company, as evidenced by the surviving notes from various meetings in the 1660s. Some of the private ships hired were deemed "inadequate" for slaving voyages.[28] During a *Heren XIX* meeting in 1669, one of the main points of contention was how the WIC could secure profits from the slave trade "currently enjoyed by the [private] ship-owners".[29] Directors from the Chamber of Zealand specifically criticised the use of third-party vessels, arguing that it encouraged smuggling by captains working for private shipowners.

Even if the WIC managed to generate some profit from subcontracting the *asiento,* the Company was unable to achieve the gains it initially anticipated. A key issue was its inability to finance operations through equity. The low share price and the precarious financial state of the WIC made capital acquisition almost impossible, except through expensive advances of capital via various forms of loans. In 1666, the directors proposed a potential solution to this acute problem by launching a special fund dedicated to the African trade. WIC shareholders were invited to invest in this fund, with its capital earmarked exclusively for the African (slave) trade north of Benin. After a relatively warm request from investors, a renewed request for subscriptions in 1668 brought the fund to a total of at least 700,000 guilders. The WIC directors diligently utilised most of this fund to finance slaving voyages to Curaçao, but the capital proved insufficient to fully sustain operations. Furthermore, as investors in the fund were entitled to one-third of the profits from the voyages it financed, the WIC ultimately failed to realise the profits it had initially envisaged under the subcontract.[30]

5 Amsterdam Merchant Networks and the *Asiento*

From the outset of the *asiento* subcontract, the WIC relied on private merchants, alone or organised in partnerships, to fulfil its contractual obligations.

28 NL-HaNA, WIC 34, 11 and 14 May 1668.

29 NL-HaNA, WIC 29, Minutes of the Zeeland Chamber of the WIC, 7 March 1669.

30 See S. van Brakel, "Eene memorie over den handel der West-Indische Compagnie omstreeks 1670", *Bijdragen en Mededelingen van het Historisch Genootschap* 35 (1914), 87–104.

Jonathan Israel describes a "consortium of Amsterdam merchants" that handled much of the WIC-related shipping and trade,[31] although the degree to which these merchants were formally organised remains unclear. Many of them had previously invested in a wide range of commercial ventures across the Atlantic and beyond, predating their indirect participation in the *asiento*.[32] It was this group of merchants, rather than the WIC itself, that brought the Dutch slave trade to its relative peak during the third quarter of the seventeenth century, when it accounted for over 20% of all transatlantic slave trade at the time. Despite its significance, this phase of Dutch involvement in the slave trade remains seriously understudied. What is evident is that private merchants capitalised on the WIC's weak financial position by assuming much of its role as a carrier of enslaved people to the Caribbean, often in direct cooperation with the Company or as independent participants in the Atlantic trade.

The Amsterdam notarial archives contain numerous deeds related to the activities of private slave traders, including affidavits, charter parties, freight contracts, bottomry loans, and insurance agreements.[33] Prominent merchants such as Henrico Mathias, Heerman Abramsz, and Michiel van Amelandt were active in these ventures. Many had significant experience trading with Spanish America. Mathias, for example, was one of the largest Dutch participants in the trade to Buenos Aires, and in 1656 – six years before the Grillo and Lomellino *asiento* – he arranged a slave transport for Jacinto Vasques, a merchant in Seville.[34] Heerman Abramsz, who had previously worked for the WIC on the West Coast of Africa, became director-general in Guinea for the Company in the 1670s.

Some of Grillo and Lomellino's agents in Amsterdam also played a personal role in organising slaving voyages. After 1662, this position was held by Francesco Feroni, a Tuscan merchant who resided in the city since the early 1640s. Feroni, who had amassed a fortune in the grain trade, later diversified his investments to include Caribbean trade.[35] He was eventually succeeded by Andrea d'Estevan. These agents likely received compensation from the *asen-*

31 Jonathan Israel, *Dutch Primacy in World Trade, 1585–1740* (Oxford: Oxford University Press, 1989), 241–242.

32 Antunes and Silva,"Amsterdam Merchants", 3–30.

33 See the Transatlantic Slave Trade Database (TSTD), which includes data on this group collected primarily by Franz Binder.

34 Klooster, *Illicit Riches*, 54.

35 Hans Cools, "Francesco Feroni (1614/16–1696)", in *Your Humble Servant. Agents in Early Modern Europe*, edited by Hans Cools, Marika Keblusek and Badeloch Noldus (Hilversum: Uitgeverij Verloren, 2006), 39–50.

tistas for their services, but they also leveraged their positions to secure additional benefits. Feroni and D'Estevan were granted permission by the WIC to send an annual ship to West Africa and then to the Caribbean to trade in enslaved Africans, exempt from all the usual rights and duties imposed by the Company on trade within its Atlantic domains. According to records from the Trans-Atlantic Slave Trade Database, Feroni owned multiple slave ships, including one that received permission to sail directly to Cartagena in 1669.[36] In 1672, D'Estevan was permitted to send two ships to Africa to procure 350 enslaved people each.[37] D'Estavan was assisted in this venture by Manuel Belmonte, a prominent member of the Portuguese Nation in Amsterdam, who remained connected to the *asiento* in different capacities, including as an investor in the so-called 'Coymans' *asiento* of the 1680s.

6 Routes and Procedures

Slave ships owned or freighted by the WIC typically began their voyages at Texel, the outport for Amsterdam, although some departed from Zealand (Middelburg or Flushing). From there, they sailed to West Africa to procure enslaved people. The WIC's main possession in Africa in the 1660s, Fort Elmina on the Gold Coast, was not ideally located for the salve trade and played only a minor role until the early eighteenth century. To address this limitation, the Company established smaller trading posts along the Slave Coast, in the Bight of Benin.

The principal trading post on the Slave Coast was Offra, located in the Kingdom of Ardra in present-day Benin. The WIC had intermittently traded for enslaved people in this region since the 1630s, with trade volumes increasing throughout the 1660s.[38] By around 1670, the WIC factory at Offra supplied between 2,500–3,000 enslaved people annually, although not all of these sales were connected to the *asiento*.[39] It is certain, however, that many enslaved Africans delivered by Dutch ships to Curaçao and subsequently transported by the *asiento* ships to Spanish America were procured in Offra. In the early

36 See TSTD, Voyage ID #11397. The vessel went from Ardra on the Slave Coast to Cartagena and Portobello, although it likely touched at Curaçao as well. Also see Vega Franco, *El Trafico de Esclavos*, 194–195.

37 NL-HaNA, WIC 16, 31 October 1672.

38 Robin Law, "The Slave Trade in Seventeenth-Century Allada: A Revision", *African Economic History* 22 (1994), 59–92.

39 Van Brakel, 'Eene memorie over den handel', 96.

1660s, Dutch ships also called at Calabary, Camarones, and Del Rey, although the WIC had no factories there, and trading was conducted directly from ships. After 1667, however, contracts between the *asentistas* and the WIC excluded enslaved people from these regions, as they were deemed unsuitable as *piezas de Indias*. According to a Dutch report from 1670, Spanish buyers considered enslaved people from this region "malicious, stubborn and prone to suicide".[40]

Another significant area for procuring enslaved people was the coastline stretching from modern-day Gabon to Namibia, referred to simply as 'Angola'. The WIC traded regularly at Malemba, Sonho, and other locations, with Loango-Boary, in present-day Congo-Brazzaville, being a major trading town. A Dutch trader based in Loango-Boary, reportedly "under the authority of the blacks",[41] facilitated the WIC's operations. This trader was not a salaried WIC employee but rather an independent Luso-African merchant residing in the town. By 1670, the WIC procured approximately 3,000 enslaved people annually from the 'Angola' coast, facilitated by Luso-African intermediaries well-versed in local coastal markets and the hinterland trading fairs. Enslaved people from Angola were highly valued by Spanish American buyers and commanded higher prices than those from the Slave Coast.[42] Dutch private slave traders like Henrico Matthias also procured slaves through Portuguese markets in West-Africa through their inter-imperial trade networks. However, this did not translate into a higher contractual price under the *asiento,* as the *asentistas* paid a standard rate of 107.5 *pesos* for each *pieza de india,* regardless of the African region of embarkation.

Having embarked an appropriate number of enslaved people, captains on Dutch ships set sail for Curaçao. If their voyage was undertaken as part of the *asiento*, they were required to report to the WIC governor on the island, who held the title of "vice-director" and acted as representative of the Company on the island. Grillo and Lomellino had appointed an agent on Curaçao to receive the contracted number of enslaved people from the WIC. This operation posed a significant logistical challenge, as accommodating and feeding large numbers of enslaved individuals was costly for an island with minimal natural resources. For the first thirty-eight days after arrival on Curaçao, the WIC was responsible for providing clothing and food to all enslaved people. After

40 Van Brakel, 'Eene memorie over den handel', 97.

41 Van Brakel, 'Eene memorie over den handel', 97–98.

42 SAA, NA 2725 (notary Vincent Swanenburgh), notarial deed 7 May 1665. Statement requested by Francesco Feroni of four men that Spanish-American merchants prefer Angolans and are willing to pay up to 20 *pesos* more for Angolan slaves than for other slaves.

this period, the *asentistas* were contractually obligated to cover all expenses, recorded as 'waiting costs', at a rate of 30 guilder-cents per day for each *pieza de india*.[43]

While awaiting transfer to the *asiento* agent, usually pending the arrival of *asentistas*' ships to complete the final maritime leg of the journey to Spanish colonies, the enslaved were housed by the WIC and could be employed on the Company's plantations. To minimize waiting times, the WIC was required to communicate the planned departure dates and routes for each slave ship delivering individuals for the *asiento,* enabling the *asentistas* to coordinate the timely arrival of their vessels to continue the trade via the inter-Caribbean slaving routes. Grillo and Lomellino maintained a fleet of five large ships for collecting enslaved people contracted with the WIC at Curaçao.

However, the onward journey from Curaçao to Spanish America did not always proceed smoothly. Two of these ships, the *St. Juan Bautista* and the *Nostra Sra. del Buen Suceso*, were involved in accidents in the late 1660s. The *asiento* ships also faced threats from Spanish colonial officials and pirates. A series of incidents in 1668 delayed the transport of approximately 3,000 enslaved Africans resulting in their prolonged detention on Curaçao. As the *asentistas* were contractually required to cover the costs of such delays, this led to substantial expenses being paid directly on the island.[44]

7 Illicit Trade and the *Asiento*

The chartering of private ships forced the WIC to grant private merchants in the Republic, particularly in Amsterdam, access to areas traditionally reserved for regulated trade under the Company's charter. Merchants, shipowners, shipmasters, and officers aboard private vessels frequently engaged in illicit trade that extended beyond their contracted activities in the slave trade, often carrying "private merchandise" to trade in West Africa. While illegal from the WIC's perspective, such practices were difficult – if not impossible – to prevent.

WIC officials in West-Africa occasionally attempted to curtail this illegal trade. For example, in 1668, the Chamber Zealand contracted Amsterdam merchants Joan Vlasblom and Heermans Abramz to use their ship, *Juffrouw Aletta,* for a slaving voyage to Ardra and Curaçao. The freight contract expli-

43 See for example the contracts in, Van Brakel, *Bescheiden tot de slavenhandel.*

44 See SAA, NA 3226 (notary Hendrick Outgers), notarial deeds 27 November, 16 December 1676.

citly forbade private trade and stipulated that the ship could only visit the Gold Coast to deliver WIC provisions to supply Elmina.[45] However, upon reaching West Africa, the ship called at Elmina under the pretext of delivering a letter and some provisions, actions described by the WIC director-general as a "frivolous pretext".[46] While at the Gold Coast, captain Jan van Arel reportedly engaged in illicit trade with both Africans and Europeans. Captains of chartered vessels often had ample time in West Africa to trade for personal gain, and relations between them and WIC officials were not always smooth.

In 1671, captain Iphraim Turner of the *Gulden Griffioen*, who was trading for enslaved people at Ardra, sailed to Elmina to complain to the director-general about delays in the procurement of slaves from the WIC factor at the Slave Coast.[47] Running out of provisions and with his crew idle, Turner voiced common grievances against what he portrayed as WIC incompetence and bad faith. However, such complaints often masked the captains' preference for greater flexibility to engage in their own illicit trade while ostensibly under contract to serve the WIC's *asiento* commitments.

Concerns about Curaçao's prominent role in the slave trade to Spanish America also extended to the Spanish Court. Although the *asiento* reduced visits by vessels from the Spanish Main seeking enslaved individuals through illegal channels, contraband goods from Curaçao continued to be imported via Grillo and Lomellino's fleet. The *asentistas* were interested not only in enslaved individuals but also in manufactured goods. Dutch merchants eagerly supplied these goods, making Curaçao a key market for European and Asian commodities that were subsequently distributed across the Caribbean, including Spanish America.[48] Royal dissatisfaction with this issue led Francesco Feroni to warn the WIC in 1668 that the persistent contraband trade through Curaçao could jeopardise the Dutch contract with the *asiento*. To placate the Spanish Crown, the WIC was instructed to issue a bylaw in Curaçao threatening heavy penalties for involvement in contraband. Feroni planned to send a copy of the

45 SAA, NA Friesma, 3087, 26 April 1668.

46 NL-HaNA, WIC 13b, accusation by Dirk Wilree, 27 September 1668. In the protest, director-general Dirk Wilree declared himself "innocent" if the illegal trade contacts of Van Arel would lead to legal procedures in the Dutch Republic. Van Arel's (unlikely) reply was that he had only traded in wood, to be used aboard the ship.

47 NL-HaNA, WIC 13b, accusation by Ephraim Turner of the *Gulden Griffioen*, 16 September 1671. Director-General Wilree blamed the delay on a local African insurgency at Ardra. He had therefore tried his best to send ships with enslaved Africans from the Gold Coast to Curaçao, "to fulfil the contract with the Genoese".

48 SAA, NA 2876 (notary Pieter Padthuijzen), 1 Januari 1667. Klooster, *Illicit Riches*, 55.

bylaw to Madrid.[49] However, it is unclear whether the bylaw was ever published, and even if it was, it is doubtful that it was ever implemented or enforced, being ultimately its effectiveness doubtful.

Subcontracts after 1667 included a clause requiring Dutch ship captains to pledge abstinence from illicit trade in both Africa and the Caribbean. Violations were punishable by confiscation of contraband and forfeiture of wages. Captains were also explicitly instructed to sail directly from Africa to Curaçao without calling at other Caribbean ports.[50] These measures demonstrated the persistence of contraband trade in the Atlantic and highlighted that the *asiento* was no exception. Complaints from Madrid about ongoing illicit trade from Curaçao resurfaced in 1672. The WIC directors, however, responded with deflection of responsibility, stating that illegal trade was conducted solely by private merchants. They assured the Spanish Court that it was free to confiscate, prosecute, and sentence any ships or crews deemed guilty of such activities.[51] While this response may seem presumptuous, it reflected the WIC directors' recognition of the near impossibility of eradicating contraband. Their stance was a calculated attempt to absolve the WIC of enforcement duties under its own charter while benefiting from increased commercial activity in Curaçao and shifting the enforcement costs of imperial political economies to the Spanish authorities.

8 Conclusion

During the entire period of the Grillo and Lomellino *asiento*, the WIC delivered 14,631 *piezas de Indias* in Curaçao (see Table 6.1). The first 2,000 resulting from the 1662 contract, were delivered over three years rather than the one year stipulated in the contract. In fact, the Company never fully met totals specified in its contracts with the *asentistas*, although it came close around 1670. In 1672, the slave trade was partially disrupted by the outbreak of hostilities between the Dutch Republic and a coalition led primarily by France and England. While the Republic ultimately survived this crisis, the *asentistas* hesitated to negotiate a new contract for the 1674 season.

This hesitation caused concern at the 1673 meeting of the *Heren XIX*,[52] reflecting the WIC's increasing reliance on the slave trade and, in particular,

49 NL-HaNA, WIC 15, 29 October 1668.

50 See for a printed copy, Eekhof, 'Twee documenten', 291–292.

51 NL-HaNA, WIC 16, 11 December 1672.

52 NL-HaNA, WIC 16, Minutes of the Amsterdam Chamber of the WIC, 5 October 1673.

the *asiento*. However, an even more urgent issue was the impending expiration of the Company's official state-granted charter. The WIC's financial situation remained dire, and its participation in the *asiento* had failed to reverse its fortunes. A fundamental problem was the chronic lack of reserve capital, which forced the directors to rely heavily on the services and capital of third parties. This reliance led to a drain on profits, which even the 1666/1668 fund for the African trade had been unable to mitigate.

Ultimately, the States General and the Company's creditors concluded that the only viable solution was the complete dissolution of the WIC. Following extensive negotiations, a new WIC was established from the remnants of its predecessor. This reorganised entity, known as 'Second WIC', inherited a reduced debt burden and was able to resume operations where the original Company had left off. Beginning in 1674, the Second WIC contracted with new *asientistas* and, with more funds at its disposal to equip its own slaving ships, the Company shared in the fate of the Royal Adventurers into Africa in its replacement by the Royal African Company two years before the restructuring of the WIC. Alike its English counterpart, also the WIC continued to serve future *asentistas*, although contrary to the English, neither the WIC nor any Dutch company was ever able to become an *asientista* in its own right.

CHAPTER 5

Deaths and Debts: The Zenith of Indirect Management?

The crisis that struck the 'Genoese' *asiento* after the death of Ambrosio Lomellino stemmed from a convergence of internal and external challenges. Central to these difficulties was the inability of the firm Grillo and Lomellino to navigate disputes surrounding Ambrosio's inheritance while ensuring that his share in the firm remained untouched and available to support the capital-intensive *asiento* contract. This issue mirrored a broader trend in early modern Europe, where firms often struggled to maintain stability after the loss of key partners, especially after prolonged periods of operation. Such difficulties were not unique to Grillo and Lomellino; they were emblematic of the challenges faced by many *asentistas* during the economically and politically tumultuous decades of the 1670s and 1680s. Nevertheless, Grillo and Lomellino were among the first to encounter these obstacles, setting a precedent for other *asiento* contractors.[1]

What exacerbated their situation, however, was the firm's inability to meet the annual payments owed to the Spanish Monarchy. These financial struggles were compounded by liquidity shortages, which hindered their capacity to pay subcontractors like the Royal African Company (RAC) and the Dutch West India Company (WIC) operating in Barbados, Jamaica and Curaçao. Additionally, they struggled to maintain the wages of personnel engaged in *asiento* operations across the Caribbean. The firm's predicament was further aggravated by the intensification of smuggling, a widespread phenomenon in trans-Caribbean trade. Smuggling involved not only independent actors but also agents and factors employed by Grillo and Lomellino in Spanish America and Curaçao, leading to frequent and often severe conflicts with local colonial authorities.[2]

The external pressures facing Grillo and Lomellino were no less significant. The increasing violence in the Atlantic, particularly between English

1 H. Barker and M. Ishizu, "Inheritance and Continuity in Small Family Businesses During the Early Industrial Revolution", *Business History* 54, no. 2 (2012), 227–244; Juan Corona, 'Succession in the Family Business: The Great Challenge for the Family", *European Journal of Family Business* 11 (2021), 64–70.

2 Klooster, "Curaçao and the Caribbean", 210.

and Dutch traders, escalated during the Second Anglo-Dutch War (1665–1667) and flared up again during the Third Anglo-Dutch War (1672–1974).[3] These moments of heightened maritime violence significantly increased the risks associated with the Atlantic trade, including the movement of goods, enslaved Africans, commodities and bullion between Europe, the West Coast of Africa, and the Caribbean. As trading costs rose due to these geopolitical tensions, the financial stability of the Spanish Crown further deteriorated. By the early 1670s, the Monarchy had faced multiple bankruptcies, placing immense pressure on all instruments within the fiscal system like the *asiento* to generate much-needed revenue.[4]

The combination of international developments, internal organisation weaknesses, and the financial troubles precipitated by Ambrosio Lomellino's death ultimately caused Domenico Grillo to default on payments owed to the Monarchy under the terms of the *asiento*. Despite this failure, the Spanish Crown exhibited leniency, extending the *asiento* to Grillo alone. This decision reflected a pragmatic approach: on the one hand, it acknowledge Grillo's past contributions and services as *asentista*, and on the other, it aimed to ensure the Crown could recover some of the fiscal revenue still owed by the firm. By allowing Grillo to continued delivering enslaved Africans to the Caribbean, the Monarchy sought to salvage the *asiento* and sustain the acquisition of labour and associated fiscal revenues, which remained vital to its colonial economy.[5]

1 Old Solutions to New Problems

Domenico Grillo's solo administration of the *asiento* proved equally unsuccessful. He was unable to settle his firm's outstanding debts while simultaneously failing to meet the obligations stipulated in the new *asiento* contract. This poor performance prompted the *Consejo de Indias* to terminate the agreement and pursue alternative contractors. In 1672, the *asiento* was granted to Antonio García and Sebastián Silíceo, two merchants who promised to revitalise the system. Yet García and Silíceo, like their predecessor, were hampered by the Crown's dire financial condition and the structural challenges inherent in the transatlantic slave trade. By the end of 1674 and without fulfill-

3 Klooster, *Illicit Riches*, chapter 2.

4 Sanz Ayan, *Los banqueros de Carlos II*, chapters 4 and 5.

5 Alejandro García-Monton, *Genoese Entrepreneurship and the Asiento Slave Trade, 1650–1700* (London and New York: Routledge, 2022), chapter 2.

ing the *asiento* at any point in time, they were declare insolvent, and by 1675, both were declared bankrupt without having successfully serviced the *asiento*.[6]

The financial collapse of García and Silíceo marked a critical juncture for the *asiento*. Their failure underscored the risks associated with entrusting private firms with the administration of such a complex and capital-intensive enterprise. The financial fragility of Grillo, García and Silíceo was disastrous not only for the firms themselves but also for the Spanish Crown, which was deprived of the fiscal revenues that the *aseinto* was intended to secure. Furthermore, the collapse of these contracts left the transatlantic trade in enslaved Africans largely in the hands of illicit operators, including Dutch, English and Spanish American private traders and companies. This not only undermined the Monarchy's control over the trade, but also facilitated the illicit extraction of silver and Spanish American commodities, exacerbating the Crown's fiscal woes.

In response to these repeated failures, the Spanish Crown turned to a more conservative and ostensibly perceived as reliable alternative, albeit not new: the direct administration of the *asiento* through the intermediation of the *consulado de mercaderes de Sevilla*.[7] The decision to entrust the *consulado* with the *asiento* reflected a return to an earlier model of management that prioritised oversight and centralization. The *consulado* was expected to issue licences to private slave traders, allowing them to purchase enslaved Africans in West Africa and deliver them directly to Spanish American ports, bypassing intermediate hubs such as Barbados, Jamaica and Curaçao. This arrangement sought to address some of the structural weaknesses of previous contracts, particularly the reliance on subcontractors and the logistical vulnerabilities associated with trans-Caribbean trade.

This return to the 1650s model still carried the risks that the slavers acquiring the licences still had to pay for them in advance and in Seville (rather than in a system of delayed payments in Spanish America and upon arrival of the ships in Spanish American ports) and that Dutch and English ships, belonging to the WIC or the RAC, and private traders would still illicitly use the English and Dutch entrepots in the Caribbean for illegal supply of enslaved labour and the illicit extraction of Spanish American commodities and silver.[8]

From 1676 to 1681, the *consulado* administered the *asiento*. The contract stipulated the transportation of 10,000 *toneladas*, instead of *piezas de Indias*,

6 Scelle, *La traite négrière*, vol. 1, 551–598.

7 Vila Vilar, "El Consulado de Sevilla", 188. Scelle, *La traite négrière*, 599–603.

8 Postma, *The Dutch in the Atlantic*, 164.

directly from Africa to the Spanish Caribbean. The *consulado* agreed to pay the Crown 112.5 *pesos* per *tonelada* disembarked in Spanish American ports as fiscal duties. This shift from accounting enslaved Africans in terms of *piezas de Indias* to *toneladas* represented a significant innovation. It aimed to attract smaller-scale slave traders by facilitating the formation of partnerships for individual voyages, akin to a mid-way system between bottomries and charterparties. This approach broadened the potential pool of participants in the *asiento*, enabling merchants from diverse backgrounds – including those from Flanders, Genoa, or Lima – to engage in the trade. Even non-subjects of the Spanish Crown could participate, provided they entered partnerships with naturalised traders. Fundamentally, however, the focus was on licence holders demonstrating, upon acquisition of the licence, their financial resilience through demonstrable solvency.[9]

Despite these reforms, significant challenges persisted. The requirement that licence holders pay for their licences in advance and in Seville – rather than deferring payments until the enslaved Africans arrived in Spanish America – placed a considerably financial burden on traders. Moreover, the entrenched problem of illicit trade continued to undermine the *asiento* and the revenue of the Monarchy. Dutch and English ships, often operated by the WIC and the RAC, remained active in the Caribbean, supplying enslaved Africans to Spanish American markets through unauthorised channels. These activities not only disrupted the legal slave trade but also facilitated the smuggling of Spanish American commodities, further eroding the Crown's fiscal base.

The WIC and the RAC responded unfavourably to Spanish authorities' ambitions to purchase enslaved Africans directly from West African markets and transport them to Spanish American ports without making use of the Dutch and English Caribbean hubs as intermediaries. One of their principal strategies to obstruct this effort was a refusal to sell enslaved individuals to *asiento*-licensed ships at their trading posts and forts in West Africa.[10] This policy left the *asiento* licence holders with a singular option: conducting their business through Portuguese-dominated markets or Luso-African intermediaries along the West African coast.

The *consulado*'s administration of the *asiento* during this period was thus marked by both continuity and change. While the shift to accounting in *toneladas* and the inclusion of a broader range of merchants represented signifi-

9 Vila Vilar, "El Consulado de Sevilla", 194. Orozco Cruz, "Barroso, Porcio y Coymans", 325. Scelle, *La traite négrière*, vol. 1, 641–654.

10 Postma, *The Dutch in the Atlantic*, chapter 3.

cant innovations, the underlying structural issues that had plagued previous contracts remained unresolved. The persistence of smuggling, the volatility of Atlantic trade, and the Crown's chronic financial instability continued to undermine the effectiveness of the *asiento*. Nevertheless, the *consulado*'s tenure demonstrated the potential for more centralised and regulated approaches to mitigate some of the risks associated with the trade, laying the groundwork for future reforms.

In conclusion, the crisis of the 'Genoese' *asiento* following Ambrosio Lomellino's death revealed the vulnerabilities of early modern firms engaged in large-scale transatlantic enterprises. The failures of Grillo and Lomellino, and García and Silíceo underscored the immense challenges of managing the *asiento* under the conditions of the late seventeenth century. While the Spanish Crown's decision to entrust the *consulado* with the *asiento* marked a shift back to the licence system of the 1650s, the broader structural problems of the trade remained unresolved.

2 New Names to Old Solutions

The late 1670s mirrored challenges faced during the 1650s, when few *asiento* licences were successfully sold. A similar pattern emerged twenty years later, with only one-third of the licences issued during the first three years of the contract being purchased by slave traders. The requirement to pay for licences in advance, combined with limited access to markets dominated by Dutch and English traders, forced licence holders to turn to Portuguese markets and traders in Africa, effectively eliminating competition and further curtailing trade. The diminished success of legal trading arrangements resulted in an uptick in smuggling and illicit trade. By this time, Curaçao and Jamaica remained crucial hubs for these clandestine exchanges. Among the many smugglers was the Coymans family of Amsterdam, whose involvement often took shape through alliances with the WIC or intermediation of one of its trusted allies, Joshua van Belle, as a Dutch merchant with an open *comptoir* in Seville.[11]

In response to the ongoing difficulties in selling licences, the *consulado* negotiated a contract in 1678 with Juan Barroso del Pozo and Francisco Petite. This agreement brought in additional partners, including Nicolàs Porcio, Bar-

11 Orozco Cruz, "Barroso, Porcio y Coymans", 131. Orozco Cruz, "Redes transnacionales de comercio", 319–323. Scelle, *La traite négrière*, 663–667. For more insights on the Coymans case see Ramona Négron, *Dutch Entrepreneurship in the Spanish Americas, 1580–1700*, PhD diss. Leiden: Leiden University, 2025.

roso's son-in-law, and Balthazar Coymans, an important member of the Coymans family from Amsterdam. Balthazar Coymans had joined forces with Pedro van Belle, brother to Joshua van Belle, to establish a commercial foothold in Spanish trade.[12] Barroso was granted a substantial permit to deliver 6,000 *toneladas* of enslaved Africans to Spanish American ports by 1681.[13] In other words, the *consulado* decided in favour of a subcontractor, or at least a partnership that acquired a large amount of the licences that had remained unsold.

Interestingly, a condition of the contract specified that 1800 *piezas de Indias* (approximately 14% of the total *toneladas*) would be delivered to *asiento* ships in Curaçao. This concession was strategically significant, as it provided a legal avenue for the WIC to re-enter the *asiento* trade, not as a direct subcontractor but through its association with the Coymans family. The Coymans', leveraging its shareholder status in the WIC and its involvement with Porcio through Balthazar Coymans, ensured that the WIC benefited indirectly from the *asiento*. This arrangement effectively reopened Curaçao as a hub for the *asiento* trade and demonstrated how entrenched mercantile networks could adapt to and influence evolving trading dynamics.[14]

The concession Barroso and Petite made to Porcio by accepting the Coymans participation yielded further advantages for the *asiento*. By 1679, the WIC reversed its earlier policy of denying access to its African trading posts, allowing Barroso's ships to operate in its markets. Elmina and the other forts in the Gold Coast were reopened to *asiento*-licensed ships as well, easing access to enslaved Africans for the Spanish American trade. The *consulado* in turn, began to favour ships and captains willing to use WIC-controlled areas in Africa instead of Portuguese markets, or Curaçao as preferred trading hub.[15]

Despite these apparent gains, the WIC re-entry into the *asiento* trade proved less seamless than anticipated. Barroso faced significant financial challenges in meeting his obligations to the Company. This was due, in part, to the limited scope of the WIC's role in his contract, as the majority of the 6,000 *toneladas* were to be transported directly from Africa to Spanish America. Barroso prioritised voyages outside WIC-controlled markets to maintain liquidity. Moreover, he assumed that the WIC would accept delayed payments, a common practice in the inter-Caribbean trade. Barroso likely anticipated that, in the event of financial difficulties, he could rely on payments in Spanish American

12 Van Belle, *Pertinent en Waarachtig Verhaal*.

13 Scelle, *La traite négrière*, vol. 1, 669–677.

14 Orozco Cruz, "Barroso, Porcio y Coymans", 129.

15 Wright, "The Coymans Asiento", 52.

commodities and silver, even though such transactions were technically illicit. In this sense, Barroso was hardly changing the terms of the relationship with the WIC that had dominated the Grillo and Lomellino practices with the Company. Like Barroso, also the Genoese firm was always able to comply with the, at times, delayed payments, and thus the assumption was that the *asentistas* would be able to repeat such practices.

Barroso's optimistic stance met with the intolerance of WIC director and Curaçao governor, who took a firm stance on delayed payments. In 1681, the situation escalated when the WIC confiscated two of Barroso's *asiento* ships over unpaid debts. One ship was retained in Curaçao as collateral, while the other, the *Jesús Nazareno* was sent to Amsterdam as a guarantee.[16] This seizure created a significant rift between the WIC and Barroso, whose financial stability was further jeopardized, when news of the incident reached Seville. With memories of earlier bankruptcies by Grillo, and Garcia and Silíceo still fresh, the *consulado* acted decisively. It executed part of the chattels (collaterals) Barroso had deposited as security for the contract, amounting to 100,000 *pesos*.

Whether Barroso was genuinely insolvent or simply misjudged the WIC's willingness to tolerate deferred payments remains unclear. The Company would have had little incentives to accept these delays as Barroso would be forced to pay in Spanish American commodities and silver directly in Curaçao if he was pressured into timely payments. However, the *consulado*'s decision to seize his assets likely exacerbated his financial troubles and the perception of his reputation and reliability in the markets. If he was not insolvent before this intervention, the *consulado*'s actions may have pushed him into bankruptcy.[17]

The WIC's uncompromising approach and the subsequent confiscation of ships created tensions within Barroso's partnership. Barroso and Petite began to question Balthazar Coymans's added value to their partnership. Despite Coymans's connections to the WIC, he had been unable to prevent the confiscation of the ships or to mediate effectively between the partnership and the Dutch company. For Barroso and Petite, Coymans's inability to leverage his social and political capital highlighted his limited utility for the enterprise. As a result, his position in relation to the *asentistas* became increasingly precarious.

The events of the late 1670s and early 1680s underscore the challenges of administering the *asiento* under conditions of persistent financial strain, geo-

16 Orozco Cruz, "Redes transnacionales de comercio", 329.

17 Klooster, "Curçao and the Caribbean", 206.

political rivalries, and entrenched mercantile networks. The WIC's initial refusal to engage with *asiento*-licensed ships highlighted the difficulties of navigating markets in West Africa without resorting to subcontracting. At the same time, the reliance on firms that were indirectly depending on subcontractors for the management of the *asiento* exposed the necessity of business networks that were vested and connected to different commercial hubs. The *asiento* stimulated the development of trans-European networks of financiers and traders in enslaved Africans, servicing contracts and subcontracts that did not necessarily concern the country or the colonies of the sovereign city or state they belonged to.

The partial return of the WIC to the *asiento* through trade between Curaçao and Spanish American ports illustrates the adaptability of these networks but also their inherent volatility. The conflicts between Barroso, the *consulado,* and the WIC reflect broader tensions between individual *asentistas,* institutional frameworks, and chartered commercial entities like the WIC. Furthermore, the increasing prevalence of smuggling during this period highlights the persistent inefficiencies and limitations of both trading networks and the Spanish Monarchy.

In conclusion, the asiento's evolution during this period reflects the complex interplay of economic, political and social forces. The participation of kinship networks like that of Barroso or Coymans, albeit it tangentially, underscores the importance of transnational networks in the shaping of trade dynamics, while the difficulties faced by the *asentatistas* attest to the challenges of navigating an increasingly competitive and fragmented Atlantic world. These developments not only shaped the trajectory of the *asiento,* but also shed light on the broader dynamics of the early modern transatlantic slave trade that arise in the eighteenth century in and outside the Spanish sphere.[18]

3 The Shortcoming of Indirect Management

In an effort to salvage the reputation of the *asentista* and prevent a complete breakdown of relationships with the Spanish authorities, Nicolàs Porcio took the bold and unprecedented step of bypassing the *consulado* in Seville to negotiate directly with the *Consejo de Indias* in Madrid. Acting as a representative to his father-in-law, Porcio began negotiations in late 1681. Simulta-

18 Han Jordaan, "Slavernij en vrijheid op Curaçao: de dynamiek van een achttiende-eeuws Atlantisch handelsknooppunt". PhD diss. Leiden: Leiden University, 2012.

neously, and presumably, he exerted pressure on Balthazar Coymans to influence the WIC through his family connections in Amsterdam, urging greater flexibility on delayed payments in Curaçao.

Porcio's arguments before the *Consejo* were strategically framed. He contended that Barroso had delivered more enslaved Africans to Spanish America than all the licence holders combined. This, he argued, was evidence of the inadequacy of the licensing system. This argument was valid as similar inefficiency arose in the 1650s in a similar licensing arrangement. By making the licensing system the problem, instead of the relationship between *asentistas* and subcontractors, Porcio's called for the return to a model where a single firm held responsibility for the entire *asiento* operation, rather than fragmenting the system through individual licences. This approach harked back to the arrangements of the 1660s under Grillo and Lomellino, when subcontracting became a cornerstone of the *asiento's* (in)success. The veiled suggestion in this line of argument was a suggestion to sign a new *asiento* with Barroso and Porcio, where they would be entrusted with running the *asiento*, reinstating subcontracting as a rule, welcoming the WIC once again as a key partner.[19]

Porcio's lobbying in Madrid caught the attention of the WIC, which was still recovering from the invasion of the Dutch Republic by the French armies in 1672, the Third Anglo-Dutch War, and its 1674 restructuring. Recognising the potential benefits of a renewed association with the *asiento,* the WIC replaced Nicolaas van Liebergen in Curaçao as a gesture of goodwill, leaving an *interim* governor.[20] This decision reflected the Company's prioritisation of a binding contract with a future *asentista* in view of its continued problems of capitalization and liquidity.

The WIC's calculated move demonstrated its willingness to adapt to evolving circumstances. The Company anticipated that if Porcio's negotiations succeeded, the *asiento* would return to a model that allowed for direct subcontracting. This arrangement would not only grant the WIC a stable revenue stream but also enable the Company to operate as an integral part of the transatlantic slave trade under legal and structured conditions.

The negotiations culminated in a significant victory for Porcio. In 1682, the *Consejo de Indias* awarded a new *asiento* contract to Barroso and Porcio, although Barroso died approximately a year later. The terms of the contract closely resembled the 1662 agreement with Grillo and Lomellino. It mandated the delivery of 10,000 *toneladas* of enslaved Africans to Spanish American

19 Scelle, *La traite négrière*, vol. 1, 648.

20 NL HaNA, 1.05.01.02, 1177 + 1.05.01.02, 617 (secrete letters with complaints about Nicolaas van Liebergen. Klooster, *Illicit*, chapter 3, 59–72.

ports over five years, of which 1000 *toneladas* encompassed still the share the *consulado* had been unable to deliver before the signing of the contract. For each *tonelada,* the *asentistas* were required to pay 112,5 *pesos* directly to the *Real Hacienda.* In other words, the *Consejo* saw the advantages to have a *estanco* or monopoly, as it had done before under Grillo and Lomellino, this time in the hope that the partnership would run the trade directly from Africa to the Spanish American ports.[21]

One notable innovation in this contract was the privilege granted to the *asentista* to outfit three ships capable of transporting bullion, up to 300 *pesos* per *tonelada,* bypassing the customary requirement for all ships to call at Cadiz or Seville. This measure was introduced to address delays in the payments for enslaved Africans in the Caribbean, particularly in Curaçao and Jamaica. In practice, it also facilitated renewed subcontracting arrangements with the RAC and the WIC, as these companies were assured payment in bullion, thus reducing their financial risks.[22]

The privilege to transport bullion represented a pragmatic decision by the Spanish Crown. It reflected the Monarchy's awareness of the precarious balance in the Caribbean trade, where the circulation of capital through the *asiento* was vital for maintaining royal revenues. This privilege also incentivised the WIC to re-enter the *asiento* under more favourable conditions. Instead of relying on representatives in Amsterdam, as Grillo and Lomellino had done by appointing Feroni and D'Estevan, Barroso and Porcio opted to negotiate directly with the Coymans House. The resulting contract, mediated by Balthazar Coymans and signed by Jan Coymans and Carel Voet, stipulated the delivery of 18,000 *piezas de Indias* (instead of *toneladas*) through Curaçao over five years. However, the contract left unresolved questions about how Coymans and Voet intended to secure the cooperation of the WIC in this ambitious endeavour.[23]

The early 1680s saw escalating violence in the Caribbean, which significantly impacted the *asiento*'s circuits. This turbulence placed increasing pressure on Porcio, prompting him to take the drastic decision to relocate the administration of the *asiento* to Spanish America. However, this move exposed him to additional challenges, particularly disputes between the WIC and Spanish American authorities. Despite the privilege of transporting bul-

21 W. R. Menkman, "Slavenhandel en rechtsbedeeling op Curaçao op het einde der 17e eeuw", *De West-Indische Gids* 17 (1935–1936), 11–26.

22 Scelle, *La traite négrière,* vol. 1, 679.

23 Wright, "The Coymans Asiento", 58–62. Van Belle, *Pertinent en Waaractig Verhaal,* appendix Litera A.

lion, the WIC continued to face difficulties in receiving timely payments for enslaved Africans delivered to Curaçao. The Company's practice of threatening to confiscate *asiento* assets in response to payment delays frequently led to conflicts with (Spanish)American captains and mariners. These grievances were often brought to the attentional of colonial officials, further complicating the *asientista*'s position.

Porcio arrived in Spanish America via Panama. However, the escalating conflict between the WIC authorities in Curaçao and the governor of Cartagena forced Porcio to visit Cartagena. Upon arrival, tensions between the *asentista* and the governor escalated. The governor of Cartagena, frustrated by the persistent complaints and threats of the WIC and the continuous extraction of bullion from local markets, ordered Porcio's arrest. This dramatic turn of events underscored the precarious position of *asentistas* and their agents, who were frequently at the mercy of local colonial officials, who in this case hoped to press Porcio into complying with the deferred payments and with bringing to a halt all attempts to use local bullion in detriment of local markets.[24]

Porcio's arrest dealt a severe blow to the reputation of the *asiento* and the *asentistas.* Although he manage to escape Cartagena and return to Panama, his credibility suffered irreparable damage. From Panama, he launched a campaign against the governor of Cartagena, which culminated in an uneasy negotiation in 1684. This confrontation illustrates the deep vulnerabilities inherent in the *asiento,* where *asentistas* were simultaneously dependent on and undermined by local authorities. The disputes between Porcio and the governor also exacerbated division within the *asiento* network. Agents and representatives in Spain, the Dutch Republic, England, and the Caribbean were forced to take sides, leading to the fragmentation of the carefully constructed system that had sustained the trade. This breakdown in coordination further undermined the *asiento*'s viability, leaving it increasingly reliant on illicit exchanges and informal arrangements.

The 1682 asiento contract represented a pivotal moment in the evolution of the system. On the one hand, it reflected the Crown's continued commitment to a monopoly model, managed by a single firm, as a means of maximising fiscal revenues and maintaining control over the transatlantic slave trade. On the other hand, the persistent challenges faced by Porcio and his partners underscored the enduring difficulties of administering such a complex enterprise in the volatile geopolitical and economic environment of the late seven-

24 Scelle, "The Slave Trade in the Spanish Colonies", 652.

teenth century. The privilege to transport bullion, while innovative, revealed the inherent contradictions in the *asiento*. It sought to address the liquidity problems that had plagued earlier contractors but inadvertently facilitated greater dependence on external actors like the WIC and the RAC. The involvement of these companies, while essential for the trade's operation, introduced additional layers of complexity and conflict, particularly in the Caribbean.

Porcio's bold decision to bypass the *consulado* and negotiate directly with the Consejo de Indias marked a turning point in the history of the asiento. While his efforts secured a new contract and temporarily restored the system's stability, the challenges he faced highlighted the structural weaknesses of the trade. The reliance on subcontracting, the precarious relationships with colonial authorities, and the persistent threat of violence and piracy in the Caribbean all contributed to the fragility of the *asiento*. Ultimately, the 1682 contract underscored the inherent tensions between the Monarchy's fiscal ambitions and the practical realities of the transatlantic slave trade. It reflected the Monarchy's willingness to innovate and adapt, but also its inability to fully resolve the systemic issues that plagued the *asiento*. The experiences of Porcio offer valuable insights into the complexities of early modern intersections of economic, political, and social forces that shaped the Atlantic world.

4 The Definite Failure of Indirect Management

The growing tensions between Nicolás Porcio and the governor of Cartagena over payments and exchanges involving the *asiento* in Curaçao did not deter Porcio from his primary focus: maintaining a steady flow of enslaved Africans to Spanish America. Porcio understood that the continued operation of the slave trade was critical to generating the revenue needed to fulfil the *asiento*'s financial obligations to the Spanish Monarchy. Following this logic, Porcio made a controversial decision to divert one of the *asiento*'s privileged ships to transport specie to Jamaica, bypassing Curaçao and the WIC entirely. This allowed him to purchase human cargoes directly from the RAC, a move that not only escalated tensions between Curaçao and Jamaica but also deepened the animosity between the RAC and the WIC, triggering further violence in the Caribbean.[25]

25 Van Belle, *Pertinent en Waarachtig Verhaal*, appendix Litera O.

While attempting to mediate the conflicts between the *asiento* and the WIC from Panama, Porcio simultaneously faced challenges in maintaining legal and operational ties with the RAC in Jamaica. His efforts to keep the asiento operational, however, drew criticism in Spain. Balthazar Coymans and Pedro van Belle, fearing the reputational damage that Porcio's financial difficulties could inflict on their shared interests, petitioned the *Consejo de Indias*. They warned of Porcio's failure to settle outstanding debts with the WIC and highlighted his struggles to sustain the slave trade, which they argued jeopardised the *asiento*'s ability to meet its instalment payments to the Monarchy.[26]

Coymans and Van Belle, presenting themselves as the only creditworthy associates of Porcio, proposed taking over the administration of the *asiento*, including the outstanding debts. They offered reassurances of their financial stability and the logistical strength of their networks. Haunted by the memory of Grillo's insolvency in the early 1670s, the Monarchy cautiously agreed to transfer the administration of Porcio's asiento to Coymans and Van Belle, allowing them to oversee its operations until the contract's expiration in 1687. Furthermore, the *Consejo de Indias*, recognising the need for fiscal stability, extended the potential duration of the asiento by two years, allowing Coymans and Van Belle to operate as independent *asentistas* in their own right until 1689, provided they met specific conditions.[27]

In return for the Monarchy's approval, Coymans and Van Belle were required to contribute 200,000 *escudos* in cash to support Spain's military in Flanders and deliver four fully equipped warships to the Armada del Mar Océano, similar clauses to those imposed on Grillo and Lomellino. Unable to leverage their credit and funds in Spain, they relied on the Coymans House in Amsterdam, mobilising a consortium of investors with longstanding ties to their family. These financiers, many with vested interests in the WIC, others members of the Portuguese and Spanish Nations of Amsterdam, facilitated the capital infusion required for the cash payment and the construction of the ships in the Zaandam shipyards.[28]

This reliance on Amsterdam-based financiers came with strings attached. Most of the investors advocated for the renewed involvement of the WIC as a subcontractor for the asiento. Coymans and Van Belle acquiesced, reestablishing ties with the WIC. However, given the WIC's limitations in supplying sufficient numbers of enslaved Africans from Curaçao, the partnership

---

26 Zahedieh, "The Merchants of Port Royal", 577.

27 Scelle, *La traite négrière*, vol. 1, 677–679.

28 Scelle, *La traite négrière*, vol. 1, 652–658. For a fully detailed build up of this contact see : Negron, *Dutch Investment*.

also continued Porcio's arrangements with the RAC in Jamaica and relied on English vessels to transport enslaved individuals across the Atlantic to the asiento's ships.[29]

Despite their experience and access to resources, Coymans and Van Belle faced significant challenges in administering the *asiento*. Recognising the logistical complexities of managing the trade across the Atlantic, Pedro van Belle relocated to the Caribbean to oversee operations on the ground, following the example given a few years earlier by Porcio. His role included navigating the delicate relationships between the WIC in Curaçao and the RAC in Jamaica, a task fraught with conflict and competition, and at the same time temper the relationship of the administration of the *asiento* local agents and Spanish American authorities. Meanwhile, Coymans remained in Spain, frequently travelling between Seville, Cádiz, and Madrid to ensure timely payments to the Monarchy and manage correspondence with the Coymans House in Amsterdam.

The partnership's operations were further complicated by the death of Balthazar Coymans in 1686, mirroring the crises faced by previous *asentistas* (Grillo and Porcio) following the deaths of their partners (Lomellino and Barroso respectively). For Pedro van Belle, this development posed two major challenges. He had to ensure that all payments to the Monarchy, as well as those owed to subcontractors like the WIC and RAC, were met without delays. This was crucial not only to preserve the *asiento*'s credibility but also to sustain the partnership's relationship with the *Consejo de Indias* and the *Real Hacienda*. Simultaneously, the death of Coymans introduced uncertainty regarding the continuity of the partnership. Van Belle needed to negotiate with Coymans' heirs in Amsterdam to ensure that his share in the firms was retained or at least transitioned smoothly, avoiding liquidation that could undermine the partnership's creditworthiness. These negotiations were critical to maintaining the *asiento*'s solvency and operational integrity.

Besides the two challenges shared with earlier *asentistas*, Van Belle's position was further weakened by the fact that he was in the Caribbean when Coymans died. The logistical constraints of seventeenth-century communication meant it took several weeks for him to learn of the event and months to travel to Spain and then Amsterdam to address the succession crisis in the partnership. Furthermore, upon his return to Spain, Van Belle faced what he called an orchestrated campaign aimed at discrediting the Coymans and Van Belle administration. The campaign questioned not only the financial stability

29 Van Belle, *Pertinent en Waarachtig Verhaal*, appendix Litera O; Zahedieh, *The Capital and the Colonies*, chapter 2; Zahedieh, "The Merchants of Port Royal", 591–593.

of the partnership but also their religious allegiance, leveraging anti-Protestant sentiment to undermine their credibility in a predominantly Catholic Monarchy. These attacks further complicated Van Belle's efforts to stabilise the *asiento* and defend its operations.[30]

The turbulence faced by Van Belle underscored broader structural issues within the *asiento*. Despite integrating the lessons of past *asentistas*, the last years of Coymans van Van Belle's administration struggled with a fragmented supply chain, where the reliance on both the WIC and the RAC highlighted the *asiento*'s dependence on external actors with competing interests. The logistical challenges of sourcing enslaved Africans from multiple markets and coordinating their transportation to Spanish America placed a significant burden on the *asentistas*. Colonial opposition increased as did the administrative complexity of the contract. Like their predecessors, Coymans and Van Belle faced resistance from colonial authorities, particularly in Cartagena, where local officials prioritised their own financial and political interests over the smooth operation of the asiento. These tensions often led to delays, confiscations, and conflicts that further strained the partnership's resources. Lastly, they had to face political and religious prejudices. As Dutch Protestants operating in a Catholic Monarchy, Coymans and Van Belle were particularly vulnerable to attacks on their loyalty and faith. This added a layer of political risk to their administration, which hindered their ability to maintain trust with their agents, but most crucially, with Spanish institutions in general.

Nicolás Porcio, who returned to Spain probably in the end of 1685, emboldened by the death of Coymans and Van Belle's absence in Amsterdam, sought to reclaim control over the *asiento*.[31] The disputes that ensued afterwards with Van Belle and the *asiento* administrator in his absence, Jan Carcau, culminated in a protracted legal battle before the *Consejo de Indias* that included the imprisonment of Carcau, the confiscation of Coymans and Van Belle assets in Spain and in the Caribbean and with the reinstatement of Porcio to the

30 Wright, "The Coymans Asiento"; Ana Crespo Solana, "Las comunidades mercantiles y el mantenimiento de los sistemas comerciales de España, Flandes y la República holandesa, 1648–1750", in *España y las 17 provincias de los Países Bajos: una revisión historiográfica (XVI–XVIII)*, edited by Manuel Herrero Sánchez and Ana Crespo Solana (Cordoba: Fundación Carlos de Amberes, 2002), 443–468.

31 Jonatán Orozco Cruz, "Mover Roma con Santiago para influir en Madrid. Agentes, estrategias y redes clientelares en la pugna por la titularidad del Asiento de esclavos entre Nicolàs Porcio y Baltasar Coymans (1685–1694)", in *Urdimbre y memoria de un imperio global: Redes de poder y circulación de agentes en la Monarquía Hispánica*, edited by Antonio Jiménez Estrella, Julián José Lozano Navarro, Francisco Sánchez-Montes González (Granada: Editorial Universidad de Granada, 2023), 481–508.

management of the *asiento*. By 1689, Porcio had regained nominal control over the *asiento*, but the system's underlying problems persisted.[32] Rising costs, escalating violence in the Caribbean, and systemic inefficiencies continued to hinder operations. Calls for a more centralized approach grew louder, as the limitations of fragmented subcontracting became increasingly apparent. The application of Bernardo Francisco Marín de Guzmán in 1692 marked a decisive shift in the evolution of Habsburg *asientos* as we address in the following chapter.

32 Scelle, *La traite négrière*, vol. 1, 700–701.

CHAPTER 6

Credible *Asentista:* Moving Away from Intermediaries

On 12 July 1696, the Spanish Monarchy contracted the *asiento* with the Portuguese *Companhia da Guiné* (Company of Guinea). Signed in Madrid, the agreement stipulated the delivery of 30,000 *piezas de Indias* in the Spanish Americas over a period of six years and eight months, from 7 July 1696 to 7 March 1703. For each *pieza*, the *Companhia* was to pay 112,5 *pesos* in import duties at the delivery ports.[1] For the Spanish Crown, the deal represented a revenue of 3,375,000 *pesos*, regardless of the number of enslaved Africans who were actually disembarked in the Spanish American colonies.[2]

This *asiento* has garnered attention for several reasons. It was the last such contract signed by the Spanish Habsburg kings and was terminated in 1701 amidst the political turmoil that engulfed Europe over the succession to the Spanish throne. From that point onwards, this *asiento* was frequently perceived as detrimental to the interests of the Spanish Monarchy. This perception, rooted in challenges related to its implementation and the terms of its dissolution, largely dictated by France, was further reinforced by mid-eighteenth century Spanish mercantilist literature. Such writings advocated for an end to the royal monopoly over the slave trade and for the exclusion of foreigners from this activity.[3]

This negative view was perpetuated by George Scelle's monumental work on the contracts that ensured the supply of enslaved people to Spanish America over a period of more than two centuries. Regarding the *asiento* with the Portuguese *Companhia*, and drawing on Spanish, Portuguese and French sources, Scelle's work established the terms of the analysis, highlighting the broader political context in explaining why the *Companhia* was awarded the contract and why the *asiento* was relinquished in 1701.[4] Additional contribu-

---

1 *Peso* or *real de a ocho* (piece of eight) was a Spanish silver coin equal to 272 *maravedís*, the common currency in Spain and the Spanish Empire.

2 *Coleccion de los tratados de paz*, part 3, 366–393.

3 Santiago Luxán Meléndez and Lía de Luxán Hernández, "Las compañías reales de esclavos y la integración de Cuba en el sistema Atlántico del tabaco español, 1696–1739", *Anuario de Estudios Atlánticos* 62 (2016), 2–4.

4 Scelle, *La traite négrière*, 2 vols. Scelle, "The Slave Trade in the Spanish Colonies ", 612–661.

© CÁTIA ANTUNES ET AL., 2026 | DOI:10.1163/9789004745094_008

tions have come from scholarship examining Portugal's geopolitical interests in Cape Verde and Guinea, with emphasis on the role of private trading companies in fostering the economic development of the region. At the same time, studies on the Portuguese South Atlantic have shed light on merchant networks operating the transatlantic slave trade.[5] While these works do not focus primarily on the *asiento* of the *Companhia*, they have provided new data and valuable insights, enhancing our understanding of this episode within the broader contract of the history of the *asiento*.[6]

Certain aspects of the 1696 contract, however, remain underexplored. This includes the Portuguese Crown's participation, whose interests and reasons for supporting the *Companhia* and its agreement with the Spanish Crown are yet to be fully understood. Similarly, little is known about the *Companhia* itself, its internal structure, membership, financial capacity, operationalisation of the slave trade, and the manner in which it was liquidated after the termination of the *asiento*.

This chapter examines the short-lived *asiento* granted to the *Companhia* against the backdrop of broader European interests in transatlantic trade with Spanish America. By adopting a multi-layered perspective that seeks to capture the intersection of three distinct agendas – the Spanish Crown's interest in securing revenue through the supply of enslaved people to its colonies,

5 Cândido da Silva Teixeira, "Companhia de Cacheu, Rios e Comércio de Guiné: documentos para a sua história", *Boletim do Arquivo Histórico Colonial* 1 (1950), 87–132; José Gonçalves Salvador, *Os cristãos-novos e o comércio no Atlântico Meridional* (São Paulo: Livraria Pioneira Editora, 1978); José Gonçalves Salvador, *Os magnatas do tráfico negreiro (séculos XVI e XVII)* (São Paulo: Livraria Pioneira Editora, 1981); António Carreira, *As companhias pombalinas do Grão-Pará e Maranhão e Pernambuco e Paraíba* (Lisbon: Editorial Presença, 1983); Luís Filipe Alencastro, *O trato dos viventes: formação do Brasil no Atlântico Sul (séculos XVI e XVII)* (São Paulo: Companhia das Letras, 2000); Ilídio Baleno, "Reconversão do comércio externo em tempo de crise e o impacto da Companhia do Grão-Pará e Maranhão", in *História geral de Cabo Verde*, edited by Maria Emília Madeira Santos, vol. 3 (Lisbon and Praia, Instituto de Investigação Científica e Tropical – Instituto Nacional de Investigação, Promoção e Património Culturais de Cabo Verde, 2002), 157–233.

6 Jorge Palacios Preciado, *La trata de negros por Cartagena de Indias, 1650–1750* (Tunja: Universidad Pedagógica y Tecnológica de Colombia, 1973); Ana Maria Rodrígues Blásquez, "Penetración portuguesa en América a través del asiento firmado por la Real Compañia de Guinea en 1696", *Temas Americanistas* 4 (1984), 50–58; Ildefonso Gutiérrez Azopardo, "El comercio y mercado de negros esclavos en Cartagena de Indias (1533–1850)", *Quinto Centenario* (Madrid, Universidad Complutense de Madrid, n.º 12, 1987), 187–210; Postma, *The Dutch in the Atlantic*; Maria Cristina Navarrete, *Génesis y desarrollo de la esclavitud en Colombia (Siglos XVI y XVII)* (Cali: Universidad del Valle, 2005); Weindl, "The Asiento de Negros", 229–257; Luxán and Luxán, "Las compañías reales", 2–4.

the Portuguese Crown's geopolitical ambitions in Guinea, and the business interests of the *Companhia*'s partners – this chapter offers a renewed interpretation of this *asiento.*

1 Aligning Interests before the *Asiento* of 1696

By the 1680s, concerns about the supply of enslaved Africans to the Americas were mounting in Madrid due to disputes between Nicolás Porcio and Balthazar Coymans, and, after the latter's death, between Porcio and Coymans' partner Pedro van Belle and assistant Jan Carcau. These tensions were compounded by increasing diplomatic friction with the Dutch Republic, which was driven by the growing centrality of Curaçao as a slave transit port for the Caribbean.[7] By July 1692, the application from Bernardo Francisco Marín de Guzmán, a merchant from Caracas, for the *asiento* could not have been more timely. In addition to his proposal to pay a higher fee for the monopoly, an agreement with Marín de Guzmán held the promise of curtailing the hegemonic role of the WIC and reducing the importance of Curaçao, Jamaica, and Barbados, as hubs of the transatlantic slave trade. Marín promised to supply the Spanish Indies primarily with enslaved people from Upper Guinea.[8] Such a clause strongly indicates that an informal agreement between Marín and the Portuguese *Companhia de Cacheu e Cabo Verde* had already been reached before he signed the *asiento.* Indeed, by October 1692, Marín had negotiated in Lisbon a contract for the supply of enslaved Africans, which terms were finalised in February 1693.[9]

This joint venture between the *Companhia de Cacheu* and Marín de Guzmán is often cited as the principal reason for the return of the Portuguese as direct investors to the *asiento* of 1696. In turn, the latter would not have materialised without the political and financial support of the Portuguese Crown and its geopolitical interests in Upper Guinea. These imperial ambitions can be traced back to the 1660s, when the Portuguese Crown shifted its strategy. Against the backdrop of intense European rivalries along the West Coast of Africa and seeking to expand its influence in a region with significant potential as a market for enslaved Africans, the Crown opted to share the risks and

7 Scelle, *La traite négrière*, vol. 1, 623–624 and vol. 2, 32–41.
8 *Coleccion de los tratados*, 307–308, clause 18.
9 Scelle, *La traite négrière,* vol. 2, 26.

rewards of such endeavours with merchants.[10] This was accomplished through charters that granted monopoly rights over trade and shipping to trading companies. In return, the Crown tasked these companies with public utility functions such as tax collection, funding royal administration and clergy, and constructing and maintaining military infrastructures.[11]

The first of these companies was the *Companhia da Guiné*, established in 1664 and whose operations were located south of Arguim, hence its alternate name, *Companhia do Porto de Palmida*. Its existence was short-lived; by 1676, the Crown had issued a second charter, shifting the focus further south to the Cacheu River delta to better articulate with the hinterland. This new partnership, led by António de Barros Bezerra and Manuel Preto Valdez, was named the *Companhia de Cacheu, Rios e Comércio da Guiné* and operated until 1682.[12]

Despite these setbacks, the Crown continued to view trading companies as viable instruments of foreign policy and market expansion. Interest in exploiting the Cacheu region also persisted among Lisbon's business elite. By the late 1680s, the prospect of supplying Nicolás Porcio's *asiento* (1688–1693) spurred renewed efforts toward establishing a permanent settlement in the region.[13] To this end, five investors formed a partnership and, in 1690, approached King Pedro II for a new charter with a seven-year duration. This partnership became the *Companhia de Cacheu e Cabo Verde*. Unlike its predecessors, the *Companhia* was not granted monopoly rights over trade and shipping. Its advantage lay in fiscal exemptions and, more significantly, in the privilege of selling enslaved people in Cacheu or elsewhere to any buyer, except the Dutch and English.[14] Through this privilege, which allowed Portuguese subjects to trade directly with foreign ports, the Portuguese Crown partially lifted the constraints of colonial exclusivity, albeit temporarily.

The 1690 charter transformed the *Companhia de Cacheu* into a credible supplier of enslaved Africans for the *asiento*. Leveraging the *Companhia*'s prerogatives, one of its partners negotiated in Madrid during the summer of 1690 to supply an unspecified number of enslaved individuals to Porcio's *asiento*.

---

10 On the European rivalries, between the Dutch, the French, the English and the Portuguese and the role chartered companies played in the western coast of Africa in the seventeenth century, see A.G. Hopkins, *An Economic History of West Africa* (New York, Columbia University Press, 1973).

11 Teixeira, "Companhia de Cacheu", 87–132; Carreira, *As companhias pombalinas*, 22–23.

12 On the dissolution of this company, see Baleno, "Reconversão do comércio", 211–212.

13 Scelle, *La traite négrière*, vol. 2, 21.

14 Arquivo Histórico Ultramarino (hereafter AHU), Conselho Ultramarino, book 296, fls. 73–74 (1690-01-03). The third clause of the charter concerns the privileges of selling slaves.

Although the terms of this agreement remain unknown, it was ratified by King Pedro II a few months later.[15] By early 1691, the *Companhia*'s agents in Cape Verde were already selling enslaved Africans to the representatives of the *asiento*, who transported them to the Spanish Americas.[16] The *Companhia de Cacheu* must have been successful in these initial operations, as evidenced by its partners beginning negotiations with Bernardo Marín de Guzmán, the new *asentista*, in the autumn of 1692.

The negotiations in Lisbon were fraught with difficulties, as the *Companhia* adopted a hard bargaining stance. The *Companhia* was aware that Marín had committed to purchasing enslaved people from the English and the Dutch in the Caribbean only as a last resource, in line with his original pledge during the *asiento* negotiations to prioritise direct transport from Africa to Spanish America. This constraint gave the *Companhia* an advantage, enabling it to secure better terms than those it had achieve with Nicolàs Porcio. Rather than acting as a mere supplier, the *Companhia* aimed to claim a more significant share of the *asiento* business. Consequently, negotiations centred on two interconnected issues: the *Companhia's* ability to directly deliver Africans to Cartagena and Veracruz, and its freedom to withdraw the corresponding revenue in silver and colonial commodities. Through this arrangement, the partners sought to maximise their earnings, both by selling enslaved people at a higher price to the *asentista* and by engaging in the export of tradable colonial goods.

After weeks of complex negotiations, an agreement was reached whereby the *Companhia* would deliver 2,500 *piezas* de *Indias* (equivalent to 4,000 enslaved individuals), less than half of the 6,000 *piezas* Marín had intended to secure, for an annual sum of 252,500 *pesos*. Signed on 6 February 1693 and ratified by King Pedro II shortly afterwards, the agreement was generally approved by King Carlos II, with the exception of the ports to which the *Companhia* was granted access. Instead of Cartagena and Veracruz, deliveries were restricted to an entrepôt to be established in either La Guaira or Cumaná by the *asentista*.[17] Despite this limitation, the deal represented progress for the Portuguese partnership, marking a step towards resuming direct trade with Spanish America, which had been interrupted since the Portuguese Restoration of 1640, and the promise of substantial profits.

---

15 Arquivo Nacional da Torre do Tombo (hereafter ANTT), Chancelaria D. Pedro II, book 35, fl. 35v (1690-10-21).

16 Scelle, *La traite négrière,* vol. 2, 15. The permission granted by the Portuguese Crown for the settlement of a Spanish vice-consul in the island of Santiago (Cabo Verde) signals this activity.

17 Scelle, *La traite négrière,* vol. 2, 22–31.

The execution of the 1693 contract required several preconditions, which the *Companhia* sought to secure before signing with Marín. First, it requested an extension of its 1690 charter for a further six years, which King Pedro II immediately granted, reflecting the deal's royal endorsement.[18] Second, the partners sought to expand the geographical scope of their operations, recognizing that the Cacheu region alone would not suffice to meet the annual supply required under the agreement with the *asentista.*

To address this limitation, they considered bidding for the Angola contract to access an additional source of labour. However, this effort met resistance from competing merchant networks in Angola and Brazil, which feared that diverting enslaved people to the Spanish America would drive up prices and lead to labour shortages in Brazil, potentially disrupting the Luso-Brazilian sugar economy.[19] The king intervened to maintain the stability of the sugar economy, and the *Companhia* withdrew its bid on the condition that it be authorised to procure up to 1,500 enslaved individuals annually from Angola and another 1,500 from the islands of Cape Verde. The remaining 1,000 enslaved people needed to meet the 4,000 stipulated in the Marín contract were to be sourced from Cacheu and the Gold Coast.[20]

In response to the demands of the 1693 contract, the *Companhia* scaled up its operations. Following its negotiated allotment with the Crown, it tapped into additional African markets. By early 1695, in addition to its offices in Santiago (Cape Verde) and Cacheu, the *Companhia* opened a new axis of operations in the Gulf of Guinea. This expansion included establishing a slave entrepôt on the island of Príncipe (modern-day São Tomé and Príncipe) and constructing two fortresses.[21] Further investments were made in acquiring new ships to increase transport capacity.[22] These investments were substantial and likely required loans, which the *Companhia* obtained from

18 Biblioteca Nacional de Portugal (hereafter BNP), Reservados, book 1205/34A.

19 AHU, Angola, box 14, doc. 109 (1693-01-29).

20 Vitorino Magalhães Godinho, "Portugal and her Empire, 1680–1720" in *The New Cambridge Modern History*, vol. 6, *The Rise of Great Britain and Russia, 1688–1715–25*, edited by J.S. Bromley (Cambridge: Cambridge University Press, 1970), 515.

21 AHU, Guiné, box 3, doc. 91; box 4, doc. 104–105; Idem, Conselho Ultramarino, Consultas, book 489, fl. 107–107v. See also, Cristina Seuanes Serafim, *As ilhas de São Tomé no século XVII* (Lisbon: Centro de História de Além Mar, 2000), 112–113.

22 Arquivo Distrital de Lisboa (hereafter ADL), Cartórios Notariais de Lisboa (hereafter CNL), Cartório do Distribuidor (hereafter CD), book 69, fl. 81, 81v and 83v (1694).

institutional and private creditors.[23] However, the death of Bernardo Marín's in 1695 dealt a significant blow to the *Companhia's* prospects.

Marín's *asiento* abruptly ended with his assassination in Curaçao around 7 May 1695 under unclear circumstances. Recognising the financial losses and frustrated expectations resulting from the contract's termination, the *Companhia de Cacheu* petitioned to take over Marín's contract based on their supply agreement. However, Madrid rejected the request, arguing that the Spanish government could not be bound by a private contract. Alternative options for the *asiento* proved equally problematic. The Dutch were ruled out due to the fallout from the so-called Coymans *asiento*, and the French were similarly excluded due to Spain's conflict with Louis XIV during the Nine Years' War (1688–1697). The English were also deemed unsuitable, as Madrid feared their ability to exploit the *asiento* to gain both legal and illicit access to the Spanish colonies' protected markets.[24] Under these circumstances, Madrid eventually welcomed a new offer from the *Companhia* in early 1696.

Meanwhile, in Lisbon, the prospect of the *asiento* spurred renewed efforts. Before presenting a new proposal to Madrid, the *Companhia* secured political and financial support from King Pedro II, which materialised in the renewal of its charter for another six years and a promise of a loan of 200,000,000 *réis* at a 4% interest rate.[25] This line of credit provided the liquidity necessary for the *Companhia* to include a loan of 200,000 *pesos* at an 8% interest rate in its offer to the Spanish Crown in the spring of 1696. This advance was to be delivered in Madrid and repaid only at the end of the contract by deducting the amount of the customs duties levied on the delivered enslaved people.

The inclusion of the loan in the proposal proved decisive, giving the Portuguese an edge over other competitors. Negotiations on the terms of the *asiento* followed shortly thereafter in Madrid between Gaspar de Andrade, representing the *Companhia,* and the inner circle of King Carlos II's advisers. For the duration of six years and eight months (1696–1703), the *Companhia* agreed to deliver 30,000 *piezas de Indias,* for which it would pay 112,5 *pesos* in duties for each *pieza*. This amount marked a return to the standard rate paid by the *asentistas* since the contracts of Grillo and Lomelino, significantly lower than the 212 *pesos* Marín had agreed to pay.[26] In return, King Carlos II granted the

23 Lisbeth Rodrigues, "O incumprimento do crédito no século XVIII: o caso da Misericórdia de Lisboa", in *Economia, finanças e instituições no Portugal moderno*, edited by Bruno Lopes and Roger Lee de Jesus (Coimbra: Imprensa da Universidade de Coimbra, 2019), 247.

24 Scelle, *La traite négrière*, vol. 2, 32–41.

25 AHU, Conselho Ultramarino, book 296, fls. 108v-110, 1696-03-17. For the loan, see Scelle, *La traite négrière,* vol. 2, 39.

26 Scelle, *La traite négrière,* vol. 1, 694.

Companhia access to seven ports – Cumaná, Caracas, Havana, Cartagena de *Indias*, Portobelo, Honduras and Veracruz – and guaranteed the right to withdraw earnings in silver and colonial goods, as well as direct navigation to Portugal.[27]

The terms of the *asiento* included a significant innovation. Breaking away with the past of indirect management, the Spanish Crown bypassed intermediaries and established a contract directly with a company that had direct access to African supply markets. However, this decision came at a cost, as it meant granting the *asiento* to foreigners rather than to Spanish subjects or foreign residents within Spanish territories. In this sense, the 1696 *asiento* signals a shift in Spain's management of its monopoly on the import of transatlantic enslaved people.[28] The change was not well received, particularly by the *Consejo de Indias* and the merchant guilds with exclusive rights over trade with Spanish America. The 1696 *asiento* suspended these colonial exclusives, albeit for this purpose alone, for both the Spanish and Portuguese Crowns. For King Carlos II, this meant allowing foreigners direct access to Spanish colonial markets, while King Pedro II authorised the transport of enslaved Africans to territories outside Portuguese jurisdiction. Given that both monarchies had pledged to uphold their colonial exclusives under the 1668 Peace Treaty, the implementation of the *asiento* required a temporary suspension of this clause, achieved through mutual agreement.[29]

Signed on 12 July 1696 in Madrid, the *asiento* was awarded to the *Companhia da Guiné*, the new name adopted by the former *Companhia de Cacheu e Cabo Verde* upon the renewal of its charter on 17 March 1696. Under this charter, the public duties of the *Companhia* were expanded to include the establishment of an additional outpost in Guinea – Bissau – demonstrating Portugal's ongoing interest in consolidating its presence in the region. The next section examines the structure of the *Companhia* and the role played by the Crown in supporting the *asiento*.

2 Partners and Capital

The businessmen who formed the original partnership behind the *Companhia de Cacheu* (1690) were motivated from the outset to supply enslaved people to the Spanish American markets. The lucrative trade with the Spanish colonies,

27 *Coleccion de los tratados*, part 3, 369–372, clauses 1, 3, and 6.

28 George Scelle already noted this shift *La traite négrière*, vol. 2, 29.

29 Scelle, *La traite négrière*, vol. 2, 41.

which had been conducted in silver during the Iberian Union of the Crowns (1580–1640), served as a powerful incentive for the partners to seek a royal charter. This primary goal was reaffirmed in 1693 and 1696, coinciding with the contract with Bernardo Marín and the subsequent prospect of obtaining the *asiento* under the *Companhia*'s own name. However, the scale of business entailed by that these agreements required the original partnership to expand. The *Companhia de Cacheu*, later renamed the *Companhia da Guiné*, embodied and combined three versions of a core partnership that replaced or added new members according to business needs. Analysing the backgrounds and prior experience of the individuals who successfully formed these partnerships, reveals not only their capacity to gather capital and expertise but also their strategies for organising the various segments of their enterprise. Meeting these requirements – capital, experience, and management – was especially critical given that the *Companhia* operated across three continents and at least two empires, while fulfilling public duties stipulated in its charters.

The core of the 1696 partnership managing the *asiento* traces its origins to the group established in 1690. At that time, the profiles of the five partners aligned with the *Companhia*'s business goals and the responsibilities outlined in its charter. Four of the five partners were experienced businessmen who brought capital, trade expertise, and extensive mercantile networks: António de Castro Guimarães, Francisco Mendes de Barros, Louis Martin and Gaspar de Andrade. Among them, António de Castro Guimarães stood out as one of the wealthiest businessmen in late seventeenth-century Lisbon, remaining involved until the partnership's liquidation in the early 1700s. Originally from a rural parish in northern Portugal and the son of a carpenter, António moved to Lisbon as a youth to train under Gaspar Pacheco, the head of one of the city's most prominent mercantile houses in the 1640s.[30] There, António acquired skills in wholesale trade, tax farming, and military provisioning, building an extensive network of business contacts. By the late 1680s, in his early sixties, he had become a prominent figure in Lisbon's business scene, with successful ventures in military provisioning and wholesale trade with Brazil. His vast business and financial network, which included New Christian merchants, extended across northwestern Europe (notably Amsterdam) and the Mediterranean (notably Genoa). This network enabled him to provide financial services, including brokering payments for the Crown, paying Portuguese diplomats across Europe, and earning royal favour that lasted until his

30 On Gaspar Pacheco, see David Grant Smith, *The Mercantile Class of Portugal and Brazil in the Seventeenth Century: A Socio-Economic Study of the Merchants of Lisbon and Bahia, 1620–1690*, PhD diss. (Austin: Texas University Press, 1979), 134 and 420.

death around 1710.[31] French diplomatic sources suggest he may also have facilitated foreign encroachment into Portugal's protected colonial markets, although this claim lacks corroboration in Portuguese sources.[32]

Francisco Mendes de Barros and Louis Martin, while less prominent, were experienced wholesale traders. Francisco Mendes de Barros, like António Castro, hailed from northern Portugal (Guimarães) and moved to Lisbon, likely joining his brother José Mendes de Barros's mercantile house. At the time of joining the *Companhia de Cacheu,* Francisco Mendes was primarily engaged in wholesale trade with Brazil and was regarded by the French ambassador as one of Lisbon's most skilled businessmen.[33] Louis Martin, a French merchant from Provence, had been based in Lisbon since at least the 1670s. He maintained an active trade between Lisbon and French ports, particularly Marseille and Bordeaux, and was involved in exploiting the brazilwood monopoly. By the late 1680s, according to the French consul, Louis Martin headed one of the two wealthiest French merchant houses in Lisbon.[34] Although Portuguese sources do not mention it, Martin shared his interest in the *Companhia* with his business partner and brother-in-law, Francisco (or François) André. Born in Lisbon to a French father and a Portuguese mother, André inherited his father's mercantile house and his partnership with Martin that dated back to the 1680s.[35] André continued his father's shipping business, actively trading with France and, as a Portuguese subject, engaging in direct trade with Brazil.[36] Together with António de Castro Guimarães, Francisco Mendes de Bar-

31 ANTT, Tribunal do Santo Ofício, Conselho Geral, Habilitações, António, bundle 12, doc. 438 (1661); ANTT, Chancelaria Afonso VI, book 39, fl. 122–122v (1679-09-01) and book 40, fl. 85 (1681-02-05); ANTT, Chancelaria D. Pedro II, book 35, fls. 159–160 (1687-05-10) and book 48, fl. 314 (1688-07-06). For an overview of the services rendered by António Castro Guimarães to the King, ANTT, Registo Geral de Mercês, D. João V, book 3, fl. 87–87v (1709-03-01). On António de Castro and his descendents, see Maria Adelaide Pereira Moraes, "Desceram do monte, atravessaram, o mar (Castro de Guimarães e seu termo), *Boletim de Trabalhos Históricos*, Guimarães, vol. 38, 1987, 61–103.

32 Claude-Frédéric Lévy, *Capitalistes et Pouvoir Au Siècle Des Lumières: Les Fondateurs Des Origines à 1715*, vol. 1 (Paris : Mouton, Reprint 2019 [ed. 1969]), 132.

33 ADL, CNL, CD, books 62–67. Lévy, *Capitalistes et pouvoir*, 132.

34 Jean-François Labourdette, *La nation française à Lisbonne de 1669 à 1790: entre colbertisme et liberalisme* (Paris: Fondation Calouste Gulbenkian – Centre Culturel Portugais, 1988), 524–525 and 670–671.

35 ANTT, Tribunal do Santo Ofício, Conselho Geral, Habilitações, Francisco, bundle, 13, doc. 414 (1676). On his partnership with Louis Martin, see Labourdette, *La nation française*, 525.

36 AHU, Pernambuco, box 7, doc. 678 (1663-03-20) and box 7, doc. 692 (1663-03-24); ANTT, Chancelaria Afonso VI, book 20, fl. 35 (1665-12-19) and book 22, fls. 406v-407 (1669-03-09); AHU, Rio de Janeiro, Castro e Almeida, box 8, doc. 1448–1449 (1682-01-26 and 1682-01-30).

ros, Louis Martin, and Francisco André formed the core of the *Companhia,* which remained intact through the restructuration processes in 1693 and 1696.

As for Gaspar de Andrade, in addition to capital, he brought valuable skills to the partnership. He had served on the Island of Madeira acting as a commissioner for the *Junta do Comércio* (Board of Trade), where he provided logistical support for the convoys linking Lisbon to the main Brazilian port cities. He combined this role with some small-scale trading within the Portuguese South Atlantic.[37] Andrade maintained good relations with António Barros Bezerra, a former partner of the *Companhia de Cacheu, Rios e Comércio da Guiné* (1676–1682), which suggests prior involvement and interests in the Cacheu region.[38] By all accounts, he seems to have possessed considerable knowledge of how the business should be conducted, making it likely that he was one of the *Companhia*'s promoters. His role within the *Companhia* between 1690 and 1701 support this assumption. From as early as 1690, he served as the executive manager (*caixa*) of the *Companhia.*[39] In this capacity, he twice represented the *Companhia*'s interests in Madrid: first in 1690 during discussions with Nicolàs Porcio regarding the supply of enslaved Africans to the Spanish Americas, and again in 1696 during final negotiations with Spanish authorities for the *asiento.*[40] Following these negotiations, Andrade was appointed head officer of the *Companhia* in Cartagena de *Indias.*

The fifth and final partner of the 1690 partnership, Domingos Monteiro de Carvalho was a career army officer who had previously served as an infantry captain in Salvador da Bahia.[41] He was tasked with overseeing operations in Cacheu and was formally appointed as its captain-general by the Crown.[42] However, his tenure lasted little over a year, ending with his death sometime in 1691.[43]

In the context of the operational expansion required by the 1693 contract with Marín, two new investors joined the partnership: Francisco Nunes de Santarém and Domingos Dantas da Cunha (see Table 6.1).[44] Alongside capital, Francisco Nunes brought extensive business connections in the Portuguese South Atlantic and Northwestern Europe, as well as a distinguished career in

37 ANTT Cabido da Sé do Funchal, bundle 24, doc. 2 (1680-09-18).
38 AHU, Cabo Verde, box 7, doc. 6 (1682-09-07).
39 AHU, Cabo Verde, box 7A, doc. 155 (1693-12-19).
40 ANTT, Chancelaria Pedro II, book 35, fl. 35v (1690-10-21); Scelle, *La traite négrière,* vol. 2, 39–40.
41 ANTT, Chancelaria Pedro II, book 58, fl. 85–85v (1690-01-17).
42 ANTT, Conselho Ultramarino, book 296, fls. 73–74 (1690-01-03).
43 AHU, Cabo Verde, box 7A, docs. 121, 123 (1690-09-12) and doc. 129 (1691-08-07).
44 BNP, Reservados, book 1205/34A (1693).

TABLE 6.1 Reconstruction of the partnerships, 1690–1696

1690	1693	1696
António de Castro Guimarães	António de Castro Guimarães	António de Castro Guimarães
Francisco Mendes de Barros	Francisco Mendes de Barros	Francisco Mendes de Barros
Louis Martin (and Francisco André)	Louis Martin (and Francisco André)	Francisco André (and Louis Martin)
Gaspar de Andrade	Gaspar de Andrade	–
Domingos Monteiro de Carvalho	–	–
	Francisco Nunes Santarém	Francisco Nunes Santarém
	Domingos Dantas da Cunha	Domingos Dantas da Cunha

SOURCES: AHU, CONSELHO ULTRAMARINO, GUINÉ, BOX. 3, DOC. 59 (1690); BNP, RESERVADOS, BOOK 1205/344; 1696 *COLECCION DE LOS TRATADOS*, PART 3, 369–372 (1693).

the royal bureaucracy, granting him access to privileged information. He was a descendant of João Nunes Santarém, a prominent financier during the reign of King João IV in the 1640s. Francisco inherited a well-established mercantile house engaged in wholesale trade within the Portuguese South-Atlantic, with networks extending to Amsterdam through the Portuguese (Jewish) Nation.[45] He concentrated his activities in the Portuguese South Atlantic, investing in the *Companhia Geral do Comércio do Brasil* (Company of Brazil, 1649–1654) and the Angola contract.[46] His prior involvement in the *Companhia Geral* justified his appointment as chief auditor of the *Junta do Comércio*, the insti-

45 João Nunes Santarém accompanied Tristão de Mendonça Furtado, ambassador to the States General in 1641, and played an important role in advancing funds to support this embassy. ANTT, Registo Geral de Mercês, Mercês da Torre do Tombo, book 12, fls. 532v-533v (1648-12-03).

46 On the Company of Brazil, see Leonor Freire Costa, Pedro Lains and Susana Münch Miranda, *An Economic History of Portugal, 1143–2010* (Cambridge: Cambridge University Press, 2016), 125–126. On his investments in the Company of Brazil, ANTT, Chancelaria Afonso VI, book 4, fls. 223v-226v (1666-12-17), book 10, fls. 226–229 (1672-10-15) and book 13, fls. 352–354v (1672-10-15). On the Angola contract, see Smith, *The Mercantile Class*, 421.

tution responsible for liquidating the *Companhia Geral,* a role he held for nearly seventeen years.[47] By the time he joined the *Companhia de Cacheu,* his expertise as an auditor and his connections within the imperial bureaucracy made him a valuable asset. In contrast, Domingos Dantas da Cunha left fewer records but was recognised as a wealthy businessman whose fortune stemmed from wholesale trade with Brazil.[48]

In the absence of Portuguese sources, we rely on correspondence from French diplomats in Lisbon to reconstruct the share capital of the 1693 partnership. A month after the contract with Marín was signed, Jean d'Estrées reported to Paris that the share capital of the *Companhia* had increased to 60,000,000 *réis*, divided into twelve shares of 5,000,000 *réis* each, with the Crown holding four shares.[49] Since the Crown does not formally appear as partner in the 1693 charter, it is likely that this share originated from a promise made in autumn 1692 to provide funds as a loan to enable the *Companhia* to meet its financial obligations.[50] The second-largest shareholder were the estate of Pedro Álvares Caldas, a prominent New Christian businessman active in the 1660s and 1670s, holding three shares. However, as with the Crown, the charter does not mention these shareholders. It is more plausible that the shares were held by Francisco Nunes Santarém, who was the administrator of Pedro Álvares' estate.[51] The remaining five partners held one share each.

By 1696, when the *Companhia* signed the *asiento*, its partnership had undergone further changes. Gaspar de Andrade, although still connected to the enterprise, seems to have withdrawn as partner, while two new members, João de Moura and Manuel Ferreira de Carvalho, signed the *asiento*.[52] However, neither of these men were among the five private shareholders of the 1696 *Companhia,* according to the French ambassador in Lisbon. More significantly, the partnership restructured to meet the financial demands of the

---

47 ANTT, Chancelaria Afonso VI, book 40, fl. 219 (1682-07-08); ANTT, Registo Geral de Mercês, Pedro II, book 2, fls. 252v-253 (1682-11-22).

48 ANTT, Tribunal do Santo Ofício, Conselho Geral, Habilitações, Domingos, bundle 6, doc. 1 (1677). Before joining the *Companhia de Cacheu,* Domingos Dantas da Cunha had exploited the tax farming contract of the *portos secos* (interior customs) of Algarve and Alentejo (Southern Portugal).

49 Lévy, *Capitalistes et pouvoir*, 132.

50 BNP, Reservados, book 1205/34A; Scelle, *La traite négrière*, vol. 2, p. 26.

51 ANTT, Chancelaria Pedro II, book 58, fl. 347–347v (1693-06-27). In support of our argument, we stress that Francisco Nunes pledged his private assets, as all other partners, for the liabilities incurred by the *Companhia* in the 1696 *asiento* contract. *Coleccion de los tratados,* part 3, 368.

52 *Coleccion de los tratados,* part 3, 367.

asiento. The share capital increased to 190,000,000 *réis*, divided into nine shares of 21,000,000 *réis,* instead of twelve. The Crown remained the largest shareholder, increasing its stake with four shares, but its participation grew from 33.3% to 44.4%, a change likely driven by the lack of private investors willing to participate in the endeavor. According to the French diplomat, the Crown even attempted, unsuccessfully, to sell its position in the *Companhia*.[53] The remaining shares, were distributed equally among António Castro Guimarães, Francisco Mendes de Barros, Francisco André (with Louis Martin), Francisco Nunes Santarém, and Domingos Dantas da Cunha.[54]

The share capital alone was insufficient to meet the operational demands of the *asiento*. For working capital, estimated at 400,000,000 *réis* according to Rouillé, the French ambassador, the royal treasury again had to intervene, as the partners were unable to raise this amount through borrowing. The Crown provided a line of credit worth 320,000,000 *réis* at an unspecified interest rate and appointed a deputy to the *Companhia*'s board of directors. Consequently, due to these capitalisation problems, the majority of both the share and working capital came under Crown control. This fact undermines claims that the *Companhia de Cacheu* was a front for foreign investors.[55] On the one hand, there were no barriers preventing foreigners to openly investing in colonial companies, as evidenced by the inclusion of Louis Martin, a Frenchmen, among the *Companhia's* core partners. On the other hand, the capitalisation processes of 1693 and 1696 offered ample opportunities for both direct and indirect investment in the partnerships of Cacheu and of Guiné, but the endeavour failed to attract new financiers, compelling the Crown to intervene. The count of Pontchartrain, minister and chancellor to Louis XIV, encouraged Saint-Malo businessmen to participate in the *asiento* through the *Companhia*, but these efforts also proved unsuccessful.[56]

3 The *Asiento* under the *Companhia da Guiné*

To operationalize the *asiento*, the *Companhia da Guiné* established an organisational structure spanning three continents. Its headquarters were located in Lisbon, where the five partners managed daily operations alongside a mag-

53 Lévy, *Capitalistes et pouvoir*, 136.

54 Scelle, *La traite négrière*, vol. 2, 46–47.

55 Stanley Stein and Barbara Stein, *Silver, Trade, and War: Spain and America in the Making of Early Modern Europe* (Baltimore: Johns Hopkins University Press, 2000), 115.

56 Lévy, *Capitalistes et pouvoir*, 133–137.

istrate representing the Crown's interests in the *Companhia*.[57] It is unclear how management tasks were divided among the partners, though it is likely that Francisco Nunes Santarém served as its treasurer. For significant financial and political matters, the *Companhia* liaised with the secretary of State, Mendo de Fóios Pereira.[58] Following the signing of the *asiento*, the *Companhia* opened an agency in Madrid, headed by Manuel Ferreira de Carvalho, a young jurist who had signed the *asiento* contract in July 1696 in the Spanish capital.[59] His role was to represent the *Companhia* before the *Consejo de Indias*, the institution overseeing the *asiento*. The Madrid agency likely included clerks to assist Ferreira de Carvalho, especially as the workload increased significantly by 1699 due to growing tensions between the *Companhia*, the *Consejo de Indias*, and the local authorities in Spanish America.[60]

Although limited information exists about the African agencies, by 1696 the partnership established operations on Santiago Island (Cape Verde), in Cacheu, and on Príncipe Island. The latter was significantly reinforced to serve as the *Companhia's* main slave entrepôt in the Gulf of Guinea. To protect this infrastructure, construction of two fortresses was underway by September 1696. These projects were financed by the *Companhia*, which also covered the salaries of the garrison, comprising sixty soldiers and five officers.[61] A fourth agency in Africa was established in Bissau as a military stronghold, with its construction and garrison salaries also funded by the *Companhia*, following the renewal of its charter in March 1696.

In Spanish America, the *Companhia* set up its headquarters in Cartagena, then the principal slave trading port and redistribution centre for the Spanish Caribbean colonies and territories under the jurisdiction of the Viceroyalty of Peru.[62] Gaspar de Andrade was appointed as general factor and arrived in Cartagena in late 1696 to oversee daily operations and managed the *Companhia*'s personnel in Cartagena and in the circum-Caribbean region. The second most significant figure in the Cartagena factory was João de Moura, one of the signatories of the 1696 *asiento*. Sources offer conflicting accounts of Moura's activities; inquisitorial records suggest he travelled aboard *Companhia*-

57 ADL, CNL, 2.º Cartório, box 63, book 317, fls. 71–72 (1696-06-27); Scelle, *La traite négrière*, vol. 2, 46.

58 AHU, Conselho Ultramarino, book 296, fls. 73–74 (1690-01-03).

59 He was 31 years old in 1996 and had qualified for a judgeship appointment. ANTT, Desembargo do Paço, Leitura de Bacharéis, letter M, bundle 18, doc. 6 (1695).

60 Scelle, *La traite négrière*, vol. 2, 55–59.

61 Serafim, *As Ilhas de São Tomé*, 102–103.

62 Alex Borucki, "Trans-Imperial History in the Making of the Slave Trade to Venezuela, 1526–1811", *Itinerario* 36, no. 2 (2012), 29–54.

outfitted ships between Africa and Spanish America, while other sources identify him as a captain operating between Cartagena and Curaçao.[63] Additional employees in Cartagena included an assistant factor (António Franco), a treasurer (João Barbosa da Costa), and a clerk. The warehouse where enslaved individuals were held also required guards and auxiliary staff, though their numbers remain unspecified.[64]

Veracruz hosted the second most important factory, despite its declining significance in the slave trade since the 1650s.[65] From 1697, three factors managed sales of enslaved Africans on behalf of the *asentistas:* Manuel Luís da Fonseca, Lucas da Costa and Damião Pereira de Araújo. By 1700, three additional employees had joined the Veracruz agency: Francisco Dantas de Vasconcelos (factor), Roque Pereira da Cunha (treasurer), and António da Luz (cashier).[66] While evidence of *Companhia* agents in La Guaira/Caracas and Havana is supported by records of enslaved Africans disembarked there between 1696 and 1702, no information exists about operations in the remaining three ports – Honduras, Portobelo, and Cumaná – authorised under the *asiento*.

The primary objective of this pluricontinental organisational structure was to ensure the day-to-day operations that were necessary to ensure the delivery of 4,500 *piezas* annually to Spanish American markets, as stipulated by the *asiento*. Following its signing, Gaspar de Andrade and his staff departed for Cartagena, while the Lisbon partners began implementing the contract. The *Companhia* expanded its transport capacity by purchasing and freighting ships, enabling the dispatch of four ships from Lisbon by April 1697.[67] Two were large vessels of approximately 700 tons each, one destined for Guinea to embark 1,000 enslaved Africans and the other for Santiago, where it was to load 500 enslaved people, by way of the Canary islands. In the Canaries, the *asentistas* were permitted to load 400 tons of local produce for the Spanish American markets.[68] The other two smaller ships also sailed to Cape Verde to enhance transport capacity, indicating the *Companhia*'s ambition for a substantial initial delivery.[69]

63 Scelle, *La traite négrière*, vol. 1, 746–747; Archivo General de Indias, Indiferente, 2778.

64 Palacios, *La trata*, p. 51. The warehouse of the Portuguese *Companhia* was located between the fortresses of San Juan de Manzanillo and San Felipe de Barajas (Gutiérrez, "El comercio y mercado", 194–195 and 201).

65 Borucki, Eltis and Wheat, "Atlantic History", p. 437.

66 Rodrígues Blásquez, "Penetración portuguesa", 50–58; Scelle, *La traite négrière*, vol. 2, 56.

67 ADL, CNL, CD, book 70, fl. 82v (1696–11); Scelle, *La traite négrière*, vol. 2, 53.

68 *Coleccion de los tratados*, part 3, 378, clause 21.

69 Scelle, *La traite négrière*, vol. 2, 53–54.

However, the *aiento's* demands exceeded the capacity of Portuguese African slave markets, prompting the partners to diversify their supply sources through their agents, Simão and Luís de Sousa. From 1697 to 1700, the Sousa brothers brokered several deliveries with European slaving companies, including the RAC, the WIC, and the Brandenburg African Company (BAC). According to French diplomatic correspondence, the deal with the RAC in 1697 involved the delivery of 3,000 *piezas* to Cartagena and Veracruz.[70] Concurrently, the Souza brothers signed contracts with the WIC in late 1697 and again in 1699 for 2,500 to 3,000 *piezas*, with probable renewal in early 1700.[71] Meanwhile, the BAC, a relative newcomer to the slave trade, approached the brothers in late 1698, offering to deliver 2,000 captives.[72]

In addition to these corporate agreements, the Sousa brothers also negotiated with Amsterdam merchants who illicitly traded within the WIC's monopoly.[73] With the exception of the BAC, which supplied captives from its St. Thomas agency in the Caribbean, all other parties committed to supplying their human cargos from Africa.

French involvement in the Portuguese *asiento* remained limited, at least formally, until the spring of 1699. Attempts by the *Compagnie du Sénégal* to secure a role, brokered by Louis Martin in Lisbon in February and December 1698, ultimately failed due to conflicting interests between the French and Portuguese monarchs. However, the French gained a foothold in the *asiento* in May 1699 through an agreement between the *Compagnie de Saint Domingue* and Gaspar de Andrade for delivery of enslaved Africans to Cuba and the Spanish colony of Santo Domingo.[74] This arrangement contravened the terms of the *asiento*, which barred the Portuguese from accessing the Santo Domingo market.

In addition to contracts with European West African trading companies, the *Companhia* also relied on independent merchants for the supply of Afri-

70 Lévy, *Capitalistes et pouvoir*, 137; Scelle, *La traite negrière*, vol. 2, 54.

71 Postma, *The Dutch*, 47.

72 Lévy, *Capitalistes et pouvoir*, 137; Scelle, *La traite négrière*, vol. 2, 54. On the BAC, see Richard Schück, *Brandenburg-Preussens Kolonial-Politik unter dem Grossen Kurfürsten und seinen Nachfolgern (1637–1721)*, 2 vols. (Leipiz: Grunow, 1889) and Waldemar Westergaard. *The Danish West Indies under Company Rule (1671–1754): With a Supplementary Chapter, 1755–1917* (New York: The Macmillan Company, 1917), 71–94.

73 On Dutch privateers in the African coast, see Ruud Paesie, *Lorrendrayen op Africa: de illegale goederen- en slavenhandel op West-Afrika tijdens het achttiende-eeuwse handelsmonopolie van de West-Indische Compagnie, 1700–1734* (Amsterdam: De Bataafsche Leeuw, 2008); Postma, *The Dutch in the Atlantic*, 79.

74 Lévy, *Capitalistes et pouvoir*, 138–141.

can captives to Spanish Americas. While evidence is limited, negotiations with non-institutional suppliers are attested in several instances of deliveries directly from Africa or via the Caribbean. These examples highlight the declining effectiveness of the monopolies held by the WIC and the RAC.[75] Among independent merchants operating out of London, figures such as James Waite, John Verhulst, and John Stafford are notable.[76] Their involvement can be traced to proposals made directly to the *Companhia* in Lisbon by Paul Methuen, the English *chargé d'affaires* to Portugal, in 1698.[77] Similarly, Jewish merchants of Iberian origin – including David Ximenes, António Álvares Machado, Manuel de Belmonte and the Sousa brothers – facilitated deliveries of enslaved individuals to Cartagena during the Portuguese *asiento*. Belmonte's participation marked a continuation of his earlier involvement with his family – Francisco de Schonenberg, a diplomat at the service of the Dutch Republic – as financiers of Balthazar Coymans' bid for the administration (and later on the tenure) of the *asiento*. Belmonte had already mediated the relationship between the WIC and the Coymans House during in the late 1670s and early 1680s.[78]

Local merchants from Curaçao and the English Caribbean, rather than the WIC or the RAC, were instrumental in supplying the *asiento*. This dynamic and international network included merchants of Portuguese origin with connections spanning Curaçao, Cartagena (notably Gaspar de Andrade), and La Guaira/Caracas.[79] Examples include Manuel Álvares Correia, Johannes Goetvrint, Filipe Henriques and David Senior.[80] Jamaican merchants, some of Portuguese Jewish origin, also leveraged long-standing trade relationships with

75 On the WIC, see Postma, *The Dutch in the Atlantic*, 79. In the late 1690s, the RAC was already licensing private traders. See Ann Carlos and Jamie Brown Kruse, "The decline of the Royal African Company: Fringe Firms and the Role of the Charter", *The Economic History Review*, 49, no. 2 (1996), 291–313.

76 On James Waite, one of the top English slave traders, see Mathew David Mitchell, *The Prince of Slavers: Humphry Morice and the Transformation of Britain's Transatlantic Slave Trade, 1698–1732* (London: Palgrave, 2020), 81; and William A. Pettigrew, *Freedom's Debt: The Royal African Company and the Politics of the Atlantic Slave Trade, 1672–1752* (Chapel Hill: University of North Carolina Press, 2013), 233.

77 Lévy, *Capitalistes et pouvoir*, 136; Donnan, *Documents illustrative of the History*, 120–121.

78 *Slave Voyages: The Transatlantic Slave Trade Database*, https://www.slavevoyages.org/ (accessed 1 May 2021).

79 On the Dutch entrepôt trade in Curaçao, see Klooster, "Curaçao and the Caribbean", 203–218.

80 Jordaan, "The Curaçao Slave Market", 223–224. *Slave Voyages: The Intra-American Slave Trade Database*, with "Time Frame – 1697–1702", "Principal Place of "Purchase" and "Principal Place of Landing" (accessed 1 May 2021).

Spanish colonies to deliver human cargos.[81] Profits were high as the Spanish paid two to three times the price offered by English planters in the Caribbean.[82] The *Companhia* engaged Santiago del Castillo, a Catalan merchant who had migrated to the Spanish Americas as Nicolàs Porcio's agent before settling in Port Royal, to mediate this trade.[83]

The first ship delivering enslaved people under the Portuguese *asiento* from Curaçao arrived in Cartagena in early 1698.[84] By May 1702,[85] the *Companhia* had introduced an estimated 12,332 enslaved Africans to the Spanish Americas, a figure exceeding Palacios Preciado's estimate of 9,853 captives disembarked in Cartagena alone during the same period (Table 6.2).[86] Our estimate is based on the *Slave Voyages Database* (hereafter SVD) and incorporates additional findings from secondary sources on arrivals in Veracruz and Cuba.[87] Notably, the SVD lacks records of slave arrivals in these ports for the observed period.[88] We only included voyages documented by Spanish state-produced sources or qualitative material linking them to the *asentistas*. Other voyages recorded in the SVD were excluded due to incomplete data, such as unspecified landing dates or locations, casting doubt on their connection to the Portuguese *asiento*. Given these limitations, it is plausible that the actual number

---

81 *Slave Voyages: The Intra-American Slave Trade Database*, with "Time Frame – 1697–1702", "Principal Place of "Purchase" and "Principal Place of Landing".

82 Zahedieh, "The Merchants of Port Royal", 580 and 589.

83 Donnan, *Documents*, vol. 1, 420; Scelle, *La traite négrière*, vol. 1, 685–686; F. J. Osborne, "James Castillo, Asiento Agent", *The Jamaican Historical Review* 8, 1971, 9–18, Aaron Alejandro Olivas, "The Global Politics of Transatlantic Slave Trade during the War of the Spanish Succession, 1700–1715", in *Early Bourbon Spanish America: Politics and Society in a Forgotten Era, 1700–1759*, edited by F. A. Eissa-Barros and A. Vásquez Varela (Leiden: Brill, 2013), 85–109.

84 Navarrete, *Génesis y desarrollo*, 56–57.

85 Up until 1 May 1702, the *Companhia* was allowed to introduce slaves, in accordance with the terms set in the 18 June 1701 dissolution treaty. *Tratados, convenios y declaraciones de paz y de comercio que han hecho con las potencias estranjeras los monarcas españoles de la casa de Borbon desde el año de 1700 hasta el dia*, edited by Alejandro del Cantillo (Madrid: Imprenta de Alegria y Charlain, 1843), 28–35.

86 Palacios Preciado, *La trata*, 70.

87 The records we are using from the *Slave Voyages Database* pertain both to the *Transatlantic and the Intra-American Slave Trade Databases*. As for the secondary sources, we use data recently compiled by Joseph Michael Hopper Clark, *Veracruz and the Caribbean in the Seventeenth Century*, PhD diss. (Baltimore: Johns Hopkins University, 2016); Luxán and Luxán, "Las compañías".

88 On the sub-representation of the intra-American traffic in the *Slave Voyages Database*, see Borucki, "Trans-Imperial History", 30–31.

TABLE 6.2 Suppliers to the Portuguese *asiento*, 1698–1702

Suppliers	1	2	3	4	5	6	7
WIC	2,427	19.68	5	2,427	19.68	–	–
Companhia da Guiné	**2,407**	**19.52**	**12**	**2,407**	**19.52**	–	–
Independent Merchants (English Caribbean)	2,010	16.30	19	–	–	2,010	16.30
Independent Merchants (Curaçao)	1,843	14.94	19	–	–	1,843	14.94
(BAC)	1,162	9.42	10	–	–	1,162	9.42
Independent Merchants (England)	1,149	9.32	5	1,149	9.32	–	–
Independent Merchants (Dutch Interlopers)	803	6.51	2	803	6.51	–	–
RAC	131	1.06	3	131	1.06	–	–
NI	400	3.24	1			400	3.24
Total	12,332	100.00	76	6,917	56.09	5,415	43.91

Key: 1. Number of slaves; 2. Number of slaves (%); 3. Number of ships; 4. Slaves from Africa; 5. Slaves from Africa (%); 6. Slaves from the Caribbean; 7. Slaves from the Caribbean (%).
SOURCES: SVD: *THE TRANSATLANTIC AND THE INTRA-AMERICAN SLAVE TRADE DATABASES*; CLARK, *VERACRUZ AND THE CARIBBEAN*, 183; LUXÁN AND LUXÁN, "LAS COMPAÑÍAS", 9.

of enslaved individuals introduced legally by the *Companhia* was higher than our estimate, a question that further research may clarify.

From 1698 to 1702, the *Companhia da Guiné* relied heavily on outsourcing to meet its contractual obligations. While it directly accounted for around one fifth of total deliveries, the WIC, RAC, and BAC collectively supplied 30,2% (Table 6.2). One of the most striking features of this *asiento* was the significant role of independent merchants, who delivered 15,8% of captives directly from Africa and 31,2% via the Caribbean.[89] This underscores the challenges faced by the WIC and RAC in maintaining their monopolies, formally and informally. The RAC, in particular, lost its monopoly in 1698 due to competition and pressure from independent traders.[90]

89 On the role of the intra-American slave trade to the Spanish Americas, centered on Curaçao and as well as on Jamaica and Barbados, see Borucki et al, "Atlantic History", 443–445.

90 Pettigrew, *Freedom's Debt*, 1–8; Mitchell, *The Prince of Slavers*, 9–11.

TABLE 6.3 Annual deliveries of enslaved Africans to the *asiento*, 1698–1702

Suppliers	1698	1699	1700	1701	1702	Total
BAC	252	910	–	–	–	1,162
Companhia da Guiné	1,665	522	165	55	–	2,407
Independent Merchants (Curaçao)	554	217	233	582	257	1,843
Independent Merchants (Dutch interlopers)	–	–	–	803	–	803
Independent Merchant (England)	504	394	251	–	–	1,149
Independent Merchants (English Caribbean)	153	773	1,084	–	–	2,010
RAC	131	–	–	–	–	131
WIC	–	–	941	1,486	–	2,427
NI			400			400
Total	3,259	2,816	3,074	2,926	257	12,332

SOURCES: *SVD*; CLARK, *VERACRUZ AND THE CARIBBEAN*, 183; LUXÁN AND LUXÁN, "LAS COMPAÑÍAS", 9.

Following the substantial initial delivery of 1698, the *Companhia's* transatlantic operations slowed significantly in subsequent years. Deliveries from Portuguese African agencies fell to approximately one-third in 1699 and became negligible during the final years of the *asiento* (Table 6.3). High transatlantic shipping costs and difficulties in procuring enslaved Africans may have contributed to this decline, though further research is needed to confirm these factors. What is clear, however, is that 1699 marked a turning point, as the *Companhia* began to incur losses due to obstacles imposed by local authorities. Despite this, the decline in its direct deliveries was largely offset by outsourcing, maintaining a relatively stable pace of slave deliveries except in 1702. Nevertheless, the average annual number of captives introduced, at 3,083, fell short of the 4,500 *piezas* stipulated in the 1696 contract.

Under the *Companhia*, Cartagena remained the primary landing site for enslaved Africans, accounting for 81,1% of disembarkations, followed by Veracruz (8,5%), La Guaira/Caracas (6,4%), Havana (3,2%), Puerto Rico (0.5%), and Santo Domingo (0.2%), with the latter two outside the authorised ports. For reasons already discussed, the relative significance of Veracruz and Havana is likely underrepresented in these estimates. Of the seven ships that landed in Veracruz between 1698 and 1701, information exists for only three.

Similarly, secondary sources only provide only aggregate numbers for enslaved Africans arriving in Cuba from Curaçao and Jamaica between 1670–1702.[91]

In the absence of the *Companhia's* accounting records, the financial results of the Portuguese *asiento* cannot be fully assessed. French diplomatic correspondence refers to shipments of coined silver, hides, cochineal, and cacao arriving in Lisbon in 1698 and 1699.[92] However, without a detailed evaluation of operational costs and incurred losses, these shipments reveal little about the *Companhia*'s profitability. Furthermore, the *asiento* enterprise unfolded against a backdrop of declining slave prices in Spanish America, a trend that likely impacted financial outcomes negatively.[93]

4 The Dissolution of the Portuguese *Asiento*

On 18 June 1701, Felipe v of Spain formally dissolved the *asiento* contract with the *Companhia de Cacheu*, nearly two years before its scheduled end on 7 March 1703. The terms of this dissolution were enshrined in a treaty signed between the two Iberian Crowns, which included the repayment of a 200,000 *pesos* loan and compensation of 120,000,000 *réis* for damages incurred by the *Companhia*. While the termination must be understood within the broader context of the War of the Spanish Succession, it is essential to note that the *asiento* had become a diplomatic flashpoint between Portugal and Spain, with disputes intensifying in Madrid and Lisbon from late 1699 onwards. These tensions originated in Spanish America and were rooted in conflicts between local authorities and the *Companhia's* representatives.

Cartagena was the epicentre of these tensions, echoing the disputes experienced by Nicolàs Porcio fifteen years earlier, although similar issues arose in Veracruz and Havana. The conflict began in March 1699 when the governor of Cartagena ordered the seizure of English ships after having delivered their human cargos. Additional grievances of the *Companhia* included the imposition of custom duties not stipulated in the 1696 contract, obstacles to exporting revenues in silver, delays in customs clearance resulting in the deaths of enslaved Africans aboard ships, and demands for immediate payment of cus-

91 Clark, *Veracruz and the Caribbean*, 183; Francisco Castillo Meléndez, "Población y defensa de la isla de Cuba (1650–1700)", *Anuario de Estudios Americanos* vol. 44 (1987), 1–87; Donnan, *Documents*, vol. 1, 121.

92 Godinho, "Portugal and Her Empire", 515.

93 Leslie B. Rout, *The African Experience in Spanish America, 1502 to the Present Day* (Cambridge: Cambridge University Press, 1976), 325.

tom duties contrary to general practice. Tensions in Cartagena escalated further with the arrival of a new governor, Juan Diaz Pimienta, who ordered the seizure of six *Companhia*-owned ships, prompting the *Companhia* to seek intervention from King Pedro II.[94]

The *asiento* became a diplomatic issue, first addressed in Madrid between the Portuguese ambassador, Diogo Mendonça Furtado, and the *Consejo de Indias*, and later in Lisbon between King Pedro II and Pierre Rouillé, the French ambassador, as part of the French efforts to align Portugal to side with France and Spain during the Spanish Succession crisis. The conflicting underpinning these tensions are evident in discussions with the *Consejo de Indias,* which received numerous petitions and memorials from both sides. Spanish American authorities justified the seizure of ships on grounds of naval defence against piracy and accused the *Companhia* of smuggling enslaved Africans, evading royal treasury dues, and introducing captives to unauthorised ports such as Santo Domingo and Puerto Rico. Viewing these actions as violations of the *asiento*, the *Consejo de Indias* instructed colonial authorities to continue collecting customs duties on introduced captives and to withhold repayment of the 200,000 *pesos* loan, further aggravating the *Companhia*.[95]

The death of Carlos II of Spain in November 1700 and the terms of his will plunged Europe into a succession crisis, uniting France and Spain under a single dynasty. As war over the Spanish throne became inevitable, Portugal emerged as a pivotal ally for both factions – France and Spain on the one side, and the maritime powers (England and the Dutch Republic) alongside the Holy Roman Empire on the other. Acknowledging Portugal's strategic importance, Louis XIV's diplomatic overtures to Lisbon included negotiations over the *asiento*. For Portugal, resolving *asiento*-related disputes became a condition for aligning with the Bourbons, as was already evident that Spain intended to dissolve the contract. Key Portuguese demands included repayment of the 200,000 *pesos* loan with interest and compensation for damages.

Louis XIV's determination to secure Portugal's alliance enabled King Pedro II to keep a strong position in the negotiations, culminating in a treaty signed on 18 June 1701. For the first time, the dissolution of a slave-trading contract became the subject of an international treaty, subsidiary to the main political alliance treaty with Spain, signed the same day.[96]

The winding up of the *Companhia's* affairs in Spanish America proved challenging, compounded by continued resistance from local authorities. Mean-

---

94 Scelle, *La traite négrière*, vol. 2, 59–64.

95 Scelle, *La traite négrière*, vol. 2, 63, 66–67.

96 Scelle, *La traite négrière*, vol. 2, 93–94.

while, Portugal shifted allegiances, joining the Great Alliance with the maritime powers on 16 May 1703, before receiving any of the agreed upon for losses incurred under the *asiento*. The issue of *asiento*-related debts resurfaced during peace negotiations in Utrecht in 1713–1714. The Spanish Monarchy acknowledged the outstanding debt, which had accrued to 600,000 *pesos*, and agreed to repay it in the peace treaty signed with Portugal on 9 February 1715.[97]

---

97 Clauses 14, 15 and 16 of the peace treaty between Spain and Portugal (*Tratados, convenios*, 164–169).

CHAPTER 7

Royal Shareholders: The End of an Era

On 23 February 1715, the affluent banker Antoine Crozat wrote to the French minister of the Navy regarding the possibility of regaining the *asiento* through his English connections.[1] This correspondence was sent two years after the Treaty of Utrecht (1713), which had ended the French *asiento* (1701–1713). The *Compagnie de l'Asiento* (also referred to as the *Compagnie de Guinée et de l'Asiento,* or the French *Asiento* Company) had been egregiously unable to fulfill its obligations and had been dissolved with debts amounting to 32,000 *livres.*[2] Nevertheless, the Minister of the Navy responded to Crozat, stating that "his Majesty approves that you continue your correspondence with those who write to you to bring this enterprise back into French hands".[3] This raises the question: why were Crozat and the Minister of the Navy so keen to recover the *asiento,* despite the company's prior poor performance?

1 The Negotiation Process and the Content of the Contract

In 1701, France successfully negotiated exclusive rights to supply enslaved Africans to Spanish America. This negotiation occurred in a unique context; only a year earlier, in November 1700, King Carlos II had designated Louis XIV's grandson, Philip of Anjou, as his heir to the Spanish throne.[4] Louis XIV's position as a strong political ally to his grandson, coupled with the latter's urgent need for financial support to secure his claim to the throne, influenced the

---

1 AN MAR/B/2/241, Letter to Crozat from Versailles, 6th of march 1715.

2 V7 203 « Compte que les directeurs généraux de la Compagnie royale de Guinée et traitté de l'assiente des nègres signé à Madrid le 27 aoust 1701. »

3 AN MAR/B/2/241, Letter to Crozat from Versailles, 6th of march 1715 : « J'ay receu M. vostre lettre du 23 du mois passé, j'ay examiné la copie de celle qui vous a esté escrite d'Angleterre par laquelle on propose de retirer des anglois de la Compagnie de l'Assiente, j'en ay rendu compte au Roy, sa majesté trouve bon que vous entriez en correspondance comme de vous mesme et sans affectation avec celuy qui vous escrit pour parvenir à remettre cette entreprsis entre les mains des françois, je vous prie de m'informer des suittes de cette négociation. »

4 This included the kingdoms of Castile, Aragon (including Catalonia), Naples and Sicily; the Duchy of Milan, the lands of the Spanish Netherlands corresponding pretty much to present day Belgium; the entire Spanish empire overseas in the Americas, the Philippines and the coast of North Africa, G. ROWLANDS, *Dangerous and Dishonest Men: The International Bankers of Louis XIV's France* (New-York: Palgrave Macmillan, 2015), 13.

© CÁTIA ANTUNES ET AL., 2026 | DOI:10.1163/9789004745094_009

favourable outcome of the negotiation. In July 1701, the French governor of Saint-Domingue, Jean Ducasse, was dispatched to the Spanish court to formalise the so-called French *asiento*.[5] As in the case of the Portuguese *Companhia*, it was an individual already active in the Atlantic trade who was sent to negotiate the contract, demonstrating a vested interest in the arrangement.

A month later, two commissioners were appointed by the Spanish administration to finalise the contract with Ducasse. Meanwhile, the Austrian Habsburgs, supported by the Dutch Republic and Great Britain, sought to secure the Duchy of Milan against Philip of Anjou's claims.[6] As a result, Philip urgently required financial backing, and the *asiento* agreement with France included a loan of 200,000 *escudos*, 50,000 of which were allocated to maintaining the garrison in Milan.[7] The *asiento* contract was signed on 14 September 1701, two months after Ducasse's arrival in Spain.

A distinctive feature of the contract was that it positioned the kings of two different countries as shareholders: Philip of Anjou, the Spanish king-to-be, and Louis XIV of France.[8] Each monarch was expected to contribute a quarter of the starting capital of 4,000,000 *livres*, jointly owning half the company's capital – a model inspired by King Pedro II's shareholding in the Portuguese *Companhia*.[9] The remaining two million *livres*, 50% of the start-up capital, were to be raised through private shareholders. Both kings were represented in the company: Jean-François Des Haguais acted for the French King, while

5 Scelle, *La traite négrière*, vol. 2, 126.

6 Rowlands, *Dangerous and Dishonest Men*, 15.

7 P. Hrodej, *L'amiral Du Casse: l'élévation d'un Gascon sous Louis XIV* (Paris : Librairie de l'Inde, 1999), 293.

8 The contract between the two Kings and the company was printed in French and Spanish in 1703, it is called "Assiento" in the Spanish sources and "traité" in the French translation: « Assiento ajustado entre las dos magestades, catholica, y christianissima, con la compania de Guinea, establecida en el reyno de Francia sobre Encargarse de la Introduccion de Negros en la America, por tiempo de diez años, que empeçaran à correr en primero de Mayo proximo venidero de mil setecientos y dos, y cimpliràn otro tal año de mil setecientos y doze. Traité fait entre les deux roys, catholique et très chrétien, avec la compagnie royale de Guinée établie en France concernant l'introduction des nègres dans l'Amérique, pendant le temps de dix années, qui commenceront le premier jour de May prochain mil sept cent deux, et finiront à un pareil jour de l'année mil sept cent douze. » ANOM F2a7.

9 Article 28 of the contract : « (...) il a été réglé, que leurs dites Majestez y seront interessées pour la moitié,& chacune d'Elles pour un quart, ainsi qu'il a été convenu ; Et d'autant qu'il seroit necessaire que Sa dite Majesté Catholique, pour pouvoir participer aux profits que cette Assiente pourra donner, fit compter & payer à ladite Compagnie un million, faisant le quart de quatre million de livres tournois (...) .» ANOM F2a7.

Charles de Salabéry represented the future Spanish King.[10] Interestingly, Salabéry was also shareholder in the *Compagnie de Saint Domingue*, a French company primarily focused on organising smuggling operations to Spanish America.[11] Many shareholders of the *Compagnie de l'Asiento* were also investors in the *Compagnie de Saint Domingue,* illustrating interconnected financial interests. Concerns about the monarchs' financial contributions were evident in the contract. Article 28 stipulated that "if Her Catholic Majesty does not provide this sum in advance, the said company will provide the advance", with repayment to the Company set at an interest rate of 8%.[12]

Under the contract, the new *asentista* was granted exclusive rights to transport 4,800 enslaved Africans to Spanish America over ten years, amounting to a total of 48,000 human beings.[13] This represented a significant increase compared to the *asiento* of Grillo and Lomellino nearly four decades earlier. Taxes owed to the Spanish Crown amounted to 33 *pesos* per enslaved African delivered, applicable to only 4,000 of the 4,800 transported annually.[14] The remaining 800 enslaved Africans were exempt from taxation, incentivising legal trade and mitigating potential losses. During wartime, the annual compulsory deliveries were reduced to 3,000 enslaved Africans, though the ten-year total remained 48,000. If the company failed to deliver the agreed numbers, it was still required to pay taxes on the total contracted amount, even if the enslaved Africans did not arrive in the Spanish colonies.[15] The Company could also benefit from a three-year extension beyond the contract's term to complete its quota without incurring additional taxes.[16] Furthermore, the *Compagnie* was required to advance one-quarter (150,000 *livres*) of the anticipated 600,000 *livres* in revenues from the Spanish American slave trade to the Spanish Crown.[17]

---

10 Hrodej, *L'amiral Du Casse,* 294.

11 Hrodej, *L'amiral Du Casse,* 294.

12 Article 28 of the contract : « Il a été convenu, que, si Sadite Majesté Catholique ne juge pas à propos de faire compter & payer par avance cette somme, ladite Compagnie en fera l'avance, bien entendu que Sadite Majesté Catholique en payera l'interest à ladite Compagnie, à raison de huit pour cent par chaque année (…) » ANOM F2a7.

13 Article 5 and 19 of the contract ANOM F2a7.

14 Article 5 of the Asiento ANOM F2a7. The price of an enslaved African was 300 piasters. When the treaty was signed piasters and écus had the same value, this was going to change in 1713. HRODEJ, P., *L'amiral Du Casse*, p. 293.

15 Scelle, *La traite négrière*, vol. 2, 272.

16 Scelle, *La traite négrière*, vol. 2, 418.

17 Lévy, *Capitalisme et* pouvoir, vol. 1, 170.

The *Compagnie* was authorised to employ ships and crews from Catholic countries allied with France and Spain.[18] It could operate out of any French or Spanish ports, provided captains registered their trade activities.[19] This arrangement granted the French direct access to Spanish American markets. In Spanish America, the *Compagnie* was permitted to call at all Atlantic coastal ports in Spanish America where royal officials were present to record the disembarkation of enslaved Africans.[20] The Spanish *Consejo de Indias* opposed even restricted access to Buenos Aires, fearing that Peruvian silver might be smuggled onto French ships. The Spanish Crown did not give access to the South Sea, though.[21]

The Company was allowed to send four to six company employees to Spanish American ports where they were regarded as subjects of the Spanish Crown and were allowed to engage in hinterland trade on behalf of the *Compagnie,* provided they complied with local laws and the terms of the *asiento.*[22] Commodities acquired could include precious metals or foodstuffs, though the latter was subject to export taxes and occupied more ship space.[23] Notably, *Compagnie* vessels were exempt from inspection by Spanish royal officials, enabling potential smuggling activities.[24]

2 The Late Establishment of the *Compagnie De L'asiento*

Although the *asiento* was signed in September 1701, preparations in France were incomplete. As Claude-Frédéric Lévi observes, the French Company's greatest challenge was its non-existence at the time of signing.[25] Initially, Pontchartrain, the Minister of the Navy, considered utilizing the *Compagnie de Saint Domingue,* established in 1698 with a royal mandate to trade enslaved Africans to the French colony of Saint Domingue. Its mission included promoting settlement, developing the sugar industry, and facilitating trade with

18 Article 8 of the contract ANOM F2a7.

19 Article 26 of the contract ANOM F2a7.

20 Articles 9 and 10 of the treaty ANOM F2a7.

21 Scelle, G., *La traite négrière aux Indes de Castille*, p. 340.

22 Article 12 of the contract ANOM F2a7.

23 Article 25 of the contract ANOM F2a7: « Elle pourra pareillement faire ses retours soit en Reaux, Barres d'Argent, Lingots d'or, ou autres fruits, denrées et marchandises provenant de la vente desdites Negres dans lesdits Ports d'Espagne et de France »

24 Olivas, "Global Politics", 92.

25 Lévy, C.F., *Capitalisme et pouvoir*, vol. 1, 170.

the Spanish empire.[26] Among its directors were Pontchartrain himself, Jean Ducasse (the *asiento* negotiator), and the influential banker Antoine Crozat and his brother- in-law Joseph Legendre. However, this Company faced significant competitive disadvantages compared to the *Compagnie de Guinée,* lacking both the right of *entrepôt* of foreign merchandise in French ports and the crucial tax exemptions on imports from the French West Indies.[27]

The directors of the company set to manage the *asiento* were determined to secure favourable terms from Louis XIV. Some sought to become shareholders of the *Compagnie de Saint Domingue* and of the *Compagnie de Guinée.*[28] A document titled "Observations to the Guinea Company", dated September 1700, advocated for the inclusion of four directors from the *Companie de Saint Domingue* and a resident of Martinique as new shareholders in the *Compagnie de Guinée,* proposing a total investment of 200,000 *livres.* This strategy, however, proved unsuccessful.[29] Undeterred, in 1700 the directors of the *Compagnie de Saint Domingue* pursed a new approach by sending one of their investors, Jean Ducasse, to Madrid to negotiate the *asiento.* In the summer of 1701, they reached an agreement with Pontchartrain to assume control over the *asiento,* provided the *Compagnie de Saint Domingue* was granted the same privileges as the *Compagnie de Guinée.*[30]

The proposal of the *Compagnie de Saint Domingue* was rejected by Michel Chamillart, the *contrôleur général des finances.* Consequently, during the negotiations in Madrid, Jean Ducasse did not represent a specific company but rather a consortium of influential businessmen: Vincent Maynon, Antoine Crozat, Pierre Thomé, Samuel Bernard, Jacques de Vanolles, Etienne Landais, Joseph Legendre d'Armigny, and Claude Foucherolles.[31] Most of these individuals – Ducasse, Maynon, Thomé, Vanolles, Landais, and Crozat – were shareholders in the *Compagnie de Saint Domingue.* As with other French chartered

26 E. Greenwald, *Marc-Antoine Caillot and the Company of the Indies in Louisiana* (Baton Rouge: Louisiana State University Press, 2016), 97.

27 Since the *arrêts* of 1682 and 1684, the measures against the entry of colonial sugar in the metropolis had increased and in 1698, sugar refined in the West Indies had been assimilated to foreign sugar which meant increase in taxes. Only the raw sugar imported for metropolitan refinery benefited from relatively low taxes. Lévy, *Capitalisme et pouvoir,* 161.

28 ANOM F2a7 : « Observations des privilèges et exemptions demandés par la Compagnie de l'Assiente »

29 ANOM F2a11 Compagnie de Guinée : « Ainsy si on agregeoit quatre de Mess de st domingue et le sr Poquet, la compagnie auroit un nouveau fond de deux cent mil livres. »

30 ANOM F2a7 Lettre de Pontchartrain à Versailles le 29 juin 1701.

31 Lévy, *Capitalisme et pouvoir,* 166.

companies of the turn of the eighteenth century, the directors and investors were primarily financiers, often holding tax collection offices in various regions and maintaining close ties with the French Crown and the Minister of the Navy for future contracts.[32]

Instead of granting the *Compagnie de Saint Domingue* the same privileges as the *Compagnie de Guinée*, Pontchartrain opted to replace the directors of the *Compagnie de Guinée* with the group of businessmen associated with Jean Ducasse.[33] On 12 September 1701, all directors of *Compagnie de Guinée* were dismissed, and the company was reconstituted as the *Compagnie de Guinée et de l'Asiento*.[34] As was customary with French chartered companies of the period, the Minister of the Navy assumed the role of director. On 19 October 1701, Pontchartrain was appointed director of the *Compagnie de Asiento* on behalf of Louis XIV.[35] To raise sufficient initial capital, Pontchartrain sought twenty associates. By the following months, fifteen shareholders were secured, largely due to Antoine Crozat, whose brother-in-law, Legendre d'Armigny, was among the eight initial investors. Crozat also enlisted three new financiers: his brother-in-law Louis Doublet and his tobacco monopoly partners, Charles Le Jougleur and Charles Pouthou.[36]

Despite the efforts, Pontchartrain aimed to attract investors from outside Crozat's network, particularly merchants from port cities such as Nantes or Bordeaux with experience in Atlantic trade. These attempts, however, were unsuccessful. A preliminary draft of the *Acte d'association* of the *Compagnie de l'Asiento*, dated 10 November 1701, included seven new shareholders, most of whom were aligned with Crozat's network. Exceptions to this were François Saupin and Claude Foucherolles. The a*cte de société* between the two Kings

32 For more details about the different investors in French chartered companies of the end of the 17th and beginning of the 18th century see, the agency of empire chap. 1.

33 ANOM F2a7, Édit de subrogation de la Compagnie de Guinée : « Sa majesté estant en son conseil a subrogé et subroge de leur consentement, les srs Maynon, Crozat, Thomé, Bernard, Vanolles, Landais, Legendre D'armigny et Foucherolles, au privilège accordé par l'édit du mois de février 1685 (...) ». ANOM F12a11 Compagnie de Guinée. Despite the strong opposition of the « Cinq grosses fermes » the edict of the 28th of October allowed the Asiento/Guinea Company the right of *entrepôt.*

34 In this chapter I refer to this company as the *Compagnie de l'Asiento* to differentiate it from the previous *Compagnie de Guinée.*

35 ANOM B24 f°210: « Arrest qui nomme Pontchartrain directeur pour le Roy dans la compagnie de l'Assiente et en son absence M. Des Haguais ? à Fontainebleau le 19 octobre 1701. »

36 J. M. Price, *France and the Chesapeake: A History of the French Tobacco Monopoly, 1674–1791, and of Its Relationship to the British and American Tobacco Trades*, vol. 1, 55.

and the Company stipulated that each of the fifteen members would hold shares worth 150,000 *livres*. The 2,250,000 *livres* raised included a 750,000-*livres* advance for the Spanish King's share.[37] Louis XIV provided ships valued at 750,000 *livres* but contributed no liquid capital. The total investment ultimately amounted to 3,000,000 *livres*.

The Company's bankers and agents in Spain, Hubert Hubrecht and Bartolomé de Flon, played key roles in financing the War of Spanish Succession and the early reign of Philip V.[38] Hubrecht, born in Zealand, in the Dutch Republic, was a merchant banker involved in wool trade, shipbuilding, and the slave trade. His partner, Flon, a key intermediary for venal offices at the Spanish court, facilitated the placement of officials sympathetic to the *Compagnie* and Bourbon interests in significant administrative positions in Spain.[39]

In April 1702, Jean Laurent Verzure, a Genoese banker, joined the Company as the representative of François de Mari, who, in turn, acted on behalf of Francesco Grillo, Marquis of Villa Franca.[40] Verzure contributed 150,000 *livres*. The final shareholder, Nicolas Doublet de Persan, joined in 1706, but both he and Étienne Landais only paid half of their shares after being compelled by Pontchartrain.[41] Doublet de Persan and Landais were not the only shareholders who struggled to pay their contributions. This financial instability became a chronic issue for the *Compagnie de l'Asiento* during the twelve-year management of the *asiento*. It is likely that other shareholders did not pay their share. The *acte de société* between the Kings and the Company explicitly stated that the Spanish King relied entirely on the Company's general capital to advance his share.

---

37 Article 1 of the Acte de société entre les deux rois et la compagnie, ANOM F2A7.

38 ANOM B26: letter to D'Aubenton on the 26 august 1705. Born in Zeeland, Hubert Hubrecht was a merchant banker active in various areas of trade: wool, ship building and slave trade. In Sanz Ayan, "Financieros holandeses de Felipe V", 565.

39 Flon was granted this position by the Philip of Anjou as means of payment for debts in Olivas, "Global Politics", 101.

40 ANOM F2a7, 19 April 1702 « Sur la requeste présentée au Roy estant en son conseil par Jean Laurent Verzure escuyer contenant que don François Grillo marquis de Francavilla de Madrid ayant ésté informé que le Roy de France et le Roy d'Espagne vouloient establir une Compagnie de l'Assiento voulut y avoir interest et ayant fait remettre au supliant la somme de 150 000livres que chaque associé devoit avancer pour estre admis dans la société il pria le supliant de paroitre de son nom, et d'en faire déclaration au proffit de Mr. François de Mari noble gennois, le suppliant ayant payé cette somme de 150 000 livres le 19 avril 1702 entre les mains du sieur Caquet caissier de la compagnie (…) »

41 ANOM F2a7, *arrêt du 10 février 1706 qui ordonne que les sieurs Persan et Landais demeurent intéressés et directeurs de l'Assiente chacun pour 75 000 livres.*

Unable to recruit new shareholders to compensate for the lack of funds, Pontchartrain demanded an additional payment of 600,000 *livres* from existing shareholders three years after the company's founding. While the directors agreed, they paid this amount in long-term bills of exchange, which did little to improve the Company's liquidity.[42] By 1704, the *Compagnie* had accrued significant debt, amounting to 1,600,000 *livres.* All profits were immediately absorbed by creditors,[43] and in 1705 the directors secured another loan of 400,000 *livres.* Without the ships promised by Louis XIV, the Company would have been unable to continue voyages to Spanish America.[44]

By 1707, the Company was on the brink of collapse. Pontchartrain intervened again, compelling shareholders to inject additional capital.[45] In 1708, the *Compagnie* sought to renegotiate its contract with the Spanish Monarchy, proposing a new clause that would require the Company to pay taxes only on the enslaved Africans it had actually transported to Spanish America, rather than on the annual contracted number.[46] This proposal was rejected, and the *Compagnie* continued to pay taxes based on the original agreement.

Given these circumstances, it can be argued that the French *asiento* primarily served as a cover mechanism for Louis XIV to support his grandson's claim to the Spanish throne. Through the *Compagnie,* the French King effectively contributed to the war effort, using the Company's capitalisation to subsidise Spain's wartime expenses.

3 Licensing and Contracting

The solution to the financial difficulties faced by the *Compagnie de l'Asiento* was to outsource part of its monopoly. Pontchartrain initially planned to allow French Atlantic port cities to manage the slave trade to the French West Indies through the issuing of licences, reserving the *Compagnie* exclusively for the *asiento.* This approach sought to avoid competition between French and Spanish colonial markets in the Americas and the Caribbean for the same supplier of enslaved Africans, informed by the precarious position of the RA and the RAC *vis-à-vis* the English planters in the Caribbean. Pontchartrain

42 Scelle, G., *La traite négrière*, vol. 2, 435.

43 ANOM B 26, Pontchartrain to Orry, 28 October 1705.

44 ANOM F2 8, Arnoul, 21 February 1705.

45 AN B2 199, Letter to the directors, 28 December 1707.

46 ANOM B31 Pontchartrain to the duke of Vendôme, 31st August 1708 and SCELLE, G., La traite négrière aux Indes de Castille, p. 439.

envisioned using Saint Domingue as a hub for trade to Spanish America, similarly to the roles of Curaçao, Jamaica and Barbados.

While Pontchartrain encouraged private French merchants from port cities to supply enslaved Africans to the French West Indies under licences issued by the *Compagnie*, accessing the Saint Domingue market remained challenging due to rampant tax evasion and fraud. The *Compagnie* maintained strict control over the island, mandating that all enslaved Africans imported by licensed French merchants to the Caribbean be sold to *Compagnie* agents in Saint Domingue at a maximum price of 400 *livres* per person. These agents then transported the human cargoes to Spanish and French colonies, managing the *asiento* shipping system between non-Spanish Caribbean ports (e.g., Curaçao, Jamaica, Barbados) and the Spanish Main.[47] Unlike earlier *asiento* contracts (e.g., Grillo and Lomellino Barroso del Pozo or Coymans), the intra-Caribbean transport under the *Compagnie* originated not from Spanish ports nor Spanish subjects serving the *asentista* but rather from French Caribbean ports manned by French subjects.

These obstacles, combined with the *Compagnie*'s tight control, deterred French private merchants from participating in the provisioning of the French West Indies. Licences to trade with Saint Domingue and other French Caribbean islands were rarely issued, and when available, they were prohibitively expensive. Additionally, the War of Spanish Succession (1701–1713) disrupted trade across Europe and the Atlantic, significantly affecting French shipping during the early eighteenth century. Within this context, Nantes was the only port city that consistently requested licences for the slave trade.[48] Consequently, colonists in the French islands, including Saint Domingue, lamented the shortage of enslaved labour and resorted to illegal trade with the nearby British and Dutch colonies, mirroring the same practices of English planters in the 1660s.[49]

Licensing ultimately proved unsuccessful, prompting the *Compagnie* to attempt outsourcing, albeit with limited success. Jean Ducasse first considered contracting part of the monopoly to the Brandenburg Company but later approached the *Companhia de Cacheu*.[50] This attempt failed as the *Compa-*

47 Scelle, G., *La traite négrière*, vol. 2, 250–251.

48 ANOM B31 fos 411–413, A Monsieur de Luzançay au sujet des propositions de traité négrière déposées par le sieur Montaudoiun, négociant à Nantes, pour la Martinique, Saint Domingue et Cayenne. Aux directeurs de la Compagnie de l'Assiento sur le même sujet. Au sieur Montaudouin sur le même sujet, 27 February 1709.

49 Scelle, *La traite négrière*, vol. 2, 257.

50 ANOM F2 7 letter of Des Haguais 22 November 1701 and answer of the Portuguese Company to Ducasse on the 26th of September 1701 AAE, Portugal, Correspondance, Ve 35, f° 482 in Scelle, *La traite négrière*, 273.

nhia prioritised the Brazilian market, where the discovery of gold mines had sharply increased the price of enslaved Africans. Another attempt to subcontract to Noelle Danycan and his partner Natales Stephanini, merchants in St. Malo, also proved unsuccessful.[51] The only marginally successful contract was with the *Compagnie du Sénégal,* which was authorised to transport 500 enslaved Africans to Martinique and then to Caracas.[52]

In October 1707, the *Compagnie* signed a contract with Louis de La Boulaye, General Intendant of the Navy and Director of the *Compagnie de Saint Domingue,* and Nicolas La Chipaudière Magon, both merchants from Saint Malo, to transport enslaved Africans to Veracruz.[53] However, their ship was seized by Spanish officials in Veracruz with French merchandise and only a few enslaved Africans, leading to accusations of interloping and a ban on selling their cargo. De La Boulaye and La Chipaudière Magon used this incident as a pretext to avoid fulfilling their contractual obligations to the *Compagnie.*[54]

A similar contract was signed between the *Compagnie* and the *Compagnie de Saint Domingue,* which agreed to supply enslaved Africans to Veracruz. Unlike the previous contract, this arrangement resulted in the *Compagnie de Saint Domingue* being ordered to pay compensation of 75,000 *livres* in damages for failing to meet its contractual obligations.[55]

Undeterred by these setbacks, Ducasse negotiated a further agreement with Jean Chourio, a resident of Saint Pierre in Martinique, to supply 150 enslaved Africans annually to various provinces (Margarita, Trinidad, Cumaná, Cumanagotte, Maracaibo, and Puerto Rico) for 45,000 *livres* per year beginning in January 1708.[56] However, according to George Scelle, the stringent terms of

51 ANOM B24, Letter of Pontchartrain to Des Haguais, 4 October 1702. In January 1702, Spanish individuals offered to take over the whole *Asiento* for 200 000 piasters yearly but the French Crown refused, since the outsourcing of the entire contract would have meant losing access to the Spanish American markets in Scelle, *La traite négrière*, vol. 2, 274.

52 ANOM B24 Pontchartrain to Daubenton, 4 October and 29 November 1702.

53 C. Frostin, "Les Pontchartrain et la pénétration commerciale française en Amérique espagnole (1690–1715)", *Revue Historique* 245, no 498 (1971), 313 ; Scelle, *La traite négrière*, vol. 2, 282.

54 ANOM F2 8, 1709, *Mémoire sur le refus que font MM.de La Boulaye etc* and ANOM F2 9, 1710, La réponse des sous-traitants.

55 AN B2 198, letter of Pontchartrain to the directors, 31 August 1707 and ANOM B35 two other letters to M. de Fontanieu, 31 Octobrer 1713 and ANOM B36 to the Company of Saint Domingue, 12 December 1714.

56 ANOM F2 8 25 Copy of the treaty made in Saint Pierre on the 25 November 1707.

this contract led Chourio to divert his human cargoes to Curaçao instead.[57] Like De La Boulaye and La Chipaudière Magon, Chourio was accused of smuggling, and his ships were banned from Veracruz by the governor.[58]

The contracts between the *Compagnie* and potential suppliers were relatively small compared to earlier *asientos* with chartered and joint stock companies and private traders. These agreements resembled licensing arrangements in many respects. The *Compagnie*, and the French King as its principal shareholder, appeared to favour a model of small subcontracts that regulated access to the Spanish American market, ensuring that it benefitted French subjects. A large-scale contract granting the entire *asiento* to a major Atlantic trading power would have curtailed French access. In 1702, a group of so-called Spanish merchants residing in Spain – likely of Dutch or English descent or acting as fronts for Dutch and English traders – offered to take over the whole *asiento* for 200,000 piasters annually. The French King rejected this proposal, as outsourcing the entire contract would have undermined France's foothold in Spanish America.[59]

With most outsourcing attempts and licensing arrangements failing, the *Compagnie* had no option but to petition the *Consejo de Indias* for permission to transport enslaved Africans from Curaçao and Jamaica. This approach reverted to traditional *asiento* shipping practices, relying on Dutch and English supply hubs.[60] The *Compagnie* argued that integrating smuggled enslaved individuals from Curaçao and Jamaica into the tax-paying trade system would benefit both the *Compagnie* and the Spanish Crown.[61] Despite initial resistance, as this proposal conflicted with the *asiento* clauses and benefited France's rivals, the petition was approved in 1706 after lengthy negotiations in Madrid.[62] In 1707, the French general factor of the *Compagnie* in Spanish America was authorised to supply Porto Belo with enslaved Africans purchased from Dutch traders.[63] By this time, most enslaved Africans disembarked in Venezuela by French ships had been acquired in Curaçao. Emboldened by the permission to import enslaved Africans from Curaçao and Jamaica, the *Compagnie* successfully petitioned the Spanish authorities for

57 Scelle, *La traite négrière*, vol. 2, 289.

58 ANOM F2a8, letter of Musnier to the Spanish King in Caracas, 1 October 1709.

59 Scelle, *La traite négrière*, vol. 2, 274.

60 Borucki, "Trans-imperial History", 37.

61 Lévy, *Capitalisme et pouvoir*, 394.

62 ANOM F2a7 « 1706 La proposition des Anglois à la Compagnie de l'Assiente est de luy fournir à la Jamaïque tous les noirs dont elle a besoin pour l'amérique espagnolle. »

63 ANOM B 28, letter of Pontchartrain to Deslandes, 3 August 1707.

two passports allowing Dutch ships to engage in the slave trade to Spanish America, despite opposition from the French *Chambre de Commerce*.[64]

Despite relying on English and Dutch redistribution hubs in the Caribbean, efforts were made to maintain control over English and Dutch trade through Saint Domingue. Pontchartrain encouraged the development of Saint Domingue as a port where the English traders could sell enslaved Africans from Jamaica using French passports, after which Spanish ships with English passports would transport the human cargoes to Spanish America. These ships would then return with Spanish American commodities to Saint Domingue.[65] The primary concern was that English and Dutch traders might dominate the Caribbean trade circuits by exporting Spanish American commodities directly to Europe, settling payments to the *Compagnie* with bills of exchange. This would deny access to payments in silver and limit potential profits from wholesale trading of Spanish American commodities in French markets. Securing access to bullion was crucial for Louis XIV and Philip of Anjou to sustain their war efforts. Unregulated inter-Caribbean trade risked strengthening English and Dutch access to silver, thereby bolstering their military advantage in Europe to the detriment of the Spanish and French armies. Despite attempts to subcontract and regulate the limited participation of Dutch and English traders in the intra-Caribbean trade, by 1708, the *asiento* had achieved less than half of its expected deliveries.[66]

4 Costs and Gains of the *Asiento*

The most apparent advantage for the Spanish Crown in contracting the *asiento* was the anticipated revenue of 400,000 *livres* annually for ten years, amounting to a total of four million *livres* from the taxes levied on the introduction of enslaved Africans in Spanish America.[67] This revenue was intended to support the war effort. Philip of Anjou, future Philip V, as shareholder, faced the same risks as other investors, particularly as the company had accumu-

64 Scelle, *La traite négrière*, 285.

65 ANOM B 28 fo.219, letter to the directors of the Asiento Company, 23 June 1706: « j'ay pensé que vous pourriez faire apporter les nègres à Léogane par des batiments anglois pour lesquels le Roy donnera des passeports et ensuite on se serviroit de ceux d'angleterre pour les batiments espagnols qui porteront ces nègres à Portobel, et rapporteront vos effets à st Domingue ou les vaisseaux de guerre de sa majesté les prendront pour les apporter seurement en France. »

66 Scelle, *La traite négrière*, vol. 2, 289.

67 Scelle, *La traite négrière*, vol. 2, 418.

lated significant debt by 1705 and most of licensing and contracting attempts had failed. While the *Compagnie* advanced Philip's share at an interest rate of 8%, the Spanish Crown risked losing 750,000 *livres* but expected to gain four million *livres* in taxes. Additionally, the French *asiento* provided Philip with opportunities to borrow funds from the *Compagnie* to support his war and political efforts to secure the Spanish throne.

The contract specified that the *Compagnie* would lend 200,000 *escudos* (600,000 *livres*) to the Spanish King, one quarter of which was to be provided immediately – a figure identical to the demands placed on Balthazar Coymans during negotiations in Madrid during the 1680s, or Grillo and Lomelino before him. Of this sum, 50,000 *escudos* were allocated for the garrison in Milan, 50,000 for 'urgent affairs', and 25,000 for the troops in Catalonia. The remainder was earmarked for repaying loans taken by the King shortly before the signing of the *asiento,* intended to provision Spanish territories and allies in Italy.[68]

As stipulated, the *Compagnie* was obligated to pay the annual 400,000 *livres* in taxes to the Spanish Monarchy, even if it failed to meet the trade or generate profits. During the first year of the *asiento*, the *Compagnie* could not send ships to Spanish America, yet the Spanish Crown had had already spent the anticipated 400,000 *livres* in tax revenues. This financial burden escalated when the *Compagnie* defaulted on subsequent annual payments, and the Crown used these debts to offset Philip of Anjou's personal liabilities, following the advice of Louis XIV.[69] In 1706, under pressure from Pontchartrain, the *Compagnie* sent 300,000 *escudos* (900,000 *livres*) to finance Spanish troop maintenance.[70] To fulfill this obligation, the *Compagnie* was forced to borrow 200,000 *livres* and sought assistance from the French King.[71] This arrangement underscores how Louis XIV leveraged the *Compagnie* to support his grandson's war efforts.

For Louis XIV, the *asiento* provided political capital and international leverage, enhancing its value beyond immediate profits. The exclusive privilege of trading enslaved Africans to Spanish America aimed to weaken Dutch and English economies in the Atlantic and Caribbean, disrupt the British-Dutch alliance in the war, and redirect private French capital into the coffers of the

68 Scelle, *La traite négrière*, vol. 2, 425.

69 He used the Compagnie to pay for his musketeers or the pensions of important members of his household in Scelle, *La traite négrière*, vol. 2,428.

70 ANOM B 28 Pontchartrain to the company directors, 5 July 1706.

71 Scelle, *La traite négrière*, vol. 2, 433.

prospective Bourbon king.[72] Although a 25% shareholder, Louis IV did not hesitate to use Pontchartrain to pressure other shareholders into financing Philip's claims or dispatching fleets, even when the *Compagnie* lacked the financial resources. In January 1707, a year after the forced loan of 300,000 *escudos* to Philip, Pontchartrain urged the directors: "you must do everything in your power to fit out these ships, whatever the costs, even if it means borrowing the necessary capital".[73]

Louis XIV and the *Compagnie de l'Asiento* directors, however, were likely more interested in gaining access to Spanish American markets for silver and commodities to supply Frech wholesale markets than in the slave trade itself. As early as 1692, the abbé d'Estrée had suggested that the French should take over the *asiento* to "under the pretext of selling slaves, sell merchandise in the Indies and bring back silver and merchandise".[74] Louis XIV hoped that access to Spanish American markets would offset the *asiento's* expenses and borrowed capital channeled through the *Compagnie*.

While the *asiento* initially seemed promising, it quickly became unattractive to shareholders and potential investors. Forced loans to the Spanish King, Pontchartrain's insistence on sending ships despite the *Compagnie*'s financial instability, and licensing and contracting difficulties made it a risky venture. Nevertheless, historians note that "it is improbable that the directors did not get any profit out of the enterprise".[75] Profits likely came from trading French goods, both legally and illicitly, in Spanish America, exporting bullion and competitive commodities to European markets, and outcompeting Dutch and Engilsh imports.[76]

In 1709, *Compagnie* directors sought to legalise French trade with Spanish America when Philip requested another loan. However, the Spanish Crown refused to relinquish its rights.[77] Despite the threat of death penalty stipulated in article 28 of the *asiento*, contraband trade was widespread among *Compagnie* captains. For instance, the ship *Le François* carried so much illicit cargo

---

72 Scelle, *La traite négrière*, vol. 2, 126.

73 AN MAR/B/2 fo. 264 : « (…) je dois vous représenter que vous devez mettre tout en œuvre pour cela quelque perte que vous puissiez faire sur les emprunts que vous ferez ou sur les estats que vous avez. »

74 AAE, letter of the abbé d'Estrée on 21 July 1692.

75 Scelle, *La traite négrière*, vol. 2, 444.

76 « Le produit des cargaisons ne proviendra pas toujours de la vente des nègres mais de marchandises dont l'interdiction sous peine de la vie ne fera reculer personne » in Hrodej, *L'amiral Du Casse*, 293.

77 AN MAR/B/3/175, letter of M. de Noizin to Pontchartrain, 31 December 1709 (à Pontchartrain)

(*pacotille*) that 470 enslaved Africans could be transported instead of the contracted 600.[78] *Le François* was intercepted in Veracruz, where Spanish officials confiscated contraband goods valued at 55,733 *piasters,* filling five or six *chaloupes* according to the Veracruz's *contadores*.[79] Captains were often hired based on recommendations from *Compagnie* directors, who sought to secure lucrative jobs for family members or men in their clientele networks.[80] This recruiting system fostered protection and potential collusion between captains and directors, further complicating the *Compagnie*'s operations and liquidity.[81]

Factors and *Compagnie* officials stationed at trading posts in South America were also involved in smuggling, either in collusion with ship captains or independently, often to the detriment of the *Compagnie*. The Spanish governor in Havana seized *Compagnie* goods as collateral for an illegal private deal conducted by one of the *Compagnie's* agents in Havana, following a longstanding practice among local governors of withholding the property rights of *asiento* agents.[82] Although the penalty for illegal activities by directors and shareholders of the *Compagnie* was forfeiture of their shares, this proved to be a weak deterrent.[83] Under the guise of strict regulations against smuggling, contraband activities were widely tolerated by French authorities.[84]

When *Compagnie* directors engaged in smuggling to Spanish America, they often operated under Pontchartrain's protection. He openly acknowledged that illegal trade with Spanish America was essential for the *Compagnie's* survival, asking whether there were any real disadvantages to tolerating and enabling directors to smuggle while feigning ignorance.[85] This tolerance is further evident in a letter from director Saupin, who petitioned the French

78 The *Pacotille* was merchandise which the crew and captains could take on board for their personal trade. It was highly regulated.

79 ANOM F2a8 « Partie d'un lettre que l'on m'a escrite de ce qui s'est passé pendant la campagne que vient de faire le français commandé par Mr Bigot ».

80 ANOM F2a7, letter from Saupin to Monseigneur, 1 july 1704.

81 Scelle, *La traite négrière*, vol. 2, 398.

82 AN MAR/B/2/264 fo.52–3, letter to M. le Cardinal de Bois in Versailles, 8 July 1722 : « Le conseil envoy à Monsieur et vostre éminence un mémoire des directeurs de la comagnie de l'assiente qui se plaignent que le gouverneur de la havanne ai fait saisir leurs effets sous prétexte d'un acte de de cautionnement que le feue s. Jouchée leur directeur avois passé pour une affaire qui n'a aucun rapport a aller de la compagnie »

83 Scelle, *La traite négrière*, vol. 2, 383.

84 ANOM F2a7 Mesures contre la fraude.

85 ANOM B28, letter from Pontchartrain to d'Aubenton 21 December 1707 in Scelle, Scelle, *La traite négrière*, vol. 2, 413.

authorities to halt prosecutions against *Compagnie* employees guilty of embezzlement:

> I have been informed that under the pretext of treaties you have made with some of the *Compagnie* directors, you are suing company officials and factors guilty of embezzlement and you take them to different courts where the judgment is often at the expense of the company, since such a behavior is entirely against his interests, the intention of the King is that you will not start anymore prosecutions without the permission of the King.[86]

Directors also derived profits from provisioning the *asiento*. In 1704, the *Compagnie* was granted the right to maintain warehouses in principal Spanish American ports. It was authorised to send ammunition, weapons for their protection, construction materials for ship repairs, and provisions for crews and enslaved Africans. Perishable foodstuffs, in particular, were allowed to be sold, albeit subject to taxation, providing another opportunity for directors to sell goods in Spanish America and receive Spanish American commodities in return.[87]

Another avenue of profit was through investments in various royal overseas enterprises. Major investors could negotiate special privileges, with Antoine Crozat serving as a prime example.[88] According to Jacob Price, between 1697 and 1701, the tobacco monopoly (1697), the *Compagnie de Saint Domingue* (1698), and the *Compagnie de l'Asiento* (1701) were controlled by a single inter-

---

86 AN MAR/B/2/235, letter to Saupin in Fontainebleau, 27 September 1713: « J'ay été informé que sous prétexte de traité que vous avez fait cy devant avec les directeurs de la compagnie de l'assiente pour poursuivre les officiers et autres personnes employées au service de cette compagnie qui se trouveroient coupables de malversations vous faites naitres des discussions sans fin lesquelles étant portées par vous en différents tribunaux, ou souvent des suittes qui retournent à la charge de cette compagnie, comme une pareille conduitte est entièrement contraire à ses intérets, l'intenetion du roy est, que vous en fassiez à l'avenir aucune poursuites n'y procédures à l'ocassion de ses sortes d'affaires que vous n'en ayiez receu la permission de sa majesté. »

87 AN B7 233 letter of d'Aubenton on the 3 December 1704 in Scelle, *La traite négrière*, vol. 2, 361.

88 Originally from Languedoc, Antoine Crozat started as clerk in the office of the treasurer of the estates of Languedoc and receiver general of the clergy of France and was appointed to the affairs of the duke of Vendôme in Paris in 1699. Around 1707, Crozat left his office of receiver of finance in Bordeaux to invest in real estate: the barony of la Fauche, the marquisate of Mouy which he bought to the prince of Ligne. Lévy, *Capitalisme et pouvoir*.

est group, prominently featuring Crozat.[89] As a director of the *Compagnie de Saint Malo,* which subcontracted the *Compagnie des Indes Orientales,* Crozat was also active in the South Sea Company, established in 1698 for illicit trade to South America.[90]

Crozat leveraged his extensive European merchant network, which provided readily available credit and goods, to secure competitive advantages. This bargaining power was evident he negotiated privileges of the *Compagnie de Guinée* in 1701. His diversified investments during the early eighteenth century further strengthened his position, enabling him to exploit the French *asiento* for personal gain.

As a director of the *Compagnie de l'Asiento* and subcontractor of the *Compagnie des Indes Orientales,* Crozat petitioned to import *piasters* directly from the South Sea, warning that without such permission, he would abandon all shipping activities to Asia. Under pressure, the directors of the *Compagnie des Indes Orientales* supported Crozat's request to the Minister of the Navy.[91] In March 1711, a ship named *Le Baron de la Fauche,* after Crozat's new title, was fitted out. While she was authorised to trade in Veracruz by the Spanish King, the ship did not reach the South Sea.[92] Instead, *Le Baron de la Fauche* was to return laden with silver, sail the South Sea, and head out to Asia to finance French operations there, bolstering its position against European competitors like the VOC and the EIC. This exceptional authorisation provoked protests from Spanish merchants, but Pontchartrain dismissed their concerns, stating, "since he (Crozat) had obtained the permission from the Spanish King, Spanish merchants should not complain that the sir Crozat would trade there".[93]

When it became evident that the *asiento* would be transferred to the British, Crozat ensured amicable relations with the new *asentistas.* During the negotiations for the Peace of Utrecht in 1713, the *asiento* was officially granted to the British on 23 March.[94] In January of the same year, Crozat dispatched the final ship under the *Compagnie de l'Asiento,* instructing it to transport a

---

89 Price, *France and the Chesapeake,* 55. Additionally when Pontchartrain writes to the directors regularly calls them "the directors of the Asiento and Saint Domingue Companies" ANOM B28 f°17 and f°36.

90 Price, *France and the Chesapeake,* 56.

91 ANOM C2 14 fos.77–78 « Si ces Mrs. Ne font point le voyage, cette compagnie qui ne subsiste que par votre protection, monseigneur, tombera complétement ».

92 AN MAR B3 197 fo.134.

93 Marine B2 227 fo.574.

94 This Asiento is legally a treaty and is mentioned in the peace treaties of Utrecht, London and Madrid in Scelle, *La traite négrière,* vol. 2, 540–543.

director of the British Company.[95] Two years later, Crozat wrote to the French Minister of the Navy outlining a strategy to regain the *asiento* through his English connections, as quoted in the beginning of this chapter. In light of the different ways to profit from the *asiento*, it does not come as a surprise that both Crozat and Pontchartrain were still interested in accessing the contract despite the poor (official) performance of the *Compagnie*.

Despite the *Compagnie de l'Asiento* being unprofitable and heavily indebted from its inception, it appears that the French and Spanish Kings, as well as its shareholders, reaped significant benefits. Philip V gained substantial fiscal revenues and favourable loans that bolstered his claim to the Spanish throne and supported his war efforts. This financial backing was instrumental in his eventual success, the victorious resolution of the War of Spanish Succession, and the establishment of the Bourbon dynasty.[96]

For Louis XIV, the *asiento* provided continuous fiscal revenue, access to bullion to fund warfare and balance payments in Asia, and, most importantly, political leverage and economic power against the Dutch and English in European and Atlantic conflicts. Lastly, the directors of the ostensibly unprofitable *Compagnie* maintained their exclusive privileges, engaging in both legal and illegal activities to secure for personal profits.

95 The ship was probably meant to trade in enslaved people since among its cargo we find "old gunpowder for slave trade", AN MAR B3 213 fo.96 and Lévy, *Capitalisme et pouvoir*, 446.

96 Olivas, "Global Politics", 101.

CHAPTER 8

Conclusion

The Spanish colonies in the Americas represented the largest single market for the importation of enslaved Africans for approximately 200 years. The scale of this market, the fiscal potential it offered to the Spanish Monarchy, and its development over time enabled the Monarchy to adapt and structure the transatlantic slave trade in a way that influenced other empires and persisted until the end of the transatlantic slave era. During this period, the Habsburg monarchs ruled for over 150 years, making them the most influential architects of the transatlantic slave trade before 1713, with the legacy of their policies enduring for another century.

The magnitude and significance of Habsburg policies on the slave trade is evident in their prioritization of the Spanish Empire's political economy as predominantly exclusive to Castilian subjects. For approximately seventy-five years, the Monarchy implemented a licensing system that permitted its subjects to trade enslaved individuals to Spanish America. However, the Spanish empire lacked outposts, forts, or settlements along the West African coast, rendering the slave trade to Spanish America an inherently transnational enterprise. During the sixteenth century, enslaved Africans were procured from markets on the West Coast of Africa, which were controlled by the Portuguese, and subsequently by the Portuguese, Dutch, English, and French in the seventeenth century.

The licensing system of the sixteenth century posed two significant challenges. Firstly, it was difficult to align the demands of Spanish American markets with the availability of slave traders willing to invest in the risky transatlantic transport of enslaved Africans to the Americas. A significant part of this challenge lay in financing the Middle Passage, which was still regarded at the time as a particularly precarious enterprise. Secondly, the system for distributing licences was largely contingent on the monarch's willingness to grant privileges to a select few, often mediated through the *consulado* in Seville, and greatly influenced by the cycles of financial need of the Monarchy.

The Union of the (Portuguese and Spanish) Crowns in 1580 under Philip II offered the Habsburg Monarchy direct access to West African markets through the Portuguese empire. Although constitutionally separated from the rest of the domains of the Monarchy, the Portuguese empire was under the direct management of the Spanish king. Unsurprisingly, the first *asiento* was granted to financiers and merchant bankers of Portuguese origin closely associated with Philip II, who became intermediaries in the sale of licences for the slave trade. These individuals, leveraging kinship networks, coordinated the supply of enslaved Africans to Spanish American colonies. They achieved this by integrating permissions to trade on the West African coast under Portuguese control and secured from Portuguese *contratadores*, with the logistical needs of the Spanish colonies, mirrored in the clauses of the *asiento*. For the first time, the trade in enslaved Africans was controlled by a cohesive group of financiers, who managed both supply and demand, articulating and, at times, integrating markets in three different continents. This control allowed the Monarchy to extract fiscal revenues in a consistent and predictable manner, which was particularly advantageous in the first decades of the seventeenth century, a period in European history plagued by warfare.

The so-called "Portuguese *asientos*" were not exclusively Portuguese in practice. Licences issued by Portuguese financiers were often utilised by ships and captains of various origins, including Spanish, Flemish, and Italian traders. This highlights the transnational nature of the trade. Consequently, the notion that *asientos* were exclusively granted to specific 'national' groups need to be reconsidered, as the operational aspects of the trade were inherently transnational, even if the financing often remained in the hands of Portuguese networks.

Importantly, while many Portuguese financiers involved in the *asientos* were of New Christian descent, they operated not as representatives of a religious or national merchant community but as independent entrepreneurs. These individuals engaged in complex kinship networks of trade and finance, reflecting their integration into a broader commercial landscape rather than alignment with a singular communal or merchant 'national' identity.

The independence of Portugal in 1640 dramatically altered the dynamics of the transatlantic slave trade. Portuguese merchants, along with Portuguese forts and settlements in West Africa, were alienated from the Spanish supply chain. Now deemed enemies of the Spanish Monarchy, the Portuguese were excluded from participation in and reap the economic benefits of the Spanish-American markets. For approximately two decades, the Spanish Monarchy relied on a licensing system that proved insufficient to meet the demand for enslaved labour in the Americas or fulfill the fiscal needs of the state.

The limitations of this system were compounded by structural issues. Licences were required to be paid for upfront in Europe, rather than through deferred payments in the Caribbean as had been the case under the Portuguese *asientos*. This policy excluded many potential traders who lacked the financial capacity to bear the full costs of the licence and the risks associated with the transatlantic journey. Consequently, only those merchants with significant financial resources could participate. By eliminating the role of intermediaries such as the *asentistas*, the Crown effectively privatised the risks of the financing and the trade, transferring the burden to smaller slave traders who lacked the financial means to sustain the system independently.

The shortage of enslaved Africans arriving in Spanish America during the 1640s and 1650s prompted complaints from the colonies. This labour deficit endangered the economic survival of individual colonies and, by extension, the Spanish Empire. At the same time, the licensing system failed to generate the fiscal revenues the Monarchy had grown accustomed to under the "Portuguese *asientos*". In this context, the Monarchy resolved to auction the *asiento* once again, this time to a private firm headed by Grillo and Lomellino, two merchant bankers of Genoese descent.

Similar to the Portuguese *asentistas*, Grillo and Lomellino were not frontmen for a Genoese merchant community in Spain. Instead, they were individual partners in a firm with limited direct involvement or expertise in the slave trade. The firm lacked access to African markets, fleets to transport enslaved Africans, and the operational knowledge to deliver human cargoes to Spanish America. However, Grillo and Lomellino introduced a significant innovation to the asiento system: subcontracting. Rather than organising the trade themselves, they contracted third parties to manage the shipment of enslaved Africans to Spanish America. This innovation brought about three major shifts in the structuring of the transatlantic slave trade.

First, Grillo and Lomellino formalised the relationship between *asentistas* and suppliers of enslaved Africans. By outsourcing all trade-related activities to third parties, they separated financial responsibilities to the Monarchy from the logistics of the slave trade. While the firm remained accountable for financial matters, it delegated all operational aspects to subcontractors.

Second, Grillo and Lomellino established contractual agreements between their private firm and chartered companies, including a joint-stock company. These companies did not hold direct rights to the *asiento* but fulfilled commercial contracts with the firm. This arrangement marked the first instance of the slave trade being organised through formal agreements between private firms and corporate entities. Within this structure, corporate entities appeared subordinate to the firm, acting primarily as providers of shipping and logistical services.

Third, Grillo and Lomellino restructured the trade routes themselves. Unlike the Portuguese *asentistas* and earlier licence holders, who relied on direct imports from Africa to Spanish America, Grillo and Lomellino prioritised an alternative circuit. This involved importing enslaved Africans directly from Africa to the Caribbean – primarily to islands outside Spanish dominion – and subsequently transferring them to the Spanish Caribbean. This restructuring effectively established the inter-Caribbean trade system that characterised the late seventeenth century and the entirety of the eighteenth century, at that point not exclusively dedicated to trade in enslaved Africans only, but to colonial commodities.

The opening of inter-Caribbean trade to meet the labour demands of Spanish America led to an additional, perhaps unintended, consequence. By creating slave-trading hubs within Dutch and English-controlled territories, Grillo and Lomellino facilitated the coexistence of three interconnected political economies – Spanish, Dutch, and English. These actors operated within their respective legal frameworks but cooperated through the slave trade. Dutch and English traders imported enslaved individuals destined for Spanish American markets via hubs such as Barbados, Jamaica, and Curaçao. Meanwhile, ships operating under the *asiento* departed from Dutch and English Caribbean territories to legally trade within the exclusive framework of the Spanish Empire, fulfilling the Crown's stipulation of service by its own subjects or privileged foreigners.

The radical innovations introduced by Grillo and Lomellino in the structuring of the transatlantic slave trade, implemented through clauses agreed with the Spanish Monarchy for the *asiento*, set the precedent for the evolution of the trade over the next 150 years. However, Grillo and Lomellino were unable to avoid a common challenge faced by private firms in the early modern period. The death of Lomellino brought significant difficulties, as Grillo had to manage the potential dissolution of the partnership due to claims on Lomellino's assets by his heirs and creditors, while simultaneously meeting the financial obligations of the *asiento* with the Spanish Monarchy. These obligations included the regular payment of fiscal revenues derived from the trade. Although partially caused by the structural complexities of the *asiento* system itself, Grillo's eventual insolvency was largely a consequence of Lomellino's passing. This insolvency also became a problem for the Spanish Monarchy.

The Monarchy, taken aback by the firm's inability to withstand the loss of a partner, reverted to direct management through the intermediation of the *Consulado* of Seville. The *consulado* reintroduced a system resembling that of the 1650s, wherein licences were sold to traders who were subjects of the king or had resided in Spain for a considerable period. While this approach ostensibly allowed broader participation from traders of various European origins and social backgrounds, in practice the requirement to pay for licences in advance in Seville limited accessibility. Few traders possessed the necessary capital to finance the journey during a time of heightened violence and instability in the Atlantic.

Moreover, legitimate licence holders faced fierce competition from illicit traders who continued to utilise Dutch and English Caribbean hubs as stopovers to supply enslaved Africans to inter-Caribbean circuits, albeit illegally. The incentive of receiving payment in Spanish silver, which had previously motivated the WIC, the RA, and the RAC to enter into contracts with Grillo and Lomellino, also drew many illicit traders into the trade. From the Spanish authorities' perspective, such activities undermined the regulated system of the *asiento*. Similarly, English authorities had to address the dual pressures of supplying two competing markets: their plantation economies in the Caribbean and the Spanish American colonies.

English colonists found themselves at a disadvantage compared to Spanish markets, which offered far higher prices for enslaved individuals. In Spanish America, prices for each enslaved person were two to three times higher than those paid in English colonies such as Barbados or Jamaica. This disparity incentivised English colonial society to engage in illegal trade with Spanish America, further complicating enforcement efforts for both Spanish and English authorities.

Given the limited number of licences sold by the *Consulado*, the monarchy took matters into its own hands. It responded positively to a proposal by Barroso del Pozo and his partners to take over the unsold licences and manage them in a manner similar to the *asiento*. Like their predecessors, Grillo and Lomellino, Barroso, and later Barroso and Porcio, as well as the Coymans and Van Belle partnerships, operated the *asiento* as a private firm. This arrangement combined subcontracting to Dutch and English chartered companies with the direct importation of enslaved Africans from Portuguese-dominated areas in Africa to Spanish America.

However, the most significant shift following the restructuring of the transatlantic slave trade, as exemplified in the 1662 *asiento* with Grillo and Lomellino, was the introduction of foreign royal participation in the Spanish *asiento*. Recognising that indirect management through subcontracting had failed to secure a steady supply of enslaved Africans for Spanish America while failing to meet the Monarchy's fiscal demands, the Spanish Crown opted for a return to direct management and direct imports from Africa by the early 1690s. To achieve this, the Monarchy contracted a new *asiento* with the Portuguese *Companhia*, whose shareholders included the Portuguese king, Peter II.

The involvement of the Portuguese monarch provided financial guarantees to the company's shareholders, while simultaneously elevating the *asiento* into the realm of diplomacy and statecraft. The participation of a king in a company operationalising the *asiento* was a calculated risk for Madrid, taken to regain direct access to African markets and to curtail the growing influence of Dutch and English trading companies and private traders, who utilised inter-Caribbean circuits for the slave trade. By contracting with the Portuguese *Companhia*, the Spanish Monarchy reaffirmed its reliance on Portuguese trading networks to integrate and coordinate West African slaving markets with Spanish American ports.

The exclusion of the Dutch West India Company and the Royal African Company from subcontracting, along with the removal of Curaçao and Jamaica from the inter-Caribbean slave trade to Spanish America, reflected the Spanish ambition to limit Dutch and English access to the profits of the slave trade in Spanish American ports. These profits, critical for sustaining Spanish imperial finances, had been redirected to fund increasing interstate violence in Europe and the Atlantic. By reclaiming control over these economic flows, the Spanish Monarchy sought to reinforce its position in an era of heightened competition and conflict.

If Peter II of Portugal was the first foreign king to hold shares in an *asiento* company, others soon followed. Louis XIV of France, along with his grandson Philip of Anjou, the future King of Spain, became shareholders in a French company established to transform the French Caribbean island of Saint Domingue into a significant hub for the slave trade, comparable to Curaçao or Jamaica. However, when this ambition failed, Saint Domingue instead became an outpost for the export of French industrial manufacturing to Spanish American markets in exchange for silver.

Louis XIV's success in this venture was twofold: he opened new markets for French manufacturers while simultaneously diverting Spanish silver into French coffers. This silver became a key financial resource for his grandson Philip's campaign to secure the Spanish throne against Dutch and English opposition in Europe and the Atlantic. The *Compagnie de l'Assiento* thus served not only as a fiscal tool for the Monarchy and a diplomatic asset in negotiations between European powers but also as a critical means to sustain the Franco-Spanish war effort. This war ultimately resulted in Philip's ascension to the Spanish throne and the consequent demise of the Habsburg dynasty in Madrid.

The Habsburg *asientos* reflect, on the one hand, the necessity of enslaved labour for the Spanish colonies in the Americas, and on the other, they provide a proxy for understanding Spain's fiscal challenges and dependence on steady and predictable revenues. The trade in enslaved Africans offered the financial stability the Monarchy desperately required during the seventeenth century. In this sense, the slave trade cannot be viewed solely through the lens of private traders or chartered corporations but rather as a crucial source of fiscal revenue for the Spanish state. Although scholars might utilise the *asiento* system to analyse the direct relationship between fiscality and the slave trade in the Spanish political economy, relatively little is known about the fiscal revenues that other powers extracted from the slave trade. The focus of scholarship has predominantly been on the individual profits of firms, chartered companies, and joint-stock enterprises, leaving the broader state-level economic implications less explored.

What the *asiento* also reveals is that the Spanish Monarchy, although focused on maintaining an exclusive empire with restricted access for non-Castilian subjects, created mechanisms, whether consciously or unconsciously, that included foreigners. The transnational nature of the *asiento* was not a choice but an imperative. This necessity extended not only to the financiers of the *asiento*, often termed *asientistas* and categorised by scholars based on their origins (e.g., Portuguese *asientos*, Genoese *asientos*, Dutch *asientos*, French *asientos*), but also to the broader networks involved. The relational dynamics of the *asiento* were far more complex than these labels suggest.

The firms and chartered companies that participated in the *asiento* were not always Spanish and did not necessarily represent a specific merchant community within Spain or abroad. Instead, these entities represented diverse interest groups that spanned various social categories rather than cohesive merchant communities. The transnationality of the *asiento* was not primarily tied to the origins of the *asentistas* but instead to their ability to seek collaborators beyond their own 'national' or cultural backgrounds, often engaging foreign partners or subcontractors to operationalise the system. Transnationality also manifested in practice, as the crews aboard ships trading under or for the *asiento* frequently included individuals from multiple European countries and, at times, people of African descent.

This individuality should not be mistaken for independence *vis-à-vis* the multiple European states directly or indirectly involved in the *asiento*. When negotiations in Madrid approached or problems arose in Europe or the Caribbean, consuls and ambassadors were call to aid firms and companies to have their ambitions fulfilled or the property rights upheld.

This integral transnationality created the framework for a complex interplay of exchanges. The *asiento* was managed by a diverse set of business organisations, including partnerships, firms, chartered companies, and joint-stock companies. The way the Monarchy structured the *asiento* enabled these organisations to outsource elements of the slave trade to other entities, creating a network of partnerships, firms, and joint-stock companies linked through contractual agreements. Interestingly, firms and partnerships seemed to have had an advantage over larger corporate entities in formalising contracts within the *asiento* system. The charterd Royal African Company (RAC) and the joint stock

Dutch West India Company (WIC) never attained the status of *asentistas*, remaining subcontractors to private firms that held the contracts. This challenges the prevailing scholarly emphasis on the centrality and importance of corporations in matters of long distance trade in the early modern period. The Spanish Monarchy appeared to regard corporations as less efficient or trustworthy than partnerships or firms in managing the *asiento*. Over forty years of contractual failures by corporate entities, with the partial exception of the Portuguese *Companhia*, reinforced this perception.

In practice, while the *asiento* may have been crucial to the survival of the RAC or the WIC, or for the development of slave-trading hubs in the Caribbean under Dutch and English control, it seems to have held less direct importance for the Spanish Monarchy and the *asiento* system itself. What the *asiento* ultimately reflects over a century is the capacity of multiple business organisations to cooperate, even within a framework designed to promote fierce competition and where the corporate organisation seems to have offered few innovative options to the challenges posed by the *asiento*.

The *asiento* presented similar challenges and posed comparable problems to all business organisations and transnational groups involved. The bottlenecks in the system lay in the need to effectively articulate and integrate African with Spanish American markets. This at times required the intermediation of Caribbean hubs controlled by the Dutch and the English. All business organisations and transnational groups sought to capture Spanish American commodities, particularly silver, which created complex and often insurmountable challenges concerning payment circuits. These challenges extended across Caribbean destinations, between the Caribbean and Europe, and within intra-European financial networks.

For the Spanish Monarchy, the *asiento* primarily functioned as an instrument of taxation. Fiscal revenues were critical for the Monarchy's survival, especially during times of war. Spain's ability to sustain its empire largely depended on the Crown's capacity to generate resources to fund armies, maintain the navy, and secure its territories in Europe and overseas. Thus, the *asiento* served as both a fiscal tool and a diplomatic instrument, playing a significant role in the complex negotiations Spain conducted with other European powers.

Ultimately, the *asiento* intertwined the financial interests of European states – particularly Spain – with the transatlantic slave trade and concomitant financial circuits. The *asientos* facilitated the integration of the political economies of multiple empires, aiming to bring illicit and informal trade to the legal sphere. While doing so, the Spanish Monarchy allowed others in

Europe, Africa, the Caribbean and the Americas to share in the perils, risks and gains of its Atlantic empire. In particular, the distribution of gains came at an undeniable and significant human cost, as it was imposed upon the lives and destinities of millions of African men, women, and children.

Bibliography

Published Sources

Aitzema, Lieuwe van. *Saken van Staet en Oorlogh in, ende omtrent de Vereenigde Nederlanden.* 15 vols. The Hague: Johan Veelt,Johan Tongerloo, ende Jasper Doll – Boeck-verkoopers, 1669.

Coleccion de los tratados de paz, alianza, neutralidad, garantía, protección, tregua, mediación, accesión, reglamento de limites, comercio, navigacion, etc. hechos por los pueblos, reyes, y príncipes de España con los pueblos, reyes príncipes, republicas, y demás potencias de Europea, y otras partes del mundo, y entre sì mismos, y con sus respectivos adversarios, y juntamente de los hechos directa, ò indirectamente contra ella. Madrid: Diego Peralta, Antonio Marin y Juan de Zuñiga, 1740.

Cantillo, Alejandro del, ed. *Tratados, convenios y declaraciones de paz y de comercio que han hecho con las potencias estranjeras los monarcas españoles de la casa de Borbon desde el año de 1700 hasta el día.* Madrid: Imprenta de Alegria y Charlain, 1843.

Donnan, E. *Documents Illustrative of the History of the Slave Trade to America*, 4 vols., Washington DC: Carnegie Institution of Washington, 1930.

Fanshawe, Richard. *Original letters of His Excellency Sir Richard Fanshaw: during his embassies in Spain and Portugal.* London: A. Roper and the Black Boy, and R. Basset at the Mitre in Fleetstreet; and W. Turner, at the Angel at Lincolns-Inn Back Gate, 1702.

Raithby, John, ed. *Statutes of the Realm. vol. 5: 1628–1680*, 246–250. *British History Online* http://www.british-history.ac.uk/statutes-realm/vol5/pp246–250 (accessed 3 May 2024).

Sainsbury, W.N., ed. "America and West Indies: May 1664". In *Calendar of State Papers Colonial, America and West Indies.* vol.5: *1661–1668*, 205–212. London: Her Majesty's Stationery Office, 1880.

Secondary Bibliography

Adelman, Jeremy, ed. *Colonial Legacies: The Problem of Persistence in Latin American History.* New York and London : Routledge, 1999.

Alencastro, Luís Felipe de. *O trato dos viventes: formação do Brasil no Atlântico Sul (séculos XVI e XVII).* São Paulo: Companhia das Letras, 2000.

Alencastro, Luis Felipe de. *The Trade in the Living: The Formation of Brazil in the South Atlantic, Sixteenth to Seventeenth Centuries*. Albany: State University of New York Press, 2018.

Alessandrini, Nunziatella and Antonella Viola. "Genovesi e fiorentini in Portogallo: Reti commerciali e strategie politico-diplomatiche (1650–1700)". *Mediterranea. Ricerche storiche*, 28 (2013): 295–322.

Álvarez-Nogal, Carlos. *El crédito de la monarquía hispánica en el reinado de Felipe IV*. Valladolid: Junta de Castilla y León, 1997.

Álvarez y Santaló, León Carlos, ed. *Estudios de historia moderna en homenaje al profesor Antonio García-Baquero*. Seville: Universidad de Sevilla, 2009.

Anstey, Roger. "Capitalism and Slavery: a Critique". *Economic History Review* 21, no. 2 (1968): 307–320.

Antunes, Cátia and Filipa Ribeiro da Silva. "Amsterdam Merchants in the Slave Trade and African Commerce, 1580s–1670s". *TSEG – The Low Countries Journal of Social and Economic History* 9, no. 4 (2012): 3–30.

Antunes, Cátia, Rob Post and João Paulo Salvado. "Het omzeilen van monopoliehandel. Smokkel en belastingontduiking bij de handel in brazielhout, 1500–1674". *TSEG – The Low Countries Journal of Social and Economic History* 13, no. 1 (2016): 23–52.

Antunes, Cátia and Filipa Ribeiro da Silva. "Windows of Global Exchange: Dutch Ports and the Slave Trade, 1600–1800". *International Journal of Maritime History* 30, no. 3 (2018): 42–441.

Armitage, David and Michael Braddick. *The British Atlantic World, 1500–1800*. Basingstoke: Palgrave Macmillan, 2002.

Aufhauser, Keith. "Profitability of Slavery in the British Caribbean". *Journal of Interdisciplinary History* 5, no. 1 (1974): 45–67.

Barbour, Violet. *Capitalism in Amsterdam in the Seventeenth Century*. Ann Arbor: University of Michigan Press, 1963.

Baskes, Jeremy. *Staying Afloat: Risk and Uncertainty in Spanish Atlantic World Trade, 1760–1820*. Stanford: Stanford University Press, 2013.

Bailyn, Bernard, "Communications and Trade: The Atlantic in the Seventeenth Century". *The Journal of Economic History* 13, no. 4 (1953): 378–387.

Baleno, Ilídio. "Reconversão do comércio externo em tempo de crise e o impacto da Companhia do Grão-Pará e Maranhão". In *História geral de Cabo Verde*, edited by Maria Emília Madeira Santos, vol. 3, 157–233. Lisbon and Praia: Instituto de Investigação Científica e Tropical – Instituto Nacional de Investigação, Promoção e Património Culturais de Cabo Verde, 2002.

Barker, H. and M. Ishizu. "Inheritance and Continuity in Small Family Businesses During the Early Industrial Revolution". *Business History* 54, no. 2 (2012): 227–244.

Bayly Christopher A. *et al.* AHR Conversation: On Transnational History, in *American Historical Review* 111 (2006): 1441–1464.

Beckert, Sven. *Empire of Cotton: A Global History*. New York : Alfred A. Knopf, 2014.

Bellen, Pedro van. *Pertinent en Waarachtig Verhaal van alle Handelingen en Directie van Pedro van Belle omtrent Den Slavenhandel, ofte, het Assiento de Negros, eerst door D. Juan Barosso y Posso, bij zijn overlijden door D. Nicolas Porsio, en daar na door Balthasar Coijmans met den Koning van Spangien aangegaan, zoo in Spangien, de West-Indijes, als op Curaçao: Dienende tot onderrichtinge van alle die gene, die bij het voorsz. Assiento, ofte de Compagnie van Coijmans en Van Belle tot Cadix, eenigsints zouden mogen wezen geinteresseert*. Rotterdam: Reinier Leers, 1689.

Bennett, Herman L. *Africans in Colonial Mexico: Absolutism, Christianity, and Afro-Creole Consciousness, 1570–1640*. Bloomington: Indiana University Press, 2003.

Bertrand, Michel. *Grandeza y miseria del oficio: Los oficiales de la Real Hacienda de la Nueva España, siglos XVII y XVIII*. México D.F.: Fondo de Cultura Economica, 2013.

Bethencourt, Francisco. *Strangers Within. The Rise and Fall of the New Christian Trading Elite*. Princeton: Princeton University Press, 2024.

Bethencourt, Francisco. "Iberian Atlantic: Ties, Networks, and Boundaries". In *Theorising the Ibero-American Atlantic*, edited by Harald E. Braun, Lisa Vollendorf. Leiden and Boston: Brill, 2013: 15–36

Bloom, Herbert I. *The Economic Activities of the Jews of Amsterdam in the Seventeenth and Eighteenth Centuries*. Williamsport: The Bayard Press, 1937.

Borucki, Alex. "Trans-imperial History in the Making of the Slave Trade to Venezuela, 1526–1811". *Itinerario* 36, no. 2 (2012): 29–54.

Borucki, Alex. "From Asiento to Spanish Networks. Slave Trading in Río de La Plata, 1700–1800". In *From the Galleons to the Highlands: Slave Trade Routes in the Spanish Americas*, edited by Alex Borucki, David Eltis, and David Wheat, 177–200. Albuquerque: University of New Mexico Press, 2020.

Borucki, Alex, David Eltis, and David Wheat, eds. *From the Galleons to the Highlands. Slave Trade Routes in the Spanish Americas*. Albuquerque: University of New Mexico Press, 2020.

Borucki, Alex, David Eltis and David Wheat, "Atlantic History and the Slave Trade to Spanish America". *The Americal History Review* 120, no. 2 (2015): 433–461.

Borucki, Alex, David Eltis, and David Wheat, "The Size and Direction of the Slave Trade to the Spanish Americas". In *From the Galleons to the Highlands: Slave Trade Routes in the Spanish Americas*, edited Alex Borucki, David Eltis, and David Wheat, 15–46. Albuquerque: University of New Mexico Press, 2020.

Bouza Alvarez, Fernando. *Portugal En La Monarquia Hispanica (1580–1640). Felipe II, Las Cortes y La Genesis Del Portugal Catolico*. PhD diss. Universidad Complutense de Madrid, 1987.

Bowser, Frederick P. *The African Slave in Colonial Peru, 1524–1650*. Stanford: Stanford University Press, 1974.

Brakel, S. van. "Eene memorie over den handel der West-Indische Compagnie omstreeks 1670". *Bijdragen en Mededelingen van het Historisch Genootschap* 35 (1914): 87–104.

Brakel, S. van. "Bescheiden over den slavenhandel der West-Indische Compagnie". *Economisch-Historisch Jaarboek* IV (1918): 47–83.

Brilli, Catia. "Los genoveses en el comercio americano de esclavos (segunda mitad del siglo XVIII)". *Rivista Storica Italiana* 127, no. 1 (2015): 159–82.

Bromley, J. S., ed. *The New Cambridge Modern History*, vol. 6. Cambridge: Cambridge University Press, 1970.

Brooks, George. *Landlords and Strangers: Ecology, Society, and Trade in Western Africa, 1000–1630*. Boulder: Westview, 1993.

Bryant, Sherwin K., Rachel Sarah O'Toole and Ben Vinson, eds. *Africans to Spanish America: Expanding the Diaspora*. Urbana/Chicago/Springfield: University of Illinois Press, 2012.

Budde, Budde, Sebastian Conrad, Oliver Janz (eds.). *Transnationale Geschiechte: Themen, Tendenzen und Theorien*. Göttingen : Vandenhoek & Ruprecht, 2006.

Sebastian Conrad, Oliver Janz (eds.), *Transnationale Geschiechte: Themen, Tendenzen und Theorien*. Göttingen : Vandenhoek & Ruprecht, 2006.

Bulmer-Thomas, Victor, John H. Coatsworth and Roberto Cortés-Conde, eds. *The Cambridge Economic History of Latin America*. 2 vols. Cambridge: Cambridge University Press, 2005.

Caldeira, Arlindo Manuel. "Angola and the Seventeenth-Century South Atlantic Slave Trade". In *Networks and Trans-Cultural Exchange: Slave Trading in the South Atlantic, 1590–1867*, edited by Filipa Ribeiro da Silva and David Richardson, 101–142. Leiden and Boston: Brill, 2015.

Cardim, Pedro, Antonio Feros and Gaetano Sabatini. "The Political Constitution of the Iberian Monarchies". In *The Iberian World. 1450–1820*, edited by Fernando Bouza Alvarez, Pedro Cardim, and Antonio Feros, 34–61. London and New York: Routledge, 2020.

Cardim, Pedro. "Portugal's Elites and the Status of the Kingdom of Portugal within the Spanish Monarchy". In *Monarchy Transformed: Princes and Their Elites in Early Modern Western Europe*, edited by Robert von Friedeburg and John Morrill, 212–243. Cambridge: Cambridge University Press, 2017.

Cardim, Pedro, Leonor Freire Costa and Mafalda Soares da Cunha. *Portugal Na Monarquia Hispânica: Dinâmicas de Integração e Conflito*. Lisbon: CHAM, 2013.

Carlos, Ann and Jamie Brown Kruse. "The decline of the Royal African Company: Fringe Firms and the Role of the Charter". *The Economic History Review* 49, no. 2 (1996): 291–313.

Carrasco González, María Guadalupe. *Comerciantes y casas de negocios en Cádiz, 1650–1700*. Cádiz: Universidad de Cádiz, 1997.

Carreira, António. *Notas sobre o tráfico português de escravos* 2a ed. Rev. Lisbon: Faculdade de Ciências Sociais e Humanas da Universidade Nova de Lisboa, 1983.

Carreira, António. *As companhias pombalinas do Grão-Pará e Maranhão e Pernambuco e Paraíba*. Lisbon, Editorial Presença, 1983.

Casado Alonso, Hilario and Ricardo Robledo Hernández. *Fortuna y negocios: formación y gestión de los grandes patrimonios (siglos XVI–XX)*. Valladolid: Universidad de Valladolid, 2002.

Castillo Meléndez, Francisco. "Población y defensa de la isla de Cuba (1650–1700)". *Anuario de Estudios Americanos* 44 (1987): 1–87.

Chakrabarty, Dipesh. *Provincializing Europe: Postcolonial Thought and Historical Difference*. Princeton: Princeton University Press, 2000.

Clark, Joseph Michael Hopper. *Veracruz and the Caribbean in the Seventeenth Century*. PhD diss. Baltimore: Johns Hopkins University, 2016.

Coatsworth, John H. "Political Economy and Economic Organization". In *The Cambridge Economic History of Latin America*, edited by Victor Bulmer-Thomas, John H. Coatsworth, and Roberto Cortés-Conde, 235–274. Cambridge: Cambridge University Press, 2005.

Coclanis, Peter A., ed. *The Atlantic Economy during the Seventeenth and Eighteenth Centuries: Organization, Operation, Practice, and Personnel*. Columbia, SC: University of South Carolina Press, 2005.

Cohen, Zelinda. "Subsídios para a história geral de Cabo Verde: os contratos de arrendamento para a cobrança de rendas e direitos reais das ilhas de Cabo Verde (1501–1560)". *Stvdia* 53 (1994): 317–364.

Cools, Hans. "Francesco Feroni (1614–16–1696)". In *Your Humble Servant. Agents in Early Modern Europe*, edited by Hans Cools, Marika Keblusek and Badeloch Noldus, 39–50. Hilversum: Uitgeverij Verloren, 2006.

Corona, Juan. "Succession in the Family Business: The Great Challenge for the Family". *European Journal of Family Business* 11 (2021): 64–70.

Cortés López, José Luis. *Esclavo y colono*. Salamanca : Universidad de Salamanca, 2004.

Costa, Leonor Freire. *O transporte no Atlântico e a Companhia Geral do Comércio do Brasil, 1580–1663*, 2 vols. Lisbon: Comissão Nacional para as Comemorações dos Descobrimentos Portugueses, 2002.

Costa, Leonor Freire. "Genoveses nas rotas do açucar: A intromissao em exclusivos coloniais portugueses (c. 1650)". In *Génova y la Monarquía Hispánica (1528–1713)*, edited by Manuel Herrero Sánchez, Yasmina Rocío Ben Yessef Garfia, Carlo Bitossi and Dino Puncuh, 915–932. Genoa: Società Ligure di Storia Patria, 2011.

Costa, Leonor Freire, Pedro Lains and Susana Münch Miranda. *An Economic History of Portugal, 1143–2010*. Cambridge: Cambridge University Press, 2016.

Crespo Solana, Ana. "Las comunidades mercantiles y el mantenimiento de los sistemas comerciales de España, Flandes y la República holandesa, 1648–1750". In *España y las 17 provincias de los Países Bajos: una revisión historiográfica* (*XVI–XVIII*), edited by Manuel Herrero Sánchez and Ana Crespo Solana, 443–468. Cordoba: Fundación Carlos de Amberes, 2002.

Curtin, Philip D. and Paul E. Lovejoy, eds. *Africans in Bondage: Studies in Slavery and the Slave Trade. Essays in Honor of Philip D. Curtin on the Occasion of the Twenty-Fifth Anniversary of African Studies at the University of Wisconsin.* Madison : University of Wisconsin African Studies Program, 1986.

Dalton, Heather. "Into Speyne to Selle for Slavys: English, Spanish, and Genoese Merchant Networks and Their Involvement with the "Cost of Gwynea" Trade before 1550". In *Brokers of Change: Atlantic Commerce and Cultures in Pre-Colonial Western Africa,* edited by Toby Green, 89–124. Oxford: Oxford University Press, 2012.

Davies, Kenneth Gordon. *The Royal African Company.* London : Taylor & Francis, 1957.

Delgado Ribas, José Maria. "The Slave Trade in the Spanish Imperial System, 1500–1800". In *Slavery and Antislavery in Spain's Atlantic Empire,* edited by Josep Maria Fradera and Christopher Schmidt-Nowara, 13–42. New York: Berghahn, 2013.

Denzel, Markus A., Jan de Vries, and Philipp Robinson Rössner (eds.). *Small Is Beautiful? Interlopers and Smaller Trading Nations in the Pre-industrial Period: Proceedings of the XVth World Economic History Congress in Utrecht.* Stuttgart: Franz Steiner Verlag, 2011.

Diène, Doudou, ed. *From Chins to Bonds. The Slave Trade Revisited.* New York-Oxford: Berghahn, 2001.

Diffie, Bailey W. and George Winius. *Foundations of the Portuguese Empire: 1415–1580.* Minneapolis: University of Minnesota Press, 1977.

Donoso Anes, Rafael. "Algunos aspectos relacionados con el control administrativo y contable de la renta de los esclavos enviados a Hispanoamérica". *Revista Española de Financiación y Contabilidad* 30, no. 110 (2001): 1093–1135.

Drelichman, Mauricio and Hans-Joachim Voth. *Lending to the Borrower from Hell: Debt, Taxes, and Default in the Age of Philip II.* Princeton : Princeton University Press, 2014.

Eagle, Marc, "Chasing the Avença: An Investigation of Illicit Slave Trading in Santo Domingo at the End of the Portuguese Asiento Period". *Slavery & Abolition* 35, no. 1 (2014): 99–120.

Eagle, Marc and David Wheat. "The Early Iberian Slave Trade to the Spanish Caribbean, 1500–1580". In *From the Galleons to the Highlands: Slave Trade Routes in the Spanish Americas,* edited by Alex Borucki, David Eltis and David Wheat, 47–72. Albuquerque: University of New Mexico Press, 2020.

Eekhof, A. "Twee documenten betreffende den slavenhandel in de 17e eeuw". *Nederlands Archief voor Kerkgeschiedenis* XI (1914): 271–298.

Eissa-Barros, F. A. and A. Vásquez Varela, eds. *Early Bourbon Spanish America: Politics and Society in a Forgotten Era, 1700–1759*. Leiden: Brill, 2013.

Elbl, Ivana. *The Portuguese Trade with West Africa, 1440–1521*, PhD diss. Toronto: University of Toronto, 1986.

Elbl, Ivana. "Cross-Cultural Trade and Diplomacy: Portuguese Relations with West Africa, 1441–1521". *Journal of World History* 3, no. 2 (1992): 165–204.

Elliott, John. H. "The Spanish Monarchy and the Kingdom of Portugal, 1580–1640". In *Conquest and Coalescence. The Shaping of the State in Early Modern Europe*, edied by Mark Greengrass. London: Edward Arnold, 1991: 48–67.

Engerman, Stanley. "The Slave Trade and British Capital Formation in the Eighteenth Century: a Comment of the Williams Thesis". *Business Studies Review* 46, no. 4 (1972): 430–443.

Esteves, Maria Luísa. "Para o estudo do tráfico de escravos de Angola (1640–1668)". *Studia* 50 (1991): 29–60

Esteves, Maria Luísa. "Para o estudo das relações comerciais de Angola com as Índias de Castela e Génova no período da Restauração (1640–1668)". *Studia* 51 (1992): 29–60.

Farnell, J.E. "The Navigation Act of 1651, the First Dutch War, and the London Merchant Community". *The Economic History Review* 16, no. 3 (1964): 439–54.

Felloni, Giuseppe. *Gli investimenti finanziari genovesi in Europa tra il Seicento e la Restaurazione*. Milano: A. Giuffrè, 1971.

Fernández Chaves, Manuel Francisco and Rafael M. Pérez García, "Las redes de la trata negrera: mercaderes portugueses y tráfico de esclavos en Sevilla (c. 1560–1580)". In *La esclavitud negroafricana en la historia de España siglos XVI y XVII*, edited by Aurelia Martín Casares and Margarita García Barranco, 5–34. Granada: Editorial Comares, 2010.

Fernández Chaves, Manuel Francisco and Rafael M. Pérez García. "La penetración económica portuguesa en la Sevilla del siglo XVI". *Espacio Tiempo y Forma, serie IV, Historia Moderna* 25 (2012): 199–222.

Fernández Chaves, Manuel Francisco and Rafael M. Pérez García, "La élite mercantil judeoconversa andaluza y la articulación de la trata negrera hacia las Indias de Castilla, ca. 1518–1560". *Hispania* 76, no. 253 (2016): 385–414.

Ferreira, Roquinaldo and Tatiana Seijas. "The Slave Trade to Latin America: A Historiographical Assessment". In *Afro-Latin American Studies: An Introduction*, edited by Alejandro de la Fuente and George Reid Andrews, 27–51. Cambridge: Cambridge University Press, 2018.

Fradera, Josep Maria and Christopher Schmidt-Nowara, eds. *Slavery and Antislavery in Spain's Atlantic Empire*. New York: Berghahn, 2013.

Friedeburg, Robert von and John Morrill, eds. *Monarchy Transformed: Princes and Their Elites in Early Modern Western Europe*. Cambridge: Cambridge University Press, 2017.

Frostin, C. "Les Pontchartrain et la pénétration commerciale française en Amérique espagnole (1690–1715)". *Revue Historique* 245, no. 498 (1971): 307–336.

Fuente, Alejandro de la and George Reid Andrews, eds. *Afro-Latin American Studies: An Introduction*. Cambridge: Cambridge University Press, 2018.

Alison Games, *The Web of Empire. English Cosmopolitans in an Age of Expansion, 1560–1660*. Oxford : Oxford University Press, 2008.

García Fuentes, Lutgardo. *El comercio español con América, 1650–1700*. Sevilla: EEHA-CSIC, 1980.

García Fuentes, Lutgardo. "Licencias para la introducción de esclavos en Indias y envíos desde Sevilla en el siglo XVI". *Jahrbuch für Geschichte von Staat, Wirtschaft und Geselschaft Lateinamerikas* 19 (1982): 1–46.

García-Monton, Alejandro. *Génova y el Atlántico (c. 1650–1680). Emprendedores mediterráneos frente al auge del capitalismo del Norte*. PhD diss. Florence: European University Institute, 2014.

García-Montón, Alejandro. "Corona, Hombres de Negocios y Jueces Conservadores. Un Acercamiento En Escala Transatlántica (s. XVII)". *Jerónimo Zurita* 90 (2015): 75–112.

García-Montón, Alejandro. "The Rise of Portobelo and the Transformation of the Spanish American Slave Trade, 1640s–1730s: Transimperial Connections and Intra-American Shipping". *Hispanic American Historical Review* 99, no. 3 (2019): 407–10

García-Montón, Alejandro. "Esclavistas italianos, linajes Navarros y nueva nobleza Borbónica: Justiniano Justiniani, el Istmo de Panamá y el Marquesado de Peñaflorida (1630–1714)". In *Identità Nobiliare Tra Monarchia Ispanica e Italia. Lignaggi, Potere e Istituzioni (Secoli XVI–XVIII)*, edited by Carmen Sanz Ayán, Daniele Edigati, Marcella Aglietti and Santiago Martinez Hernández, 55–69. Roma: Edizioni di storia e letteratura, 2019.

García-Montón, Alejandro. "Seducing Smugglers: The Spanish Empire's Incentives for Inter-Imperial Official Slave Trade, 1640–1670", unpublished paper presented at workshop: *Slavery, Trade, Law, and Empires in the Early Modern Atlantic*, Austin: University of Texas at Austin, 11 April 2019.

García-Montón, Alejandro. *Genoese Entrepreneurship and the Asiento Slave Trade, 1650–1700*. London and New York: Routledge, 2022.

Gehring, Charles T. and J.A. Schiltkamp. *Curaçao Papers, 1640–1665*. Interlaken, NY, 1987.

Gimenez Fernandez, Manuel. *Bartolomeo de las Casas. Capellan de S.M. Carlos I. Poblador de Cumana (1517–1523)*, 2 vols. Madrid : Consejo Superior de Investigaciones Cientificas – Escuela de Estudios Hispanoamericanos, 1984.

Godinho, Vitorino Magalhães. "Portugal and her Empire, 1680–1720". In *The New Cambridge Modern History*. vol. 6: *The Rise of Great Britain and Russia, 1688–1715–25*, edited by J.S. Bromley, 509–539. Cambridge, Cambridge University Press, 1970.

Goslinga, Cornelis, *The Dutch in the Caribbean and on the Wild Coast, 1580–1680*. Assen: Van Gorcum B.V. 1971.

Grafe, Regina and Alejandra Irigoin. "A Stakeholder Empire: The Political Economy of Spanish Imperial Rule in America". *Economic History Review* 65, no. 2 (2012): 609–51.

Green, Toby. *The Rise of the Trans-Atlantic Slave Trade in Western Africa, 1300–1589*. New York: Cambridge University Press, 2012.

Green, Toby, ed. *Brokers of Change: Atlantic Commerce and Cultures in Pre-Colonial Western Africa*. Oxford: Oxford University Press, 2012.

Green, Toby. *The Rise of the Trans-Atlantic Slave Trade in Western Africa, 1300–1589*. New York: Cambridge University Press, 2012.

Greengrass, Mark, ed. *Conquest and Coalescence. The Shaping of the State in Early Modern Europe*. London: Edward Arnold, 1991.

Greenwald, E. *Marc-Antoine Caillot and the Company of the Indies in Louisiana*. Baton Rouge: Louisiana State University Press, 2016.

Gruzinski, Serge. *Les quatre parties du monde. Histoire d'une mondialisation*. Paris: Éditions de la Martinière, 2004.

Gruzinski, Serge. *The Eagle and dragon: Globalization and European Dreams of Conquest in China and America in the Sixteenth Century*. Cambridge: Cambridge Polity Press, 2014.

Gutiérrez Azopardo, Ildefonso. "El comercio y mercado de negros esclavos en Cartagena de Indias (1533–1850)". *Quinto Centenario*, 187–210. Madrid: Universidad Complutense de Madrid, 1987.

Hair, P. E. H. "Columbus from Guinea to America". *History in Africa* 17 (1990): 113–129;

Hall, Gwendolyn Midlo. *Slavery and African Ethnicities in the Americas: Restoring the Links*. Chapel Hill: University of North Carolina Press, 2009.

Hamm, Brian. "Constructing and Contesting Portuguese Difference in Colonial Spanish America, 1500–1650". *Anais de História de Além-Mar* XVII (2016): 303–36.

Harms, Robert W. *River of Wealth, River of Sorro: The Central Zaire Basin in the Era of the Slave and Ivory Trades, 1500–1891*. New Haven: Yale University Press, 1981.

Hedinger, David and Nadin Heé. "Transnational History – Connectivity, Cooperation and Competition". *Journal of Modern European History* 16, no. 4 (2018): 429–452.

Heijer, Henk. *Goud, ivoor en slaven. Scheepvaart en handel van de Tweede Westindische Compagnie op Afrika, 1674–1740*. Zutphen: Walburg Pers 1997.

Heijer, Henk den. "The Dutch West India Company, 1621–1791". In *Riches from Atlantic Commerce. Dutch Transatlantic Trade and Shipping, 1585–1817*, edited by Johannes Postma and Victor Enthoven, 77–112. Brill: Leiden, 2003.

Heijer, Henk den. *De geoctrooieerde compagnie.* Deventer: Wolters Kluwer, 2005.

Heijmans, Elisabeth. *The Agency of Empire: Personal Connections and Individual Strategies in the Shaping of the French Early Modern Expansion (1686–1746).* PhD diss. Leiden: Leiden University, 2018.

Heijmans, Elisabeth. *The Agency of Empire: Connections and Strategies in French Overseas Expansion (1686–1746).* Leiden: Brill, 2020.

Henriques, Isabel Castro. "A Rota dos Escravos. Angola e a rede do comércio negreiro (sécs. XV a XIX)". In *A rota dos escravos. Angola e a rede do comércio negreiro,* edited by João Medina and Isabel Castro Henriques. Lisbon: Cegia, 1996.

Herrero Sánchez, Manuel and Ana Crespo Solana, eds. *España y las 17 provincias de los Países Bajos: una revisión historiográfica (XVI–XVIII).* Cordoba: Fundación Carlos de Amberes, 2002.

Herrero Sánchez, Manuel, Yasmina Rocío Ben Yessef Garfia, Carlo Bitossi and Dino Puncuh, eds. *Génova y la Monarquía Hispánica (1528–1713).* Genoa: Società Ligure di Storia Patria, 2011.

Herzog, Tamar. "Una Monarquía, dos territorios. la frontera entre españoles y portugueses: España y Portugal durante (y después) de La Unión". In *Espanã y Portugal En El Mundo (1581–1668)*, edited by Carlos Martínez Shaw and J. A. Martínez Torres, 139–155. Madrid: Polifemo, 2014.

Linda Heywood, "Slavery and its transformations in the Kingdom of Kongo, 1492–1800". *The Journal of African History* 50, no 1 (2009): 1–22.

Hopkins, A.G. *An Economic History of West Africa.* New York: Columbia University Press, 1973.

Hrodej, P. *L'amiral Du Casse: l'élévation d'un Gascon sous Louis XIV.* Paris : Librairie de l'Inde, 1999.

Iglesias Rodríguez, Juan José and Isabel María Melero Muñoz, eds. *Hacer historia moderna: Líneas actuales y futuras de investigación.* Sevilla: Editorial Universidad de Sevilla, 2020.

Israel, Jonathan. *Dutch Primacy in World Trade, 1585–1740.* Oxford: Oxford University Press, 1989.

Jordaan, Han. "The Curaçao Slave Market. From the Asiento Trade to Free Trade, 1700–1730," in *Riches from Atlantic Commerce Dutch Transatlantic Trade and Shipping, 1585–1817*, edited by Johannes Postma and Victor Enthoven, 219–257. (Leiden; Boston: Brill, 2003).

Jordaan, Han. *Slavernij en vrijheid op Curaçao: de dynamiek van een achttiende-eeuws Atlantisch handelsknooppunt.* PhD diss. Leiden: Leiden University, 2012.

Karras, Alan L. *Smuggling: Contraband and Corruption in World History.* Lanham, MD: Rowman & Littlefield, 2010.

Klein, Herbert. *The Atlantic Slave Trade.* Cambridge: Cambridge University Press, 1990.

Klooster, Wim. "Slavenvaart op Spaanse kusten. De Nederlandse slavenhandel met Spaans Amerika, 1648–1701". *Tijdschrift voor de Zeegeschiedenis* (1997): 121–140.

Klooster, Wim. *Illicit Riches: Dutch Trade in the Caribbean, 1648–1795*. Leiden: KITLV Press, 1998.

Klooster, Wim. "Curaçao and the Caribbean Transit Trade". In *From Atlantic Commerce: Dutch Transatlantic Trade and Shipping,* 1585–1817, edited by Johannes Postma and Victor Enthoven, 203–218. Leiden: Brill, 2003.

Klooster, Wim. "Inter-imperial Smuggling in the Americas, 1600–1800". In *Soundings in Atlantic History: Latent Structures and Intellectual Currents, 1500–1830*, edited by Bernard Bailyn and Patricia L. Denault, 141–180. Cambridge, MA: Harvard University Press, 2009.

Klooster, Wim. *The Dutch Moment: War, Trade, and Settlement in the Seventeenth-Century Atlantic World.* Ithaca, NY: Cornell University Press, 2016.

Koot, Christian. *Empire at the Periphery. British Colonists, Anglo-Dutch Trade, and the Development of the British Atlantic, 1621–1713*. New York: New York University Press, 2011.

Labourdette, Jean-François, *La nation française a Lisbonne de 1669 a 1790: entre colbertisme et liberalisme.* Paris: Fondation Calouste Gulbenkian – Centre Culturel Portugais, 1988.

Lamikiz, Xabier. *Trade and Trust in the Eighteenth-Century Atlantic World: Spanish Merchants and Their Overseas Networks.* Woodbridge: The Boydell Press, 2013.

Lamikiz, Xabier. "Fiscalidad y fraude en la reactivación de la Carrera de Indias, 1660–1700". In *Dinero del Rey: finanzas y cambio fiscal en la Monarquía Hispánica, siglos XVI–XVII*, edited by Ramón Lanza García, 213–248. Granada: Comares, 2021.

Lane, Kris. "Africans and Natives in the Mines of Spanish America". In *Beyond Black and Red. African-Native Relations in Colonial Latin America*, edited by Matthew Restall, 156–186. Albuquerque: University of New Mexico Press, 2005.

Lanza García, Ramón, ed. *Dinero Del Rey: Finanzas y Cambio Fiscal En La Monarquía Hispánica, Siglos XVI–XVII*. Granada: Comares, 2021.

Law, Robin, "The Slave Trade in Seventeenth-Century Allada: A Revision". *African Economic History* 22 (1994): 59–92.

Lévy, Claude-Frédéric. *Capitalistes et Pouvoir Au Siècle Des Lumières: Les Fondateurs Des Origines à 1715*. 2 vols. Paris : Mouton, reprint 2019 [ed. 1969].

Lopes, Bruno and Roger Lee de Jesus, eds. *Finanças, economia e instituições no Portugal moderno.* Coimbra: Imprensa da Universidade de Coimbra, 2019.

López Belinchón, Bernardo. *Honra, libertad y hacienda: hombres de negocios y judíos sefardíes.* Alcalá de Henares: Instituto Internacional de Estudios Sefardíes y Andalusíes – Universidad de Alcalá, 2001.

Luxán Meléndez, Santiago and Lía de Luxán Hernández. "Las compañías reales de esclavos y la integración de Cuba en el sistema Atlántico del tabaco español, 1696–1739". *Anuario de Estudios Atlánticos* 62 (2016): 1–22.

Mark, Peter and José da Silva Horta. *The Forgotten Diaspora. Jewish communities in West Africa and the Making of the Atlantic World.* New York: Cambridge University Press, 2011.

Martín Casares, Aurelia and Margarita García Barranco, eds. *La esclavitud negroafricana en la historia de España siglos XVI y XVII.* Granada: Editorial Comares, 2010.

Martínez-Montiel, Luz María. "The Influence of Blacks in the Americas". In *From Chins to Bonds. The Slave Trade Revisited,* edited by Doudou Diène, 376–394. New York-Oxford: Berghahn, 2001.

Marzagalli, Silvia and Hubert Bonin, eds. *Négoce, ports et océans, XVIe-XXe siècles: mélanges offerts à Paul Butel.* Bordeaux : Presses Universitaires de Bordeaux, 2000.

Maxwell, Kenneth R. "Hegemonies Old and New: the Ibero-Atlantic in the Long Eighteenth Century". In *Colonial Legacies: The Problem of Persistence in Latin American History,* edited by Jeremy Adelman, 69–90. New York and London : Routledge, 1999.

Melaffe, Rolando. *Negro Slavery in Latin America.* Berkeley : University of California Press, 1975.

Mello, Evaldo Cabral de. *Olinda restaurada: guerra e açúcar no Nordeste, 1630–1654.* Rio de Janeiro: Topbooks, 1998.

Menard, R.R. *Sweet Negotiations: Sugar, Slavery, and Plantation Agriculture in Early Barbados.* Charlottesville: University of Virginia Press, 2006.

Mendes, António de Almeida. "Portugal e o tráfico de escravos na primeira metade do século XVI". *Africana Studia* 7 (2004): 13–30.

Mendes, António de Almeida. "The Foundations of the System: A Reassessment of the Slave Trade to the Spanish Americas in the Sixteenth and the Seventeenth centuries". *Extending the Frontiers: Essays on the New Transatlantic Slave Trade Database,* edited by David Eltis and David Richardson, 63–94. New Haven : Yale University Press, 2008.

Mendes, António de Almeida, Carlos Martínez Shaw, and J. A. Martínez Torres, "Sueños y invenciones en el Atlántico en la ocasión Africana y Ibérica. Estrategias de unión y desunión de los imperios de España y Portugal en los viejos mundos (siglos XV–XVII)". In *España y Portugal En El Mundo (1561–1668),* edited by Carlos Martínez Shaw and José Antonio Martínez Torres, 195–218. Madrid: Polifemo, 2014.

Menkman, W. R. "Slavenhandel en rechtsdebeeling op Curaçao op het eind der 17e eeuw". *De West-Indische Gids* 17 (1935–1936), 11–26.

Mitchell, Mathew David. *The Prince of Slavers: Humphry Morice and the Transformation of Britain's Transatlantic Slave Trade, 1698–1732.* London, Palgrave, 2020.

Moraes, Maria Adelaide Pereira. "Desceram do monte, atravessaram, o mar (Castro de Guimarães e seu termo)". *Boletim de Trabalhos Históricos* 38 (1987): 61–103.

Mouta, Fernando Jorge Cruz. ""Por Virtud Del Asiento": The Naval Logistics of the Slave Trade to the Spanish Indies (1604–1624)". *International Journal of Maritime History* 31, no. 4 (2019): 707–28

Moutoukias, Zacarías. *Contrabando y control colonial en el siglo XVII: Buenos Aires, el Atlántico y el espacio peruano*. Buenos Aires: Centro Editor de América Latina, 1988.

Navarrete, Maria Cristina. *Génesis y desarrollo de la esclavitud en Colombia (Siglos XVI y XVII)*. Cali: Universidad del Valle, 2005.

Negron, Ramona. *Dutch Entrepreneurship in the Spanish Americas, 1580–1700*. PhD diss. Leiden: Leiden University, 2025.

Newson, Linda A. "Africans and Luso-Africans in the Portuguese Slave Trade on the Upper Guinea Coast in the Early Seventeenth Century". *The Journal of African History* 53, no. 1 (March 2012): 1–24.

Newson, Linda A. and Susie Minchin. *From Capture to Sale: The Portuguese Slave Trade to Spanish South America in the Early Seventeenth Century*. Leiden and Boston: Brill, 2007.

Odegard, Odegard. "Recapitalization or Reform? The Bankruptcy of the First Dutch West India Company and the Formation of the Second West India Company, 1674". *Itinerario* 43, nr. 1 (2019): 88–106.

Olivas, Aaron Alejandro Olivas. "The Global Politics of Transatlantic Slave Trade during the War of the Spanish Succession, 1700–1715". In *Early Bourbon Spanish America: Politics and Society in a Forgotten Era, 1700–1759*, edited by F. A. Eissa-Barros and A. Vásquez Varela, 85–109. Leiden: Brill, 2013.

O'Malley, Gregory E. *Final Passages: The Intercolonial Slave Trade of British America, 1619–1807*. Chapel Hill: University of North Carolina Press, 2014.

Oostindie Gert and Jessica Roitman (eds.). *Dutch Atlantic Connections, 1680–1800. Linking Empires, Bridging Borders*. Leiden : Brill, 2014.

Orozco Cruz, Jonatán. "Redes transnacionales de comercio en el asiento de negros: La compañía de Juan Barroso del Pozo y Nicolás Porcio (1675–1682)". In *Hacer historia moderna: Líneas actuales y futuras de investigación*, edited by Juan José Iglesias Rodríguez y Isabel María Melero Muñoz, 319–331. Sevilla: Editorial Universidad de Sevilla, 2020.

Orozco Cruz, Jonatán, "Barroso, Porcio y Coymans: redes y entramados mercantiles en la articulación de los asientos de negros de finales del siglo XVII (1675–1692)". In *Tratas atlánticas y esclavitudes en América, siglos XVI–XIX*, edited by Manuel Fernández Chaves and Rafael Pérez García, 125–140. Sevilla: Editorial Universidad de Sevilla, 2021.

Orozco Cruz, Jonatán. "Mover Roma con Santiago para influir en Madrid. Agentes, estrategias y redes clientelares en la pugna por la titularidad del Asiento de esclavos entre Nicolàs Porcio y Baltasar Coymans (1685–1694)". In *Urdimbre y memoria de un imperio global: Redes de poder y circulación de agentes en la Monarquía Hispánica*, edited by Antonio Jiménez Estrella, Julián José Lozano Navarro, Francisco Sánchez-Montes González, 481–508. Granada: Editorial Universidad de Granada, 2023.

Ortiz Arza, Javier. "Introducción al estudio de los navegantes vascos de la carrera de Indias y su participación en la trata atlántica de esclavos del siglo XVI". *Brocar. Cuadernos de Investigación Histórica* 43 (2019): 41–72.

Ortiz Arza, Javier. "Los libros-registro de esclavos, el sistema de licencias y la trata con Hispanoamérica en el siglo XVI: análisis y aspectos metodológicos a través del caso vasco". *Anuario de Estudios Americanos* 77, no. 2 (2020): 579–611.

Osborne, F. J. "James Castillo, Asiento Agent". *The Jamaican Historical Review* 8 (1971): 9–18.

Otte, Enrique and Conchita Ruiz-Burruecos. "Los portugueses en la trata de esclavos negros de las postmerias del siglo XVI". *Moneda y Crédito* 85 (1963): 3–31.

Otte, Enrique. *Sevilla, siglo XVI: materiales para su historia económica*. Sevilla: Centro de Estudios Andaluces, 2008.

Paesie, Ruud. *Lorrendrayen op Africa: de illegale goederen- en slavenhandel op West-Afrika tijdens het achttiende-eeuwse handelsmonopolie van de West-Indische Compagnie, 1700–1734*. Amsterdam De Bataafsche Leeuw, 2008.

Palacios Preciado, Jorge. *La trata de negros por Cartagena de Indias, 1650–1750*. Tunja: Universidad Pedagógica y Tecnológica de Colombia, 1973.

Palmer, Colin A. "The Company Trade and the Numerical Distribution of Slaves to Spanish America, 1703–1739". In *Africans in Bondage: Studies in Slavery and the Slave Trade. Essays in Honor of Philip D. Curtin on the Occasion of the Twenty-Fifth Anniversary of African Studies at the University of Wisconsin*, edited by Philip D. Curtin and Paul E. Lovejoy, 27–42. Madison : University of Wisconsin African Studies Program, 1986.

Peralta Rivera, Germán. *Los mecanismos del comercio negrero*. Lima: Kuntur Editores, 1990.

Pereira, Edgar. *A Contractor Empire. Public-Private Partnerships and Overseas Expansion in Habsburg Portugal (1580–1640)*. PhD diss. Leiden: Leiden University, 2020.

Pérez García, Rafael M. and Manuel Francisco Fernández Chaves. "Sevilla y la trata negrera atlántica: envíos de esclavos desde Cabo Verde a la América española, 1569–1579". In *Estudios de historia moderna en homenaje al profesor Antonio García-Baquero*, edited by León Carlos Álvarez y Santaló, 597–622. Sevilla: Universidad de Sevilla.

Pérez García, Rafael M. "Metodología para el análisis y cuantificación de la trata de esclavos hacia la América española en el siglo XVI". In *Los vestidos de Clío: métodos y tendencias recientes de la historiográfica modernista española (1973–2013)*, edited by Ofelia Rey Castelao and Fernando Suárez Golán, 829–830. Santiago de Compostela: Universidad de Santiago de Compostela, 2013.

Perez Guerra, Angél, ed. *Primeras Jornadas de Andalucía y América*. 2 vols. La Rábida: Instituto de Estudios Onubenses, 1981.

Pettigrew, William A. *Freedom's Debt: The Royal African Company and the Politics of the Atlantic Slave Trade, 1672–1752*. Chapel Hill: University of North Carolina Press, 2013.

Pike, Ruth. *Enterprise and Adventure. The Genoese in Seville and the Opening of the New World.* Ithaca: Cornell University Press, 1966.

Postma, Johannes M., *The Dutch in the Atlantic Slave Trade, 1600–1815*. Cambridge : Cambridge University Press, 1992.

Postma, Johannes and Victor Enthoven, eds. *Riches from Atlantic Commerce. Dutch Transatlantic Trade and Shipping, 1585–1817*. Leiden: Brill, 2003.

Price, J.M. *France and the Chesapeake: A History of the French Tobacco Monopoly, 1674–1791*. 2 vols. Ann Arbor: University of Michigan Press, 1973.

Quiroz, Alfonso W. "The Expropiation of Portuguese New Christians in Spanish America, 1635–1649". *Ibero-Amerikanisches Archiv* 11, no. 4 (1985): 407–65.

Ramos Pérez, Demetrio. "El negocio negrero de los Welser y sus habilidades monopolistas". *Revista de Historia de América* 81 (1976): 7–81.

Rawley, James A. and Stephen D. Behrend. *The Transatlantic Slave Trade: A History, revisited edition*. Lincoln and London: University of Nebraska Press, 1981.

Reinert, Sophus and Pernille Røge (eds.). *Political Economy of Empire in the Early Modern World.* New York: Palgrave Macmillan, 2013.

Rey Castelao, Ofelia and Fernando Suárez Golán, eds. *Los vestidos de Clío: métodos y tendencias recientes de la historiográfica modernista española (1973–2013)*. Santiago de Compostela: Universidad de Santiago de Compostela, 2013.

Restall, Matthew, ed. *Beyond Black and Red. African-Native Relations in Colonial Latin America.* Albuquerque: University of New Mexico Press, 2005.

Robles, Gregorio de. *América a fines del siglo XVII: Noticia de los lugares de contrabando.* Valladolid: Casa-Museo de Colón, 1980.

Rodrigues, Lisbeth. "O incumprimento do crédito no século XVIII: o caso da Misericórdia de Lisboa". In *Finanças, economia e instituições no Portugal moderno*, edited by Bruno Lopes and Roger Lee de Jesus, 229–260 Coimbra: Imprensa da Universidade de Coimbra, 2019.

Rodrigues, Miguel Geraldes. *Between West Africa and America. The Angolan Slave Trade in the Portuguese and Spanish Atlantic Empires (1560–1641)*. PhD diss. Florence: European University Institute, 2019.

Rodrígues Blásquez, Ana Maria. "Penetración portuguesa en América a través del asiento firmado por la Real Compañia de Guinea en 1696". *Temas Americanistas* 4 (1984): pp. 50–58.

Rodríguez Hernández, Antonio José. "Los judeoconversos y el negocio de la guerra: la leva de Manuel Cortizos por vía de Factoría (1648)". *Hispania* 76, no. 253 (2016): 473–510.

Roper, Lou H. *Advancing Empire: English Interests and Overseas Expansion, 1613–1688.* New York: Cambridge University Press, 2017.

Rout, Leslie B. *The African Experience in Spanish America, 1502 to the Present Day.* Cambridge: Cambridge University Press, 1976.

Rowlands, G. *Dangerous and Dishonest Men: The International Bankers of Louis XIV's France*. New-York: Palgrave Macmillan, 2015.

Rupert, Linda Rupert. *Creolization and Contraband: Curaçao in the Early Modern Atlantic World*. Athens and London: The University of Georgia Press, 2012.

Salvador, José Gonçalves. *Os cristãos-novos e o comércio no Atlântico Meridional*. São Paulo: Livraria Pioneira Editora, 1978.

Salvador, José Gonçalves. *Os magnatas do tráfico negreiro (séculos XVI e XVII)*. São Paulo: Livraria Pioneira Editora, 1981.

Santana Pérez, Germán. "Mercaderes hispanos en África subsahariana antes de la Unión Ibérica, 1503–1580". In *Los negocios de la esclavitud: tratantes y mercados de esclavos en el Atlántico Ibérico, siglos XV–XVIII*, edited by José Luis Belmonte Postigo, Manuel F. Fernández Chaves and Rafael M. Pérez García, 71–92. Sevilla: Universidad de Sevilla, 2019.

Santos, Maria Emília Madeira, ed. *História geral de Cabo Verde*. 3 vols. Lisbon and Praia: Instituto de Investigação Científica e Tropical – Instituto Nacional de Investigação, Promoção e Património Culturais de Cabo Verde, 2002.

Sanz Ayan, Carmen*Los banqueros de Carlos II*. Valladolid: Universidad de Valladolid, 1988.

Sanz Ayan, Carmen. "Financieros holandeses de Felipe V en la Guerra de Sucesión: Huberto Hubrecht". In *España y las 17 provincias de los Países Bajos: una revisión historiográfica (XVI–XVIII)*, edited by Manuel Herrero, Sánchez and Ana Crespo Solana, 563–582. Cordoba: Fundacion Carlos de Amberes: 2002.

Sanz Ayan, Carmen. "Consolidación y destrucción de patrimonios financieros en la Edad Moderna: Los Cortizos (1630–1715)". In *Fortuna y negocios: formación y gestión de los grandes patrimonios (siglos XVI–XX)*, edited by Hilario Casado Alonso and Ricardo Robledo Hernández, 73–98. Valladolid: Universidad de Valladolid, 2002.

Sanz Ayan, Carmen. "Procedimientos culturales y transculturales de integración en un clan financiero internacional: los Cortizos (siglos XVII y XVIII)". In *Las redes del imperio: élites sociales en la articulación de la Monarquía Hispánica, 1492–1714*, edited by Bartolomé Yun Casalilla, 65–94. Madrid: Marcial Pons, 2009.

Sanz Ayan, Carmen. *Un Banquero en el Siglo de Oro. Octavio Centurion, el financier de los Austrias*. Madrid: La Esfera de los Libros, 2015.

Sanz Ayan, Carmen, Daniele Edigati, Marcella Aglietti and Santiago Martinez Hernández, *ed*. *Identità Nobiliare Tra Monarchia Ispanica e Italia. Lignaggi, Potere e Istituzioni (Secoli XVI–XVIII)*. Roma: Edizioni di storia e letteratura, 2019.

Scelle, Georges. *La traite négrière aux Indes de Castille: contrats et traités d'assiento*. 2 vols. Paris: Librairie de la Société du Recueil J.-B. Sirey & Du Journal du Palais, 1906.

Scelle, Georges Scelle. "The Slave Trade in the Spanish Colonies of America: the Asiento". *The American Journal of International Law* 4, no. 3 (1910): 612–661.

Schaub, Jean-Frédéric. *Portugal na Monarquia Hispânica (1580–1640)*. Lisbon: Livros Horizonte, 2001.

Schück, Richard. *Brandenburg-Preussens Kolonial-Politik unter dem Grossen Kurfürsten und seinen Nachfolgern (1637–1721)*. 2 vols. Leipiz: Grunow, 1889.

Schultz, Kara D. " 'The Kingdom of Angola Is Not Very Far from Here'†: The South Atlantic Slave Port of Buenos Aires, 1585–1640". *Slavery & Abolition* 36, no. 3 (2015): 424–44.

Schultz, Kara D. "Interwoven: Slaving in the Southern Atlantic under the Union of the Iberian Crowns, 1580–1640". *Journal of Global Slavery* 2, no. 3 (2017): 248–72.

Seijas, Tatiana and Pablo M. Sierra. "The Persistence of the Slave Market in Seventeenth-Century Central Mexico". *Slavery & Abolition* 37, no. 2 (2016): 307–33.

Serafim, Cristina Seuanes. *As ilhas de São Tomé no século XVII*. Lisboa: Centro de História de Além Mar, 2000.

Serrano Mangas, Fernando. *Los Galeones de la Carrera de Indias 1650–1700*. Sevilla: EEHA-CSIC, 1985.

Shaw, C. M. "The Overseas Spanish Empire and the Dutch Republic Before and After the Peace of Munster". *De Zeventiende Eeuw* 13 (1997): 131–139.

Shaw, C. M. and J. A. Martínez Torres, eds. *Espanã y Portugal En El Mundo (1581–1668)*. Madrid: Polifemo, 2014.

Sheridan, Richard. "The Plantation Revolution and the Industrial Revolution, 1625–1775". *Caribbean Studies* 9, no. 3 (1969): 5–25.

Sierra Silva, Pablo Miguel. "Portuguese 'Encomenderos de Negros' and the Slave Trade within Mexico, 1600–1675". *Journal of Global Slavery* 2, no. 3 (2017): 239–41.

Sierra Silva, Pablo Miguel. *Urban Slavery in Colonial Mexico*. Cambridge: Cambridge University Press, 2018.

Silva, Filipa Ribeiro da. *Dutch and Portuguese in Western Africa: Empires, Merchants and the Atlantic System, 1580–1674*. Leiden and Boston: Brill, 2011.

Silva, Filipa Ribeiro da and David Richardson, *Networks and Trans-Cultural Exchange: Slave Trading in the South Atlantic, 1590–1867*. Leiden and Boston: Brill, 2015.

Smith, David Grant *The Mercantile Class of Portugal and Brazil in the Seventeenth Century: A Socio-Economic Study of the Merchants of Lisbon and Bahia, 1620–1690*. PhD diss. Texas: Texas University Press, 1979.

Soule, Emily Berquist. "From Africa to the Ocean Sea: Atlantic Slavery in the Origins of the Spanish Empire". *Atlantic Studies* 15, no. 1 (2018): 16–39.

Stein, Stanley and Barbara Stein. *Silver, Trade, and War: Spain and America in the Making of Early Modern Europe*. Baltimore, Johns Hopkins University Press, 2000.

Stein, Tristan. "Tangier in the Restoration Empire". *The Historical Journal* 54, no. 4 (2011): 985–1011.

Strum, Daniel. *The Sugar Trade: Brazil, Portugal and the Netherlands (1595–1630)*. Stanford, California and Rio de Janeiro: Stanford University Press-Versal Editores, 2013.

Studnicki-Gizbert, Daviken. *A Nation upon the Ocean Sea: Portugal's Atlantic Diaspora and the Crisis of the Spanish Empire, 1492–1640*. New York: Oxford University Press, 2007.

Subrahmanyam, Sanjay. "Connected Histories: Notes Toward a Reconfiguration of Early Modern Eurasia". *Modern Asian Studies* 31, no. 3 (1997): 735–762.

Subrahmanyam, Sanjay. "Holding the World in Balance: The Connected Histories of the Iberian Overseas Empires, 1500–1640". *The American Historical Review* 112, no. 5 (2007): 1359–85.

Svalastog, J.M. "Challenging Porous Frontiers: Atlantic Merchants and the Potential of the Indian Ocean, 1640–1650". *Journal of Early American History* 9, no. 2–3 (2019): 145–62.

Svalastog, J.M., *Mastering the Worst of Trades: England's Early Africa Companies and Their Traders, 1618–1672, Mastering the Worst of Trades*. Leiden: Brill, 2021.

Teixeira, Cândido da Silva. "Companhia de Cacheu, Rios e Comércio de Guiné: documentos para a sua história". *Boletim do Arquivo Histórico Colonial* I (1950): 87–132.

Temperley, Howard. *British Anti-Slavery, 1833–1870*. London : Longmans, 1972.

Thomas, Hugh. *The Slave Trade: the Story of the Atlantic Slave Trade: 1440–1870*. New York: Simon & Schuster, 1999.

Thomas, Robert and Richard Bean. "The Fishers of Men: Profits of the Slave Trade". *The Journal of Economic History* 34, no. 4 (1974): 885–914.

Thornton, A. P. "Spanish Slave-Ships in the English West Indies, 1660–85". *The Hispanic American Historical Review* 35, no. 3 (1955): 374–385.

Thornton, A. P. "The Organization of the Slave Trade in the English West Indies, 1660–1685". *The William and Mary Quarterly* 12, no. 3 (1955): 399–409.

Torrão, Maria Manuel Ferraz. "Rotas Comerciais, Agentes Económicos, Meios de Pagamento". In *História Geral de Cabo Verde*, edited by Maria Emília Madeira Santos, vol. 2, 17–124. Lisbon and Praia: Instituto de Investigação Científica Tropical and Instituto Nacional de Cultura de Cabo Verde, 1995.

Torrão, Maria Manuel Ferraz. "De Santiago para a costa da Guiné: a transferência do centro geográfico dos negócios e a manutenção da elite comerciante. As transacções da Companhia de António Fernandes Landim e de Francisco Dias Mendes de Brito (1629–1630)". *Arquipélago* 2 (1997): 83–118.

Torrão, Maria Manuel Ferraz. "Os Portugueses e o trato de escravos de Cabo Verde com a América espanhola no fim do século XVI. Os contratadores do trato de Cabo Verde e a Coroa, uma relação de conveniência numa época de oportunidades (1583–1600)". In *Portugal Na Monarquia Hispânica: Dinâmicas de Integração e Conflito*, edited by Pedro Cardim, Leonor Freire Costa, and Mafalda Soares da Cunha, 93–106. Lisbon: CHAM, 2013.

Torres Ramirez, Bibiano. *La Compañia Gaditana de negros*. Seville : Escuela de Estudios Hispano-Americanos de Sevilla, 1973.

Torres Sánchez, Rafael. *Military Entrepreneurs and the Spanish Contractor State in the Eighteenth Century*. Oxford: Oxford University Press, 2016.

Ventura, Maria da Graça Mateus. *Negreiros Portugueses na rota das Indias de Castela: 1541–1556*. Lisbon: Colibri, Instituto de Cultura Ibero-Atlântico, 1998.

Ventura, Maria da Graça Mateus. *Os portugueses no Peru ao tempo da União Ibérica: mobilidade, cumplicidade e vivências*. 2 vols. Lisbon: Imprensa Nacional-Casa da Moeda, 2005.

Valladares, Rafael. *Banqueros y vasallos: Felipe IV y el medio general (1630–1670)*. Cuenca: Universidad de Castilla La Mancha, 2002.

Vega Franco, Marisa. *El trafico de esclavos con America (asientos de Grillo y Lomelin, 1663–1674)*. Sevilla: EEHA-CSIC, 1984.

Vila Vilar, Enriqueta. "Los asientos portugueses y el contrabando de negros". *Anuario de Estudios Americanos* 30 (1973): 557–609.

Vila Vilar, Enriqueta. "La sublevacion de Portugal y la trata de negros". *Ibero-Amerikanisches Archiv* 2, no. 3 (1976): 171–92.

Vila Vilar, Enriqueta. *Hispanoamérica y el comercio de esclavos: los asientos portugueses*. Seville: Estudios Hispanoamericanos de Sevilla, 1977.

Vila Vilar, Enriqueta. "El consulado de Sevilla, asentista de esclavos: una nueva tentativa para el mantenimiento del monopolio comercial". In *Primeras Jornadas de Andalucía y América*, edited by Angél Perez Guerra, vol. 1, 181–196. La Rábida: Instituto de Estudios Onubenses, 1981.

Vries, Jan de. "The Dutch Atlantic Economies". In *The Atlantic Economy during the Seventeenth and Eighteenth Centuries: Organization, Operation, Practice, and Personnel*, edited by Peter A. Coclanis, 1–29. Columbia, SC: University of South Carolina Press, 2005.

Coclanis, Peter A., ed. *The Atlantic Economy during the Seventeenth and Eighteenth Centuries.*

Weindl, Andrea. "The Asiento de Negros and International Law". *Journal of the History of International Law / Revue d'histoire Du Droit International* 10, no. 2 (2008): 229–57.

Westergaard, Waldemar. *The Danish West Indies under Company Rule (1671–1754): With a Supplementary Chapter, 1755–1917*. New York: The Macmillan Company, 1917.

Wheat, David. "The First Great Waves: African Provenance Zones for the Transatlantic Slave Trade to Cartagena de India, 1570–1640". *The Journal of African History* 52, no. 1 (2011): 1–22.

Williams, Eric. *Capitalism and Slavery.* Chapel Hill : The University of North Carolina Press, 1944.

Wills, J. E. *1688. A Global History*. New York: W.W. Norton, 2001.

Wimmler, Jutta. *The Sun King's Atlantic: Drugs, Demons and Dyestuffs in the Atlantic World*. Leiden : Brill, 2017.

Wright, I. A. "The Coymans Asiento (1685–1689)". *Bijdragen voor Vaderlandse Geschiedenis en Oudheikunde* 6 (1924): 23–62.

Yun Casallila, Bartolomé. " 'Localism', Global History and Transnational History: A Reflection from the Historian of Early Modern Europe'. *Historisk Tidskrift* 127 (2007): 659–678.

Yun Casalilla, Bartolomé, ed. *Las redes del imperio: élites sociales en la articulación de la Monarquía Hispánica, 1492–1714*. Madrid: Marcial Pons, 2009.

Zahedieh, Nuala. "The Merchants of Port Royal, Jamaica, and the Spanish Contraband Trade, 1655–1692". *The William and Mary Quarterly* 43, no. 4 (1986): 570–593.

Zahedieh, Nuala. "Making Mercantilism Work: London Merchants and Atlantic Trade in the Seventeenth Century". *Transactions of the Royal Historical Society* 9 (1999): 143–158.

Zahedieh, Nuala. *The Capital and the Colonies: London and the Atlantic Economy 1660–1700*. Cambridge: Cambridge University Press, 2010.

Zook, G.F. *The Company of Royal Adventurers Trading into Africa*. Cornell University: Lancaster, Pa., Press of the New Era Printing Co., 1919.

Index

www.ingramcontent.com/pod-product-compliance
Lightning Source LLC
Chambersburg PA
CBHW071841290126
38984CB00004B/423
* 9 7 8 9 0 0 4 7 4 5 0 8 7 *